주한미군지위협정(SOFA)

서명 및 발효 20

주한미군지위협정(SOFA)

서명 및 발효 20

_____

| 머리말

미국은 오래전부터 우리나라 외교에 있어서 가장 긴밀하고 실질적인 우호 · 협력관계를 맺어 온 나라다. 6 · 25전쟁 정전 협정이 체결된 후 북한의 재침을 막기 위한 대책으로서 1953년 11월 한미 상호방위조약이 체결되었다. 이는 미군이 한국에 주둔하는 법적 근거였고, 그렇게 주둔하게 된 미군의 시설, 구역, 사업, 용역, 출입국, 통관과 관세, 재판권 등 포괄적인 법적 지위를 규정하는 것이 바로 주한미군지위협정(SOFA)이다. 그러나 이와 관련한 협상은 계속된 난항을 겪으며 한미 상호방위조약이 체결로부터 10년이 훌쩍 넘은 1967년이 돼서야 정식 발효에 이를 수 있었다. 그럼에도 당시 미군 범죄에 대한 한국의 재판권은 심한 제약을 받았으며, 1980년대 후반 민주화 운동과 함께 미군 범죄 문제가 사회적 이슈로 떠오르자 협정을 개정해야 한다는 목소리가 커지게 되었다. 이에 1991년 2월 주한미군지위협정 1차 개정이 진행되었고, 이후에도 여러 사건이 발생하며 2001년 4월 2차 개정이 진행되어 현재에 이르고 있다.

본 총서는 외교부에서 작성하여 최근 공개한 주한미군지위협정(SOFA) 관련 자료를 담고 있다. 1953년 한미 상호방위조약 체결 이후부터 1967년 발효가 이뤄지기까지의 자료와 더불어, 이후 한미 합동위원회을 비롯해 민 · 형사재판권, 시설, 노무, 교통 등 각 분과위원회의 회의록과 운영 자료, 한국인 고용인 문제와 관련한 자료, 기타 관련 분쟁 자료 등을 포함해 총 42권으로 구성되었다. 전체 분량은 약 2만 2천여 쪽에 이른다.

2024년 3월
한국학술정보(주)

| 일러두기

· 본 총서에 실린 자료는 2022년 4월과 2023년 4월에 각각 공개한 외교문서 4,827권, 76만 여 쪽 가운데 일부를 발췌한 것이다.

· 각 권의 제목과 순서는 공개된 원본을 최대한 반영하였으나, 주제에 따라 일부는 적절히 변경하였다.

· 원본 자료는 A4 판형에 맞게 축소하거나 원본 비율을 유지한 채 A4 페이지 안에 삽입 하였다. 또한 현재 시점에선 공개되지 않아 '공란'이란 표기만 있는 페이지 역시 그대로 실었다.

· 외교부가 공개한 문서 각 권의 첫 페이지에는 '정리 보존 문서 목록'이란 이름으로 기록물 종류, 일자, 명칭, 간단한 내용 등의 정보가 수록되어 있으며, 이를 기준으로 0001번부터 번호가 매겨져 있다. 이는 삭제하지 않고 총서에 그대로 수록하였다.

· 보고서 내용에 관한 더 자세한 정보가 필요하다면, 외교부가 온라인상에 제공하는『대한 민국 외교사료요약집』1991년과 1992년 자료를 참조할 수 있다.

| 차례

정/리/보/존/문/서/목/록

기록물종류	문서-일반공문서철	등록번호	948 9621	등록일자	2006-07-27
분류번호	741.12	국가코드	US	주제	

문서철명	한.미국 간의 상호방위조약 제4조에 의한 시설과 구역 및 한국에서의 미국군대의 지위에 관한 협정 (SOFA) 전59권. 1966.7.9 서울에서 서명 : 1967.2.9 발효 (조약 232호) ★원본

생산과	미주과/조약과	생산년도	1952 - 1967	보존기간	영구

담당과(그룹)	조약	조약		서가번호	--

참조분류	

권차명	V.50 실무교섭회의 합의의사록, 제10-37차, 1963

내용목차	★ 일지 :
	1953.8.7 이승만 대통령-Dulles 미국 국무장관 공동성명
	            - 상호방위조약 발효 후 군대지위협정 교섭 약속
	1954.12.2 정부, 주한 UN군의 관세업무협정 체결 제의
	1955.1월, 5월 미국, 제의 거절
	1955.4.28 정부, 군대지위협정 제의 (한국측 초안 제시)
	1957.9.10 Hurter 미국 국무차관 방한 시 각서 수교 (한국측 제의 수락 요구)
	1957.11.13, 26 정부, 개별 협정의 단계적 체결 제의
	1958.9.18 Dawling 주한미국대사, 형사재판관할권 협정 제외 조건으로 행정협정 체결 의사 전달
	1960.3.10 정부, 토지, 시설협정의 우선적 체결 강력 요구
	1961.4.10 장면 국무총리-McConaughy 주한미국대사 공동성명으로 교섭 개시 합의
	1961.4.15, 4.25 제1, 2차 한.미국 교섭회의 (서울)
	1962.3.12 정부, 교섭 재개 촉구 공한 송부
	1962.5.14 Burger 주한미국대사, 최규하 장관 면담 시 형사재판관할권 문제 제기 않는 조건으로
	            교섭 재개 통고
	1962.9.6 한.미국 간 공동성명 발표 (9월 중 교섭 재개 합의)
	1962.9.20~ 제1-81차 실무 교섭회의 (서울)
	  1965.6.7
	1966.7.8 제82차 실무 교섭회의 (서울)
	1966.7.9 서명
	1967.2.9 발효 (조약 232호)

마/이/크/로/필/름/사/항

촬영연도	★롤 번호	화일 번호	후레임 번호	보관함 번호
2006-11-24	I-06-0072	03	1-366	

0001

0103

March 8, 1963

I. Time and Place : 2:00 to 4:5 p.m. March 8, 1963
at the Foreign Minister's
Conference Room

II. Attendants:

ROK Side:

Mr. Whang, Ho Eul   Director
Bureau of Political Affairs
Ministry of Foreign Affairs

Mr. Shin Kwan Sup   Director
Bureau of Costums Duty
Ministry of Finance

Mr. Koo, Choong Whay   Chief, America Section
Ministry of Foreign Affairs

Col. Lee, Nam Koo   Chief, Military Affairs Section
Ministry of National Defense

Mr. Chu, Mun Ki   Chief, Legal Affairs Section
Ministry of Justice

Mr. Lee, Jae Sul   Chief of the Foreign Exchange
Division,
Ministry of Finance

Mr. Lee, Kyung Hoon   2nd Secretary
Ministry of Foreign Affairs

Mr. Kang, Suk Jae   3rd Secretary
Ministry of Foreign Affairs

Mr. Kim, Yoon Taik   3rd Secretary
Ministry of Foreign Affairs

US Side:

Mr. Philip C. Habib   Counselor of the Embassy
for Political Affairs

Brig. Gen. J.D. Lawlor   Deputy Chief of Staff
8th Army

Mr. William J. Ford   First Secretary of the
Embassy

0162

한·미국 간의 상호방위조약 제4조에 의한 시설과 구역 및 한국에서의 미국군대의 지위에 관한 협정(SOFA)
전59권. 1966.7.9 서울에서 서명 : 1967.2.9 발효(조약 232호) (V.50 실무교섭회의 합의의사록, 제10-37차, 1963) (2/2)

9

Col. G.G. O'Connor	Deputy Chief of Staff 8th Army
Capt. R.M. Brownlie	Assistant Chief of Staff USN/K
Col. W.A. Solf	Staff Judge Advocate 8th Army
Mr. Benjamin A. Fleck (Rapporteur and Press Officer)	First Secretary of the Embassy
Mr. Robert A. Lewis	Second Secretary and Consul of the Embassy
Lt. Col. R.E. Hiller	Staff Officer, JAG 8th Army
Lt. Col. W.A. Burt	J-5
Kenneth Campen	Interpreter

1. In opening the meeting, Mr. Whan announced that there had been some changes in the personnel of the Korean negotiating team as a result of personnel shifts in the Ministry of Foreign Affairs. He announced that Mr. O Won Young would no longer participate in the negotiations and that Mr. O's successor had not yet been selected. Mr. Lee Chang Bum, having been assigned to an overseas post, had been replaced by Mr. Kim Yoon Taik, who was present for the first time at this meeting. Mr. Whang also introduced Mr. Lee Jae Sul, Chief of the Foreign Exchange Division, Ministry of Fiance, who was attending this meeting for the purpose of participating in discussion of the article on Foreign Exchange Controls and the article on Military Payment Certificates. Mr. Habib replied by welcoming Mr. Whang to the negotiating table as Chief Negotiator for the Korean side. He also welcomed Mr. Kim and Mr. Lee.

한·미국 간의 상호방위조약 제4조에 의한 시설과 구역 및 한국에서의 미국군대의 지위에 관한 협정(SOFA)
전59권. 1966.7.9 서울에서 서명 : 1967.2.9 발효(조약 232호) (V.50 실무교섭회의 합의의사록, 제10-37차, 1963) (2/2)

2. Mr. Whang then stated that the trip which the entire group had made on March 6 to certain of the areas and facilities occupied by the U.S. armed forces had been very useful and enlightening in understanding the actual situation and some of the problems encountered by U.S. armed forces in Korea. Mr. Habib stated that he hoped that there would be additional such trips in the future, to other facilities and areas.

Navigational Aids

3. Substantive discussion began with consideration of the Agreed Minute, proposed by the U.S. side at the previous meeting, to the article dealing with air traffic control and navigational aids. Mr. Whang stated that the Korean side had considered the U.S. proposal. He pointed out that it referred to one of the article dealing with facilities and areas, which had not yet been agreed to. Therefore, the Korean side wished to propose an alternative Agreed Minute which did not refer to the facilities and areas article. Mr. Whang thereupon tabled the Korean Agreed Minute, stating that there was no great difference in substance between the two drafts.

4. Mr. Habib replied that there was a substantial difference. While the U.S. draft refers to the facilities and areas article, the Korean draft refers to the Joint Committee article. He pointed out that reference to paragraph 1(a) of the draft article "A" on facilities and areas was much more relevant than reference to the

0166

미문서-16③

0310

0167

한·미국 간의 상호방위조약 제4조에 의한 시설과 구역 및 한국에서의 미국군대의 지위에 관한 협정(SOFA)
전59권. 1966.7.9 서울에서 서명 : 1967.2.9 발효(조약 232호) (V.50 실무교섭회의 합의의사록, 제10-37차, 1963) (2/2)　13

Joint Committee, since the subject of the Agreed Minute was the provision of facilities. He pointed out that paragraph 1(a), Article "A", refers to the Joint Committee but provided a focal point in the SOFA for provisions regarding facilties.

5. Recapitualating the previous discussion of the navigational aids article, Mr. Habib said that the Korean side had originally agreed with the language of the U.S. draft, except for requesting that the article should explicitly provide for mutual consultation with regard to the installation of new facilities, specifically new facilities established outside existing areas and facilities. In an effort to satisfy the request of the Korean side, the U.S. side had drafted and tabled an Agreed Minute which provides for the establishment of new navigational aids outside of existing areas and facilities under the provisions of the pertinent article relating to facilities and areas which itself refers to the Joint Committee. He said that the U.S. draft thus provides a satisfactory answer to the question previously raised by the Korean side, while the Korean draft Agreed Minute goes beyond the position previously taken by the Korean side. He expressed the hope that the Korean side would reconsider the matter and accept the U.S. draft.

6. Mr. Whang asked whether the word "permanent" in the U.S. draft is meant to exclude arrangements between the two governments through the Joint Committee regarding the construction of temporary navigational aids from the

0168

provisions of the article. Mr. Habib replied that
under operational or exercise conditions, temporary
aids might be needed. He pointed out, however, that
the problem raised by the Korean side to which this
Agreed Minute addresses itself is that of the establishment
of permanent aids outside of existing facilities and
areas. Mr. Whang stated that the installation of permanent
aids would benefit not only the U.S. armed forces but
also the ROK nationals and those of third countries.
However, it appeared that temporary aids were not covered
by the Agreed Minute. Mr. Habib pointed out that they
were covered by the article itself, particularly by the
last two sentences of paragraph 2. The Agreed Minute
had been drafted to cover the specific problem raised by
the Korean side.

7. Mr. Whang reminded the negotiators that the
Korean side had originally suggested the insertion
of the phrase "through agreement between the appropriate
authorities of the two Governments" at the end of the
first sentence of paragraph 2. As a compromise to this
suggestion, he continued, the U.S. side tabled its draft
of the Agreed Minute providing inter alia that installation of navigational aids would be effected in
accordance with "the procedures established under
paragraph 1 of Article___" instead of through "agreement between
the appropriate authorities of the two Governments."
Since the U.S. side made it clear that the "Article"
referred to in its draft of the Agreed Minute meant the
first Article dealing with the facilities and areas, and

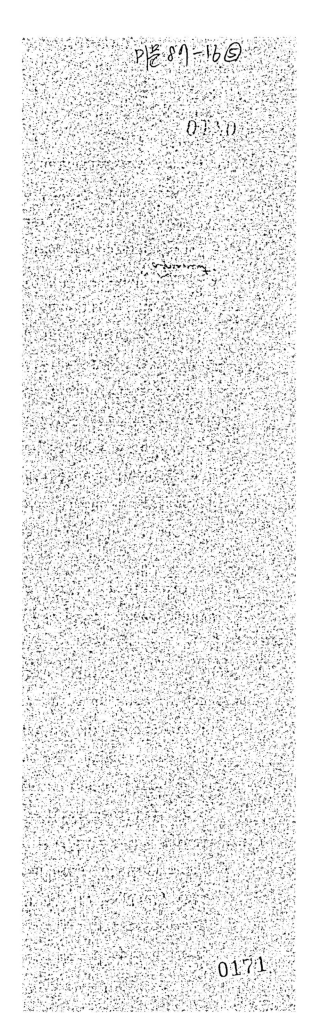

the phrase "the procedures established under paragraph 1 of Article ___" was considered to indicate that the installation of navigational aids would be effected in accordance with the agreements between the two Governments through the Joint Committee, the Korean side proposed, in its draft of the Agreed Minute, to use the phrase "arrangements between the two Governments through the Joint Committee". Mr. Whang stated that the Korean side would take the matter under further consideration. He again pointed out that the article on facilities and areas to which the U.S. draft Agreed Minute refers has not yet been agreed upon. He suggested that further discussion of this matter be deferred until agreement has been reached on the relevant paragraph of the facilities and areas article. Mr. Habib replied that if the Korean side so desired, the U.S. side had no objection. However, the U.S. side did not think it necessary to delay approval of the navigational aids article until agreement was reached on the facilities and areas article.

Foreign Exchange Controls

8. Turning to the article dealing with foreign exchange controls, Mr. Whang stated that Mr. Lee of the Ministry of Finance would present the position of the Korean side. Mr. Habib stated that Mr. Ford would explain the position of the U.S. side.

9. Mr. Ford tabled the U.S. draft of an Agreed Minute. He stated that the most pertinent point in

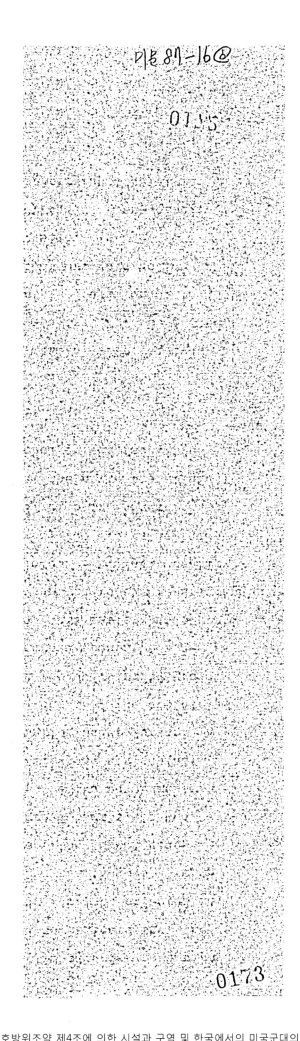

in the Agreed Minute was that the final sentence
incorporated language taken directly from the comprehensive aid agreement between the United States and the
Republic of Korea, which had been signed on February 8,
1961 and had gone into effect on February 28, 1961.
He pointed out that this agreement determines the rate
at which aid funds are converted from dollars to won.
He said that the two governments had been operating under
this agreement for two years and there had been no
difficulties whatsoever in its administration. He said
the language of this agreement was more specific and
much tighter than the corresponding language in the
Korean draft.

   10. Mr. Whang replied that the Korean side's
explanation at the previous meeting of the term "basic
rate of exchange" might have been misunderstood. He
asked the U.S. side to consider the Korean draft in that
light. Mr. Ford replied that Mr. Whang's explanation
illustrated the difficulty which lay in the Korean draft.
He pointed out that the buying rate and the selling
rate are two different rates and that one is higher
than the other.   He then asked which was the basic rate?

   11. Mr. Lee replied that, as Mr. Ford had pointed
out, the buying and selling rates are different. When
the buying rate is 129.50, the selling rate is 130.50,
but the basic rate is 130 to the dollar. Mr. Habib
stated that the point at issue was not the mechanics of
buying and selling foreign exchange ; what the
negotiators were interested in were the terms on which

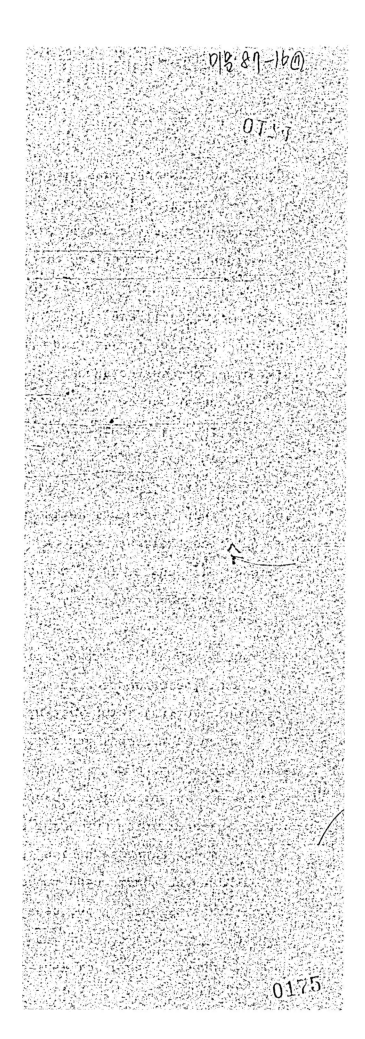

any transaction takes place, regardless of whether it is a purchase or a sale. He pointed out that the language of the U.S. draft was clear - it provided for the highest rate, either buying or selling, which was not unlawful. These are the terms under which other U.S. Government agencies do business in Korea and the U.S. side is unable to see why the U.S. armed forces should not operate under the same terms. The U.S. draft, Mr. Habib continued, is more relevant to the types of transactions which will be conducted under the SOFA. He said the U.S. side was prepared to hear any further comments which the Korean side might wish to make, but since the U.S. draft had just been tabled, the Korean side might desire to have time in which to consider it.

12. Mr. Lee pointed out that since Korean law provides for a unitary rate of exchange, the use of the term "highest rate" was not adequate. Mr. Habib replied that the U.S. draft took that into account by referring specifically to the "highest rate which is not unlawful". Mr. Whang said the Korean side would consider the U.S. draft for further discussion at a later date.

Military Payment Certificates

13. Each side table a draft of an article dealing with military payment certificates (MPC) and a few minutes were devoted to study of the drafts. Mr. Habib then explained the U.S. draft. He pointed out that the first sentence specifies that MPC may be used by

0176

authorized personnel for "internal transactions". He()]..()
said that no limitation of these transactions within
facilities and areas, such as had been included in the
Korean draft, had been put in the U.S. draft because
during field exercises and maneuvers outside the
designated facilities and areas, it may be desirable
to set up mobile and temporary post exchanges.
Furthermore, it might also prove desirable to establish
such facilities in tourist hotels or similar establish-
ments. In any event, he pointed out, inclusion of the
term "internal" limits the transactions to the extent
desired by both sides.

14. Mr. Habib continued his explanation of the U.S.
draft by pointing out that in paragraph 1(b) there is
contained the phrase "to the extent authorized by U.S.
law" which does not appear in the Korean draft. It was
included in the U.S. draft, he explained, because of
the U.S. Supreme Court decisions which affected the
jurisdiction of the U.S. armed forces over civilians.
In effect, he said, the U.S. draft stated that the U.S.
authorities will exercise the authority which they
possess. He then asked the Korean side to explain its
draft, including the Agreed Minute.

15. Mr. Lee stated that the Agreed Minute had been
included in order to provide for a way in which to
dispose of the MPC in custody of the ROK Government at
the time the SOFA comes into force. Mr. Habib remarked
that disposition of MPC held by the ROK Government had
been the subject of discussions between the two governments

0177

in the past. He pointed out that there was a very simple
the Korean Government solves it problem; Just use to pick up the MPC in a bundle and
way in which return it to the U.S. authorities the next
day. Mr. Habib then asked if the same motive lay behind
the inclusion in paragraph 1(d) of the Korean draft of
the phrase "after the date of coming into force of this
Agreement". Mr. Lee replied in the affirmative.
Mr. Habib suggested that the points just discussed
appeared to be the only points of difference in the two
drafts. He suggested that the drafts be studied by
both sides and discussed at the next meeting. The
Korean side agreed.

Facilities and Areas
16. Turning to the drafts of the facilities and
areas articles, Mr. Whang stated that the phrase "as
provided for in this Agreement" had been included in
paragraph 1 of the Korean draft because of the Korean
desire to have the Agreement provide for compensation
for use of privately-owned facilities and areas. He
said that the positions of both sides on the question
of compensation had previously been made clear and that
the Korean side felt the retention of this phrase to be
necessary. He also pointed to the use of the phrase
"wherever located" in the U.S. draft in contrast to the
use of the phrase "necessary to" in the Korean draft.
Since there was no intention on the part of the Korean
side to limit the extent of the furnishings, equipment
and fixtures, he believed that the phrase "necessary to"
really meant the same thing as "wherever located".

0179

17. In reply, Mr. Habib stated that in regard to Mr. Whang's first point, the U.S. side desired exclusion of the phrase "as provided for in this Agreement" for the same reason that the Korean side desired its inclusion. The U.S. side has made clear, he continued, that payment of compensation is not envisaged in the U.S. draft of the Agreement. In previous discussion of this point, Mr. Chin had stated that the Korean side was well aware of the U.S. position. Mr. Chin had pointed out that the Korean position was based not on legality but on the desire of the Korean Government for strengthening the friendly ties existing with the United States Government.

18. Mr. Habib stated that a Status of Force Agreement has one major purpose: that is to set out the conditions under which the armed forces of one nation are permitted to be on the territory of another nation. It sets out the respective rights, duties, obligations, privileges and immunities and other guarantees and undertakings of the respective governments and the personnel involved. It is devoted to the subject of stationing of forces. It has been the consistent policy of the U.S. Government, he continued, that facilities and areas made available to U.S. forces for mutual defense should be furnished to the United States without cost. The U.S. Government has adhered to this policy in all of its mutual defense negotiations on the agreed assumption that areas and facilities made available for use by

0181

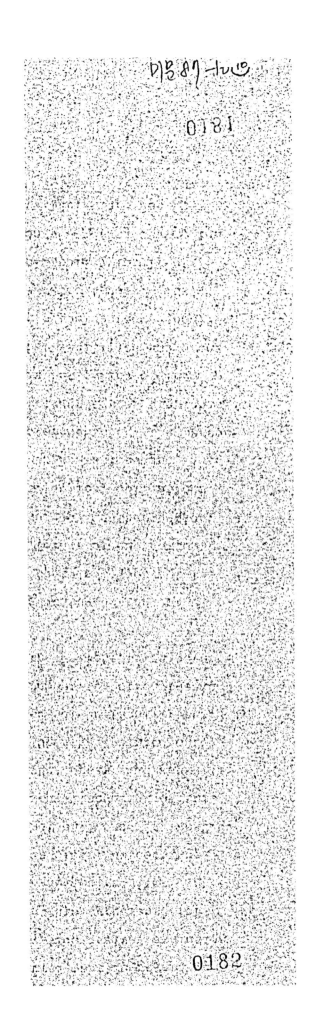

U.S. forces constitute one of the host country's constributions to mutual security. The U.S. side continues to hold that view, Mr. Habib concluded.

19. Mr. Whang replied that the Korean side was fully aware of the U.S. position. Mr. Chin had said that the request for compensation was based more on the desire for promotion of friendly ties than on legality, Mr. Whang reiterated that there had been no change in the Korean position.

20. Mr. Habib asked how the payment of compensation would fulfill the function of promoting friendly ties in any way that all the other existing U.S. programs in Korea do not. He said the SOFA is not intended to be a vehicle for making financial contributions. It has a specific purpose and we should concentrate on that purpose. In all previous discussion of this point, he continued, the U.S. side had made it clear, and will continue to make it clear, that payment of compensation is outside the scope of this SOFA. It was then agreed to defer any further discussion of this subject until consideration was again given to draft article "B".

21. Turning to paragraph 3 of the Korean draft, Mr. Whang recalled that the U.S. side had expressed the opinion that the phrase "for the purpose of this Agreement" was redundant since it is followed by the phrase "under this Agreement". He said the Korean side agreed and that the phrase "for the purpose of this Agreement" may be stricken from the Korean draft while retaining the phrase "under this Agreement". He asked for any further comment

한·미국 간의 상호방위조약 제4조에 의한 시설과 구역 및 한국에서의 미국군대의 지위에 관한 협정(SOFA)
전59권. 1966.7.9 서울에서 서명 : 1967.2.9 발효(조약 232호) (V.50 실무교섭회의 합의의사록, 제10-37차, 1963) (2/2)   29

by the U.S. side. Mr. Habib stated that the language of the corresponding paragraph in the U.S. draft (paragraph 1(b)) was more specific in its reference to the preceding paragraph. He also questioned the necessity for the phrase "shall be surveyed and determined" in the Korean draft. He pointed out that survey documents are already in existence and will be used by the Joint Committee. Furthermore, an extensive joint survey was carried out with the Ministry of National Defense in 1962. He expressed the opinion that the language of this paragraph should establish the principle set forth in the first sentence of both drafts, namely that the facilities and areas granted to the United States under the SOFA should be those in use at the time of entry into force of the Agreement. He suggested that once having established the principle, the negotiators should leave the bookkeeping to the Joint Committee.

22. Continuing the discussion of Paragraph 3 of the Korea draft, Mr. Whang replied that the Korea side wished to make a clear record of all facilities and areas in use. In some cases, he said, no survey had been made when the facility was originally made available. The survey could be made by the Joint Committee but the purpose of this language was to give guidance to the Joint Committee. Mr. Habib replied that this was taken care of by the next paragraph. He then stated that the U.S. side wished to substitute the word "agreements" for the word "arrangements" in paragraph 2 of the U.S. draft. He expressed the opinion that the wording of the U.S. paragraph

한·미국 간의 상호방위조약 제4조에 의한 시설과 구역 및 한국에서의 미국군대의 지위에 관한 협정(SOFA)
전59권. 1966.7.9 서울에서 서명 : 1967.2.9 발효(조약 232호) (V.50 실무교섭회의 합의의사록, 제10-37차, 1963) (2/2)

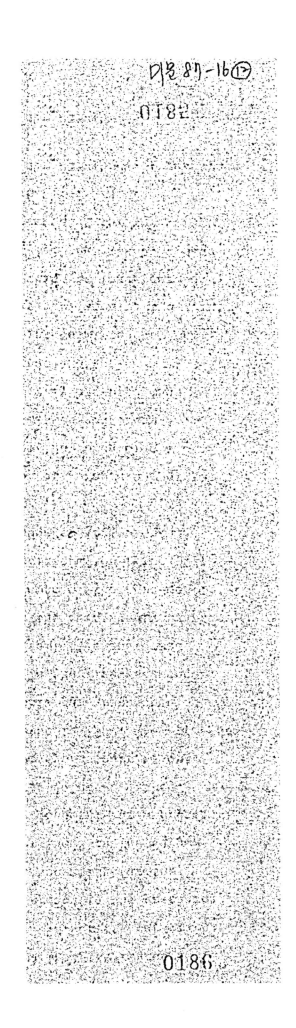

was preferable to that of the comparable paragraph in the Korean draft (paragraph 6.). He pointed out that paragraph sets out the guidelines for the Joint Committee. *The Joint* article itself says clearly that the Joint Committee shall be the means for consultation between the two governments. Obviously, he said, this had special reference to the entire question of facilities and areas. He reminded the Korean side that the U.S. side had deleted even more specific language from the draft of the Joint Committee article at the request of the Korean side. He said the Joint Committee may decide that it is not necessary to survey all of the facilities and areas. However, the U.S. side is prepared to have the Joint Committee review all of the facilities in order to determine the necessity for such a survey.

23. Mr. Whang stated that the Korean side would consider the position set forth by the U.S. side. Mr. Habib remarked that the two sides appeared to agree on the substance but not on the wording of this paragraph. Mr. Whang suggested that in addition to changing "arrangements" to "agreements" the phrase "referred to in paragraph 1" be added. Mr. Habib pointed out that the additional phrase was unnecessary because the phrase "such agreements" referred to the agreements mentioned in the previous paragraph. He added that the phrase "or portions thereof" in the U.S. draft was intended to facilitate the return of portions of a facility if the return of the entire facility was not feasible or possible. The U.S. side believed this phrase to be a useful addition to the paragraph. Mr. Whang agreed to this addition of the phrase

한·미국 간의 상호방위조약 제4조에 의한 시설과 구역 및 한국에서의 미국군대의 지위에 관한 협정(SOFA) 전59권. 1966.7.9 서울에서 서명 : 1967.2.9 발효(조약 232호) (V.50 실무교섭회의 합의의사록, 제10-37차, 1963) (2/2) 33

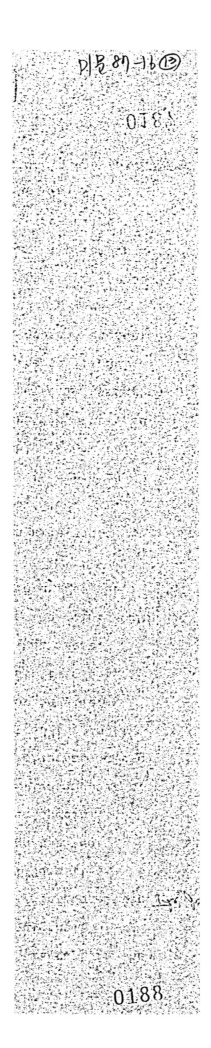

and accepted the text of the U.S. draft of paragraph 2.

24. Turning to paragraph 3 of the U.S. draft and paragraph 7 of the Korean draft, Mr. Whang referred to the use of the word "promptly" in the Korean draft and said that since the U.S. forces were prepared to return facilities promptly, the U.S. side should not object to the inclusion of this word in the text of the article. Mr. Habib replied that the U.S. draft took care of this, inasmuch as the phrase "under such conditions as may be agreed through the Joint Committee" was all-inclusive. He pointed out that the phraseology of the U.S. draft was responsive to the requirements of the ROK Government. He said that "promptly" requires interpretation and judgment, whereas the U.S. language was very specific and not subject to varying interpretation. Mr. Whang replied that with the understanding that the language of the U.S. draft was all-inclusive, the Korean side accepted the text of paragraph 3 of the U.S. draft.

25. Turning to paragraph 4 of the U.S. draft and paragraph 8 of the Korean draft, Mr. Whang asked for clarification of the meaning of the phrase "and the Government of the Republic of Korea is so advised." in the U.S. draft. Mr. Habib replied that quite simply the phrase was intended to avoid debate on the question of the exact timing of making facilities available to the ROK Government. He said it was intended to be a facilitating phrase and had no other meaning. It placed on the U.S. Government an obligation to establish a precise date for making the facilities available.

26. Mr. Whang said he understood the explanation and then asked what the implication was of the word "harmful". Mr. Habib replied that "harmful" was intended to mean the temporary use of a facility by Korean nationals in such a manner as to damage the facility or render it unusable at a later date by the U.S. armed forces. For instance, he said, if the temporary Korean users of a facility tore down buildings which were needed for later use by the U.S. armed forces, that would be "harmful" use of the facility and would be prohibited by the terms of this paragraph. Mr. Whang agreed and stated that the Korean side accepted the text of paragraph 4(a) and (b) of the U.S. draft.

27. At this point, it was decided to adjourn the meeting. The next meeting was scheduled for March 19 at 2:00 p.m..

28. Points of Agreements:

Facilities and Areas Article A. Par. 2, 3 and 4.

한·미국 간의 상호방위조약 제4조에 의한 시설과 구역 및 한국에서의 미국군대의 지위에 관한 협정(SOFA)
전59권. 1966.7.9 서울에서 서명 : 1967.2.9 발효(조약 232호) (V.50 실무교섭회의 합의의사록, 제10-37차, 1963) (2/2)   37

주한미군지위협정(SOFA) 서명 및 발효 20

March 19, 1963

I. Time and Place : 2:00 to 4:35 p.m. March 19, 1963
at the Foreign Minister's
Conference Room.

II. Attendants:

ROK Side:

Mr. Whang, Ho Eul   Director
Bureau of Political Affairs
Ministry of Foreign Affairs

Mr. Shin Kwan Sup   Director
Bureau of Costums Duty
Ministry of Finance

Mr. Koo, Choong Whay   Chief, America Section
Ministry of Foreign Affairs

Col. Lee, Nam Koo   Chief, Military Affairs Section
Ministry of National Defense

Mr. Lee, Jae Sul   Chief of the Foreign Exchange
Division,
Ministry of Finance

Mr. Lee, Kyung Hoon   2nd Secretary
Ministry of Foreign Affairs

Mr. Kang, Suk Jae   3rd Secretary
Ministry of Foreign Affairs

Mr. Kim, Yoon Taik   3rd Secretary
Ministry of Foreign Affairs

US Side:

Mr. William J. Ford   First Secretary of the
Embassy

Col. G.G. O'Connor   Deputy Chief of Staff
8th Army

Capt. R.H. Brownlie   Assistant Chief of Staff
USN/K

한·미국 간의 상호방위조약 제4조에 의한 시설과 구역 및 한국에서의 미국군대의 지위에 관한 협정(SOFA)
전59권. 1966.7.9 서울에서 서명 : 1967.2.9 발효(조약 232호) (V.50 실무교섭회의 합의의사록, 제10-37차, 1963) (2/2)   39

Col. W.A. Solf	Staff Judge Advocate 0100
	8th Army
Mr. Benjamin A. Fleck (Rapporteur and Press Officer)	First Secretary of the Embassy
Mr. Robert A. Lewis	Second Secretary and Consul of the Embassy
Lt. Col. R.E. Miller	Staff Officer, JAG 8th Army
Lt. Col. V.A. Burt	J-5
Kenneth Campen	Interpreter

Foreign Exchange Controls

1. Mr. Whang opened the meeting by reminding the negotiators that discussion had been completed on the text of the article dealing with foreign exchange controls. He stated that there were still two unresolved points in regard to the Agreed Minute, however. The first of these was the difference between the wording "including those activities provided in Article ___" in the U.S. draft and the wording "by those organizations provided in Article ___" in the Korean draft. The second was the difference between "the highest rate in terms of the number of Korean Won per United States Dollar which, at the time the conversion is made, is not unlawful in the Republic of Korea" in the U.S. draft and "the basic rate of exchange" in the Korean draft.

2. With regard to the first point, Mr. Whang stated that no agreement had yet been reached with regard to the use of "activities", as proposed by the U.S. side, or "organizations" as proposed by the Korean side.

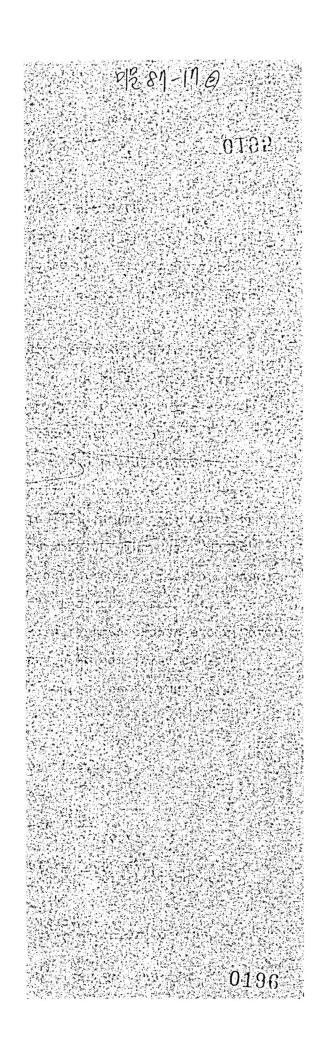

0140

He said this point would be settled when final agreement was reached on the text of the customs article.
He suggested, therefore, that the negotiators withhold
discussion on this matter until that time. Mr. Ford
agreed and pointed out that the reference to "activities
provided in Article ___" was a reference to the non-
appropriated fund activities article, which had not yet
been tabled.

3. Mr. Whang said Mr. Lee Chae Sul would explain the
position of the Korean side in regard to the second
point. Mr. Lee said that he wished to point out that
the Korean Foreign Exchange Law was first passed on
November 30, 1961. At the previous meeting, he recalled,
Mr. Ford had said the U.S. side would like to have the
rate spelled out in language similar to that of Article
6 (c) of the Comprehensive Aid Agreement (The Agreement
on Economic Cooperation, signed at Seoul on February 8,
1961). However, he said, the situation has changed
since the Aid Agreement was entered into. The Republic
of Korea now has a unitary rate of exchange. The Korean
side suggested amendment of its draft to read "effective
official rate of exchange".

4. Mr. Ford replied that the unitary exchange rate
had been adopted by the ROK government on February 1,
1961. On January 1, 1961, the official rate moved
from 650 hwan (650 won) to the dollar to 1000 hwan
(100 won) to the dollar. When the unitary rate became
effective on February 2, the rate was set at 1300 hwan
(130 won) to the dollar. This was part of a package

한·미국 간의 상호방위조약 제4조에 의한 시설과 구역 및 한국에서의 미국군대의 지위에 관한 협정(SOFA)
전59권. 1966.7.9 서울에서 서명 : 1967.2.9 발효(조약 232호) (V.50 실무교섭회의 합의의사록, 제10-37차, 1963) (2/2)   43

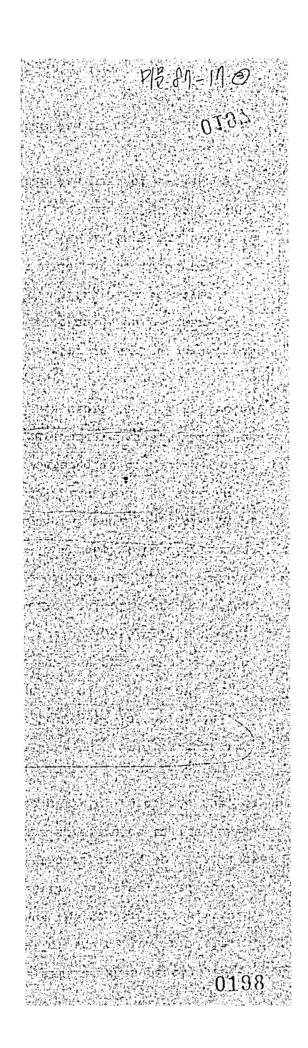

designed to stabilize the Korean economy. Another 0.00 element of the stabilization program was the conclusion of the Agreement on Economic Cooperation, commonly known as the Comprehensive Aid Agreement. This was a government to government agreement, signed by the Foreign Minister and the Ambassador. One element of the agreement was the rate at which United States dollars would be convertible into hwan. The wording of this provision had been given very careful attention by both sides and had been agreed upon. It is clear, unambiguous, and not subject to misinterpretation. There can be no dispute regarding its meaning. This provision, Mr. Ford continued, has worked very well in the context of the unitary rate system. It is difficult to understand why it should now be changed. Not a single question regarding it has been raised in over two years. If the language is changed now, he pointed out, a situation might arise in which one agency of the U.S. Government would be purchasing won at one rate while another agency would be purchasing won at a different rate. If the language had proved unsatisfactory to the ROKG, Mr. Ford suggested, the first step would have been to seek an amendment to the aid agreement rather than to put revised language into the SOFA. The U.S. side, he continued, does not understand the reason why the language should be changed. He asked the Korean side to reconsider its position, so that both the aid agreement and the SOFA might contain standard language.

한·미국 간의 상호방위조약 제4조에 의한 시설과 구역 및 한국에서의 미국군대의 지위에 관한 협정(SOFA)
전59권. 1966.7.9 서울에서 서명 : 1967.2.9 발효(조약 232호) (V.50 실무교섭회의 합의의사록, 제10-37차, 1963) (2/2)

45

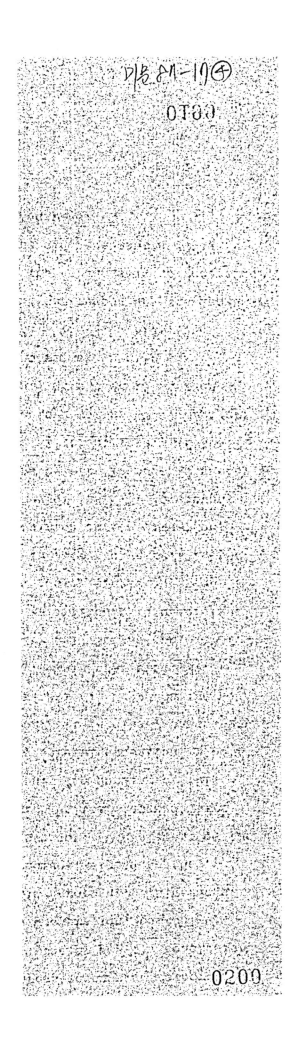

5.   In reply, Mr. Lee Chae Sul stated that it was
true that the unitary exchange rate had been adopted
in February, 1961 and set at 1300 hwan (130 won) to
the dollar. He pointed out that at the time the
Comprehensive Aid Agreement was signed there had been
no foreign exchange regulations setting the unitary
rate, which at that time was decided through mutual
consultation. Such a regulation was adopted on December
30, 1961. Therefore, the situation was now different,
because of the existence of the regulation. Mr. Ford
had asked why the wording of the aid agreement should be
changed. The wording of the U.S. draft, Mr. Lee stated,
would create the misunderstanding among the Korean
people that there is more than one rate. If there had
been an exchange regulation in existence at the time
the aid agreement was negotiated, the language of the
aid agreement would have been different, he said. He
then suggested adoption of the phrase "effective official
exchange rate". He asked the U.S. aide to reconsider
its position so as not to confuse the Korean people.

6.   Mr. Ford pointed out that the fact that the
ROKG was adopting a unitary rate was well known at the
time the Comprehensive Aid Agreement was negotiated.
Mr. Ford said that althought Mr. Lee had said that the
exchange regulations came into effect in December, 1961,
it must be assumed that these regulations were written
to be in conformity with the inter-governmental agreement
which the ROKG had entered into only a few months
previously. This assumption is strengthened by the fact

0201

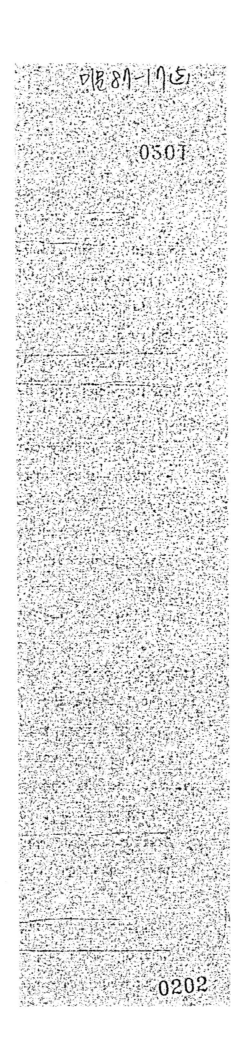

6

0307

that there has been no complaint during the more than
two years in which the aid agreement has been in effect.
There thus appears to be no conflict between the aid
agreement and the ROKG regulations. Mr. Ford stated
that Mr. Lee had alleged that there might be misunderstanding regarding the language of the U.S. draft agreed
Minute. It is clear, Mr. Ford said, that there has been
no such misunderstanding during the past two years.
The language has stood the test of time, Mr. Ford
continued, and this is not the point at which to shift
to new wording. The wording proposed by Mr. Lee was
open to misunderstanding because the word "effective" in
the phrase "effective official exchange rate" implies the
existence of more than one rate.

Mr. Lee replied that it appeared that misunderstanding
would arise if either the original Korean wording or the
original U.S. wording were accepted. The ROK proposal
of "effective official exchange rate" was intended to
mean the legal rate. There could, therefore, be no
misunderstanding regarding the language.

8. Mr. Ford reiterated that there has been no
misunderstanding regarding the meaning of the language
of the Comprehensive Aid Agreement. In the light of two
years of experience with this language, it would be a
mistake to abandon it now. Mr. Ford pointed out that an
intolerable situation would arise if one U.S. Government
agency should buy at one rate while another agency was
buying at a different rate. Standard language in both
the aid agreement and the SOFA would avoid the possibility

0203

한·미국 간의 상호방위조약 제4조에 의한 시설과 구역 및 한국에서의 미국군대의 지위에 관한 협정(SOFA)
전59권. 1966.7.9 서울에서 서명 : 1967.2.9 발효(조약 232호) (V.50 실무교섭회의 합의의사록, 제10-37차, 1963) (2/2)

49

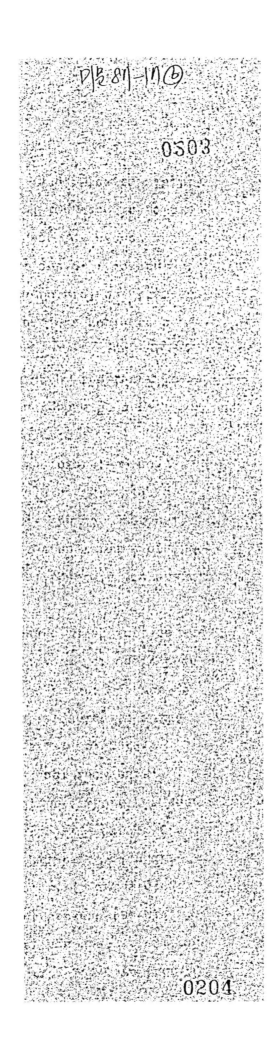

7

0301

of such a situation developing. Mr. Ford said he knew of no conflict between the two, but if such conflict did exist, he assumed that it would be resolved in favor of the treaty. However, the fact that there has been no disagreement in two years indicates that no conflict, in fact, exists.

9. Mr. Whang said that Mr. Ford was assuming that one agency could convert at one rate and another agency at a different rate. However, he said, there is a foreign exchange law and a unitary rate in effect. Therefore, the situation envisioned by Mr. Ford could not arise. Mr. Whang expressed the opinion that the substance of both sides' drafts was the same; only the language differed. Both drafts referred to the rate which is now 130 won to the dollar. The Korean language was intended to avoid any misunderstanding that there was a multiple rate. He suggested that inasmuch as the foregoing discussion would appear in the summary record, there could be no misunderstanding of the positions of two sides. He urged the U.S. side to consider and accept the Korean proposal.

10. Mr. Ford replied that the Comprehensive Aid Agreement had taken fully into account the existence of a unitary rate of exchange. He said if the Korean proposal were adopted, we would have a situation of two agreements made within two years of each other, containing differing language. He asked the negotiators to consider the possibility of future difficulties arising out of such a situation. He said the language of the

0205

aid agreement had served well and the U.S. side urged
that it be used in the SOFA also. Mr. Whang remarked
that discussion of this article had consumed too much
time. He suggested that Mr. Ford and Mr. Lee discuss
this question privately and report at the next meeting.

Military Payment Certificates

11. Turning to the draft article regarding military
payment certificates, Mr. Whang stated that the Korean
side assumed that "persons authorized by the United
States" to use MPC are persons authorized to do so by
U.S. law. He asked for identification of such persons.
Mr. Ford replied that these are persons authorized to
use MPC by U.S. armed forces regulations. Mr. Whang
asked if there were any persons included in addition to
members of the armed forces, the civilian component,
and their dependents. Mr. Ford replied that in addition
to the types of persons listed by Mr. Whang there were
U.S. Government officials, invited contractors and the
dependents of both. These were merely illustrative
examples, he said, and not all-inclusive.

12. Mr. Lee Chae Sul pointed out that the phrase
"within the facilities and areas in use by the United
States forces" in the Korean draft was not included
in the U.S. draft. He expressed the opinion that if
this phrase were omitted, both sides would be confronted
by difficulties, since the scope of MPC transactions
would not be defined. On the other hand, if such a
restriction were established, the U.S. personnel would
be inconvenienced. The Korean side believed that the

0207

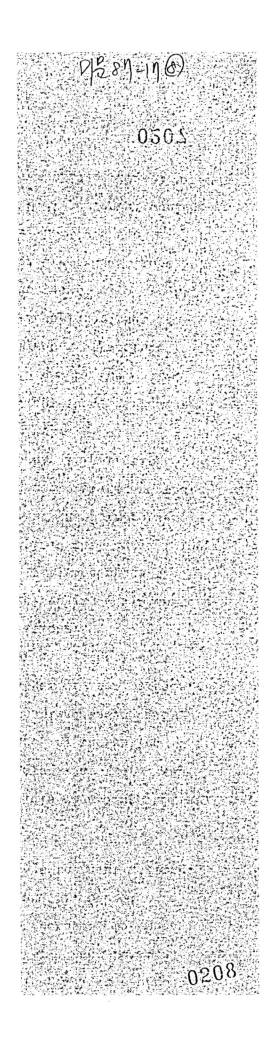

use of MPC must be made available during exercises and maneuvers and also in hotels and tourist attractions. Therefore, he continued, it is desirable to find some way in which to authorize the use of MPC in certain areas outside established areas and facilities through mutual agreement. Since the phrase in question had been omitted from the U.S. draft, the U.S. side must have given prior consideration to this problem. The Korean side, he said, would like to hear the views of the U.S. side.

13. Mr. Ford replied that the governing phrase in the U.S. draft is the phrase "for internal transactions". As Mr. Habib had pointed out during a previous meeting, the temporary use of MPC outside of areas and facilities was desirable as a factor in maintaining the morale of the troops. In regard to preventing abuse, Mr. Ford referred to the second sentence of paragraph 1 (a) of the U.S. draft, which provides that "The Government of the United States will take appropriate action to insure that authorized personnel are prohibited from engaging in transactions involving military payment certificates except as authorized by United States regulations". He also referred to the next sentence, which lays certain obligations upon the ROK Government. The U.S. side, he concluded, believes that the controls provided for in these two sentences are sufficient to prevent any significant abuse of MPC utilization outside of established areas and facilities. When special problems arise, he added, they can be discussed by the Joint Committee.

0209

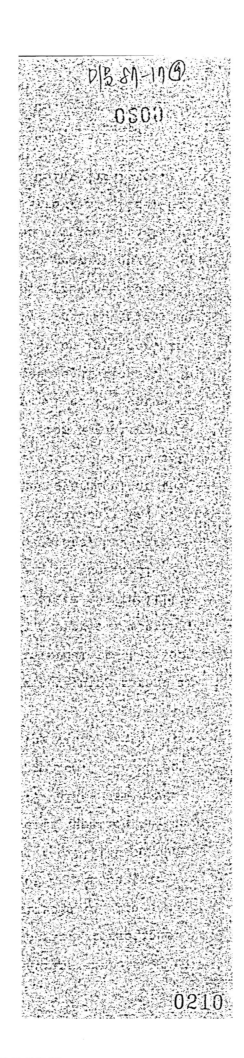

10

14. Mr. Lee replied that Korean law also prohibits unauthorized use of MPC by Koreans. However, even now, before agreement on the use of MPC, the U.S. authorities have placed limitations on the amount of Won Sold to MPC holders. Furthermore, there are quite a few existing facilities where there is no provision for the official sale of won to authorized holders of MPC. The Korean side, he said, feared that the continued existence of such restrictions would cause difficulties. Although the U.S. draft provides for appropriate action to prevent abuse, the Korean side desired clarification of how such abuse was to be prevented, at the same time providing for convenient facilities for the exchange of won.

15. In reply, Colonel Solf stated that the U.S. armed forces would continue to take all appropriate administrative, disciplinary, and penal measures against those persons under their control and jurisdiction to prevent the illegal use of MPC. He added that the U.S. side expected the ROK Government to do the same. Mr. Whang stated that the Korean side did not wish to inconvenience the U.S. armed forces by limiting use of MPC to existing areas and facilities. However, the Korean side believed that some agreed procedures should be worked out for establishing MPC facilities at places such as tourist hotels so that the troops would not be inconvenienced. In this respect, he asked whether the U.S. side had any specific plans as to when and where such MPC facilities are to be established. Colonel Solf replied that the U.S. armed forces had no specific proposals in mind at this time. It is recognized, however,

0211

한·미국 간의 상호방위조약 제4조에 의한 시설과 구역 및 한국에서의 미국군대의 지위에 관한 협정(SOFA)
전59권. 1966.7.9 서울에서 서명 : 1967.2.9 발효(조약 232호) (V.50 실무교섭회의 합의의사록, 제10-37차, 1963) (2/2)   57

that at some future time it may be considered to be
mutually advantageous to establish such facilities at
locations to be mutually agreed to. The U.S. language
is intended to provide the necessary flexibility for
making such arrangements. The U.S. side agreed, of
course, that any procedures of the kind proposed by the
Korean side would have to be mutually acceptable.

16. Turning to paragraph 1(b) of the U.S. draft,
Mr. Whang asked for clarification of the remarks made
by Mr. Habib at a previous meeting regarding the phrase
"to the extent authorized by United States law".
Colonel Solf explained that, in a series of decisions
affecting the jurisdiction of courst-martial, the United
States Supreme Court had held that in time of peace
civilians accused of crimes against the United States are
liable solely to the jurisdiction of United States
civil courts.

17. Mr. Whang asked what court had jurisdiction
over such categories of persons as invited contractors
or third-country nationals. In reply, Colonel Solf
stated that U.S. citizens could be tried in U.S. civil
courts. He pointed out that while the U.S. armed forces
might not have court-martial jurisdiction over such
persons, they still retained all administrative jurisdiction,
including discharge, deprivation of access to facilities,
and deprivation of privileges. Mr. Whang asked specifically if invited contractors would be subject to trial
by court-martial. Colonel Solf replied that if they
are civilians, they are not subject to trial by court-
martial during time of peace. Mr. Whang stated that it

0213

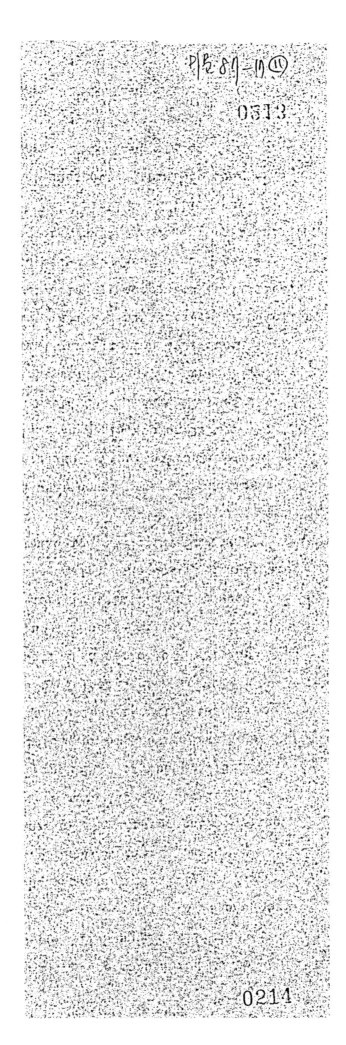

appeared that there would be people authorized to use
MPC who would not be liable to trial or punishment if
they abused this privilege. Colonel Solf replied that
the administrative sanctions at the disposal of the U.S.
armed forces were quite effective in dealing with such
abuses. He pointed out that the U.S. armed forces would
retain administrative control over all such persons.

18. Mr. Whang then referred to the phrase in paragraph 1 (d) of the Korean draft which would state no
obligation will be due to the Government of the Republic
of Korea "after the date of coming into force of this
agreement". He said that this phrase had been inserted
in the Korean draft in order to obtain payment for the
amount of MPC currently in the custody of the ROK Government.

19. Mr. Ford replied that the redemption of this
MPC impossible. He stated that there is no way in which
the ROK Government can receive payment for MPC held by
it. He pointed out that the wording of Paragraph 1(d)
of the ROK draft provides specifically that there would
be no obligation to the ROK Government after the SOFA
goes into effect; why then should there be any obligation
before it goes into effect? Mr. Lee Chae Sul replied
that a different situation exists in Korea than in any
other country. He pointed out that the U.S. armed forces
have been present in Korea since 1945 and that during
this period a huge amount of MPC had been accumulated by
the ROK Government. He said the ROK Government was
anxious to dispose of this accumulation but that it
felt a moral obligation to the Korean people who had

0215

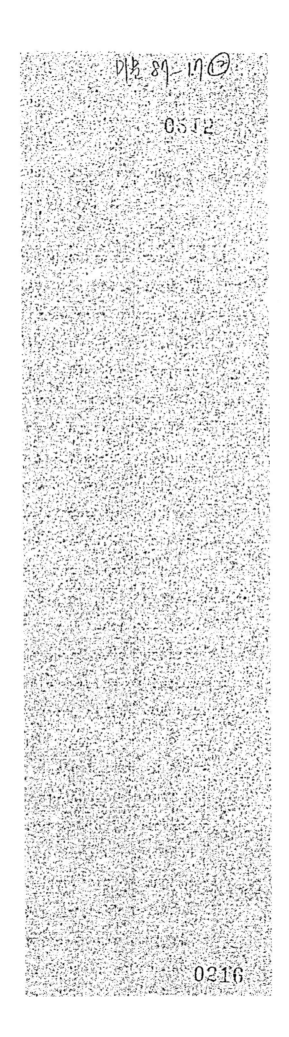

earned it through sales or services to Americans. The thousands of Korean who had turned in the MPC should be reimbursed; otherwise they would be placed in the position of having rendered goods and services to the U.S. armed forces without compensation.

20. At this point, Mr. Ford read into the record the following statement:

"a. Military Payment Certificates are issued by the United States Government solely for internal use in United States military areas and facilities and such other places as may be agreed. MPC are issued for the use of persons authorized by the United States and such use is subject to the specific regulations of the United States Government.

"b. MPC are the property of the United States Government. MPC are not a currency of the United States and do not constitute a valid claim against the United States Government for redemption when in the possession of unauthorized holders.

"c. MPC are not convertible into dollars or instruments, except by authorized holders in circumstances specified in United States Government regulations.

"d. MPC may be held temporarily in the possession of unauthorized persons or agencies in the following cases:

"1. Pending the return to an authorized person who was illegally deprived of possession of the MPC through loss or theft;

"2. During the time necessary for a law enforcement agency to hold the MPC in its possession for use in judicial proceedings;

"3. During the time necessary for a law enforcement agency to process seized MPC for return to the appropriate United States authority.

"e. Authorized holders of MPC may use them only in internal transactions to purchase approved goods and services from U.S. authorized sources, and such authorized holders may not use them for the purchase of goods and services except as I have indicated.

0217

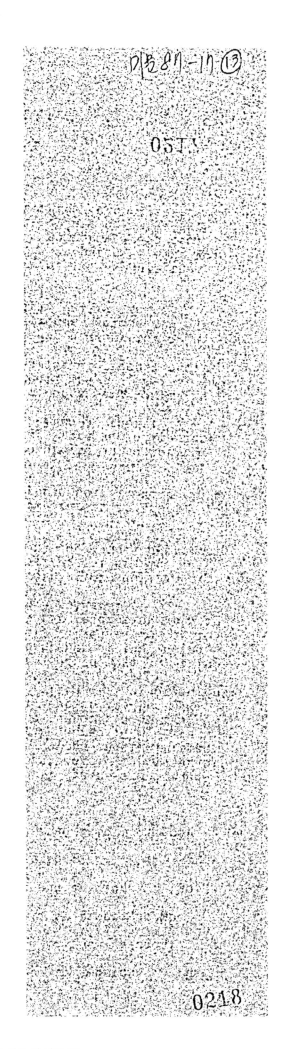

"f. Since MPC are issued by the United States Government for use by authorized persins for specific purposes, the use of MPC by unauthorized persons or for unauthorized purposes is not recognized by the United States Government.

"f. The MPC in the possession of any Korean Government agency should therefore be returned to the appropriate United States authorities. The Embassy has for some time been requesting the Korean Government to return the MPC confiscated by Korean law-enforcement agencies.

"h. In view of the special character of MPC and the fact that these requests have been made for their return, we do not consider this matter a subject for discussion in the context of these negotiations.

21. Turning to paragraph 2 of both drafts, Mr. Whang stated that since there did not appear to be any difference in language, the Korean side accepted the text of paragraph 2 of the U.S. draft. He pointed out that in the Korean draft, there appeared an additional sentence (as subparagraph (c)), which referred to the preceding sentences. Mr. Ford voiced the opinion that the sentence was unnecessary, inasmuch as mutual obligations on both governments appear in the text of paragraph 1. Mr. Whang replied that the sentence had been intended to refer only to paragraph 2. Mr. Ford said that the U.S. side believed such a reference to be unnecessary, since it was implicit in the text of paragraph 2 that the U.S. Government would take whatever measures were necessary to ensure the implementation of the provisions of the pragraph. Mr. Whang stated that with that understanding, the Korean side withdrew the proposed subparagraph (c).

14

22. Mr. Ford said that he wished to state for the record that nothing in the Foreign Exchange Controls Article or in the Military Payment Certificate Article is intended to preclude future discussions between the ROK and U.S. Governments concerning the possibility of the future substitution of U.S. coins or currency for MPC, should it appear desirable and feasible. Mr. Ford said he wished to make it clear, however, that no such discussions are presently contemplated.

23. Mr. Whang reminded the negotiators that the ROK side had proposed an Agreed Minute to the MPC Article, providing for disposal of MPC in the custody of the ROK Government at the time of entry into force of the SOFA, in accordance with mutually agreed upon procedures. Mr. Ford said the U.S. side thought that it had been agreed during the discussion just held that inasmuch as matter was currently being handled in other channels it was outside the scope of the SOFA negotiations. Mr. Whang suggested that the both sides discuss further this matter at the next meeting.

Definitions

24. Turning to the Definitions Article, Mr. Ford reminded the negotiators that they were very close to final agreement. With regard to the language of the proposed Agreement Minute /1 referring to subparagraph (a), Mr. Ford stated that the U.S. side was prepared to agree to the latest Korean proposal. However, the U.S. side now questioned the need for the Agreed Minute and proposed that the language of the subparagraph itself

be changed instead. Mr. Ford proposed that the Agreed
Minute be deleted and that subparagraph (a) be altered
by deleting the language following the words "except
for" and inserting in its place the following language:
"personnel of the U.S. armed forces attached to the U.S.
Embassy and personnel for whom status has been provided
in the Military Advisory Group Agreement of January 26,
1950, as amended". Mr. Whang said the Korean side
agreed to this change and noted that full agreement had
been reached on the text of the Definitions Article.

25. It was agreed to hold the next meeting on
March 29, at 2 p.m.

26. Points of agreement:
    Definitions Article (as revised).

외교-17(16)

0553

0221

0030

March 29, 1963

1. Time and Place: 2:00 to 3:40 p.m. March 29, 1963
                     at the Foreign Minister's
                     Conference Room

II. Attendants:

   ROK Side:

   Mr. Whang, Ho Eul   Director
                              Bureau of Political Affairs
                              Ministry of Foreign Affairs

   Mr. Koo, Choong Whay   Chief, America Section
                              Ministry of Foreign Affairs

   Col. Lee, Nam Koo   Chief, Military Affairs Section
                              Ministry of National Defense

   Mr. Chu, Mun Ki   Chief, Legal Affairs Section
                              Ministry of Justice

   Mr. Park, Bong Jin   Chief of the Customs Section
                              Ministry of Finance

   Mr. Kee, Kyung Hoon   2nd Secretary
                              Ministry of Foreign Affairs

   Mr. Kang, Suk Jae   3rd Secretary
                              Ministry of Foreign Affairs

   Mr. Kim, Yoon Taik   3rd Secretary
                              Ministry of Foreign Affairs

   U.S. Side:

   Brig. Gen. J. D. Lawlor   Deputy Chief of Staff
                              8th Army

   Mr. William J. Ford   First Secretary of the
                              Embassy

   Capt. R.H. Brownlie   Assistant Chief of Staff
                              USN/K

   Col. W. A. Solf   Staff Judge Advocate
                              8th Army

   Mr. Banjamin A. Fleck   First Secretary of the
     (Rapporteur and   Embassy
      Press Officer)

   Mr. Robert A. Lewis   Second Secretary and Consul
                              of the Embassy

0225

```
Lt. Col. R. E. Miller          Staff Officer, JAG
                               8th Army
Lt. Col. W. A. Buft            J-5
```

Military Post Offices

1. Mr. Lewis began the substantive discussion by
tabling the U.S. draft of the article dealing with
Military Post Offices. He stated that a military post
office is numerically designated as a branch of a
United States Post Office and is activated, manned, and
operated by military authorities to provide postal
services to authorized organizations and personnel. He
pointed out that the U.S. draft article provides for
the establishment and operation of military post offices
in Korea, for the transmission of mail between these
facilities and other U.S. post offices, and for the
furnishing of related financial services. Following
Mr. Lewis' opening remarks, the Korean side tabled its
draft of this article.

2. After a period of comparison of the two drafts,
Mr. Whang stated that paragraph 1 in both drafts was
identical, except for the use of the word "Korea" in
the U.S. draft and the term "Republic of Korea" in the
Korean draft. He urged the U.S. side to agree to the
latter wording. Mr. Lewis replied that this created
a small technical problem for the U.S. side in that
approval for the change would have to be sought from
Washington. He agreed that the U.S. side would take
the Korean language under consideration.

3. Mr. Whang asked for clarification of the
scope of paragraph 2 of the U.S. draft. He said the

0227

0228

Korean side would like to know who was included in the term "other officers and personnel of the United States Government, and their dependents, ordinarily accorded such privileges abroad". Mr. Lewis replied that this term included such persons as U.S. Embassy personnel, retired military personnel, civilian crews of Military Sea Transport Service ships bringing supplies to the U.S. armed forces in Korea, American Red Cross personnel (who are members of the civilian component), and the dependents of these persons. He said this was an illustrative listing and should not be considered to be exhustive or all-inclusive.

4. Mr. Whang asked whether relief organizations, such as KAVA and CARE, or religious organizations would be included. Mr. Lewis replied that personnel of such organizations would not be authorized the use of MPO facilities when the SOFA came into force.

5. Mr. Whang stated that the SOFA was intended to provide solely for members of the armed forces, the civilian component, and their dependents. However, from Mr. Lewis' remarks, it appeared that many other persons would be authorized to use the MPO facilities. Therefore, he said, the korean side would study the U.S. draft and consult with other agencies of the ROK Government before expressing any views.

6. Mr. Lewis called the attention of the Korean side to the fact that language similar to that in the U.S. draft was a commenly-accepted provision in other Status of Forces Agreements. He urged the Korean side to study some of the Status of Forces

0229

Agreements now in force, particularly that between the U.S. Government and the Government of Japan, in which this provision appears as an Agreed Minute. Mr. Whang replied that the Korean side understood and wished to study the matter further in order to ascertain whether the proposed language was in conflict with any current Korean laws or regulations, in which case either the proposed language or the laws and regulations might have to be changed.

Facilities and Areas

7. Turning to the draft articles relating to facilites and areas, Lt. Col. Miller reminded the negotiators that at a previous meeting they had already discussed the U.S. draft article "A". He suggested that discuswion begin on draft article "B", corresponding to paragraphs 10, 11, and 12 of the Korean draft article.

8. Mr. Whang stated that there were two points of difference between paragraph 1 of the U.S. draft and paragraph 10 of the Korean draft. The first was the second sentence of the U.S. draft, reading "in an emergency, measures necessary for their safeguarding and control may also be taken in the vicinity thereof". The second was the use in the third sentence of the U.S. draft of the phrase "United States armed forces" whereas the phrase used in the Korean draft was "Government of the United States". With regard to the first point, he said the Korean side would prefer to cover the question of emergency measures in an Agreed Minute. However, the

0231

미등 81-18 ④

0531

0232

Korean side would not object to retaining the sentence
in the text of the Agreement. Then he proposed the
addition of the following words to the second sentence
of paragraph 1 of the U.S. draft: "within the extent
that Korean nationals and their property are not unduly
impaired". With regard to the second point of difference, Mr. Whang said any request based on this provision would be made to the Government of the ROK.
Therefore, for the sake of balance, the party making the
request should be identified in the language of the
Agreement as the Government of the United States. He
said the Korean side understood that the request would
be made, in actual fact, by the U.S. armed forces but
the language proposed by the Korean side would be
prefereable in the Agreement.

   9.   Replying first to the second point made by
Mr. Whang, Lt. Col. Miller pointed out that the term
"Government of the United States" appeared three
times in paragraph 10 of the Korean draft. He said
the nature of the government to government relationship was well spelled out in the Joint Committee
Article, which established the Joint Committee as the
focal point of consultation between the two governments.
He called the attention of the negotiators to the
sentence in the Joint Committee Article which reads
"In particular, the Joint Committee shall serve as
the means for consultation in determining the facilities
and areas in the Republic of Korea which are required
for the use of the United States in carrying out the
purposes of this Agreement". He said this made it clear
that relations on a government to government basis were

0233

to be conducted through the Joint Committee. In actual practive, any request would probably originate with the U.S. armed forces and be passed by them to the U.S. component of the Joint Committee, which in turn would take it up with the Korean component. The request would then become a government to government matter. Lt. Coll. Miller said the language of the U.S. draft makes this process lcear and avoids repetition of the term "Government of the United States". However, the U.S. side would take under consideration the position of the Korean side.

10. General Lawlor asked the Korean side to whom it referred when it used the term "government of the United States", if not to the U.S. armed forces. Mr. Whang replied that the SOFA would be concluded between the two governments. The United States, as one of the parties to the Agreement, obviously would be represented primarily by the U.S. armed forces. But the Korean side believed that the text of the Agreement in this instance would reflect the government to government relationship. In response to General Lawlor's further inquiry, Mr. Whang stated that the term "Government of the United States" in this context was not intended by the Korean side to be limited to the U.S. Embassy or any other US Government agency. He confirmed that the difference between the two drafts was one of language rather than substance.

11. Reverting to Mr. Whang's first point, Lt. Col. Miller said that the U.S. side preferred to have language regarding emergency actions incorporated in the body of

0235

미문 84-18

0532

미문 0236

the text rather than in an Agreed Minute. He pointed
out that the situation in Korea was unique in that the
armed forces are constantly in a state of readiness
against the resumption of hostilities. With regard to
an emergency, no one knows in advance what measures
might be necessary. One of the principal problems,
however, would be subversive activities and attempts
to infiltrate. He assured the Korean side that if the
U.S. armed forces were obliged to take emergency
measures, they would hold property damage to an absolute
minimum. He said the additional language suggested by
the Korean side was implicit in the U.S. language.
However, the U.S. side would take the Korean proposal
under consideration.

12. Mr. Whang stated that the Korean side was
sure that in the event of an emergency the U.S. armed
forces would take all measures necessary to safeguard
Korean property. This being the case, the Korean side
did not see why the U.S. side should object to the
proposed additional language. Lt. Colonel Miller
replied that the U.S. draft called for all measures
"necessary". This would include everything covered by
the language proposed by the Korean side. He pointed
out that the word "necessary" placed limits on the
actions which could be taken by the U.S. armed forces,
since they would be authorized to take only those actions
which are actually necessary and not all actions which
they might think desirable.

13. Turning to paragraph 2, Mr. Whang stated
that inasmuch as there was no substantive difference
between subparagraph (a) of the U.S. draft and the first

0237

0238

sentence of paragraph 11 of the Korean draft, the Korean side accepted the text of subparagraph (a) of the U.S. draft, with the proviso that the differnce between "United States" and "Government of the United States" be resolved at a later date.

14. With regard to subparagraph (b), Mr. Whang stated that the Korean side agreed with the U.S. draft, except for the phrase "designated military communications authorities". He pointed out that the relevant competent authority of the ROK Government was the Ministry of Communications, not the Korean military establishment. Lt. Colonel Miller replied that the U.S. side was willing to delete the word "military". The phrase "designated communications authorities" would more accurately descrive the actual situation, he said. Mr. Whang said that because of the highly classified and technical nature of the subject, the Korean side was willing to accept the text of subparagraph (b) of the U.S. draft, with the word "military" deleted.

15. Mr. Whang recalled that at the 11th meeting, Mr. Habib, with reference to subparagraph (c) of the U.S. draft, had stated that one of the agreement envisioned under the terms of this subparagraph would provide for notification by the United States to the International Frequency R$_e$gistration Board of frequencies used in Korea by the U.S. armed forces. Mr. Whang said that according to Resolution No. 5 adopted by the Administrative Radio Conference of the ITU held at Geneva in 1959, the host country should notify the IFRB. Lt. Colonel Miller stated that the U.S. side was referring only to frequencies used by the U.S. armed forces. He said the U.S. forces were currently

0239

notifying the IFRB of these frequencies and what the
U.S. side had in mind was merely a continuation
of the present practice, which apparently is acceptable
to the IFRB. Mr. Whang replied that the ROK Government
is a member of the ITU and the ITU had adopted the
resolution to which he had referred. Therefore, it
was appropriate that the ROK Government do the notifying
from now on.

16. The U.S. side agreed to look inot this matter
further. Lt. Colonel Miller stated that the question
of who should notify the IERB of frequencies in use
did not affect the agreement of both sides on the
language of subparagraph (b) of the U.S. draft. Mr.
Whang said that was correct and stated that the Korean
side had agreed to subparagraph (a) and (b) of paragraph
2 of the U.S. draft.

17. Turning to subparagraph (c) of the U.S. draft,
Mr. Whang pointed out that no similar paragraph appeared
in the Korean draft. He said the Korean side had no
objection in principle to the subparagraph but wished to
hear any further comment which the U.S. side might wish
to make. Lt. Colonel Miller replied that the U.S. side
believed that both parties to the SOFA would have
obligations under the provisions of this article. Subparagraph (c) had been inserted in the U.S. draft as a
counterbalance to subparagraph (a). The latter subparagraph spells out the obligations of the United States
Government and subparagraph (c) would spell out the obligations of the ROK Government. Mr. Whang stated that
inasmuch as both sides were already cooperating "in the
utmost spirit of coordination and cooperation", as stated
in subparagraph (b), the Korean side agreed to the

한·미국 간의 상호방위조약 제4조에 의한 시설과 구역 및 한국에서의 미국군대의 지위에 관한 협정(SOFA)
전59권. 1966.7.9 서울에서 서명 : 1967.2.9 발효(조약 232호) (V.50 실무교섭회의 합의의사록, 제10-37차, 1963) (2/2)

text of subparagraph (c) of paragraph 2 of the U.S. draft.

18. Mr. Whang stated that since paragraph 3 of the U.S. draft and paragraph 12 of the Korean draft were identical, the Korean side agreed to the text of the U.S. draft.

Article "C"

19. Turning to Article "C" of the U.S. draft, Mr. Whang noted that paragraph 1 was practically identical with the first sentence of paragraph 13 of the Korean draft, the only difference being the use of "United States" in one and "Government of the United States " in the other. With the proviso that this conflict of language be resolved at a later date, he said the Korean side agreed to the text of paragraph 1 of the U.S. draft.

20. Mr. Whang suggested that discussion on the remainder of paragraph 13 of the Korean draft be deferred until a later date. He said that the views of both sides on this subject had already been fully exchanged and it was unlikely that agreement could be reached on the working level.

21. With regard to paragraph 14 of the Korean draft, Mr. Whang recalled that the U.S. side had stated that the phrase "supply or other materials left thereon" was unnecessary. He pointed out that this paragraph correlated with paragraph 2 of the U.S. draft. In explanation of the phrase in question, he said that there was no question about the fact that equipment brought into Korea by the U.S. armed forces is the property of the U.S. armed forces and can be removed from Korea by

0243

those forces. However, the Korean side, wished to point out that after a particular facility has been returned to the ROK Government by the U.S. armed forces, the ROK Government must not be held responsible for the protection of any U.S. owned supplies or materials temporarily left at the facility.

22. In reply, Lt. Colonel Miller stated that a Property Disposal Agreement already exists, which provides for disposition of equipment, supplies, or materials which the U.S. forces do not wish to remove from Korea. He suggested that this question be discussed elsewhere since the U.S. side did not believe it relevant to the facilities and areas articles.

23. Turning to paragraph 3 of the U.S. draft, Mr. Whang asked for an explanation of the special arrangements referred to therein. Lt. Colonel Miller explained that this paragraph provides the authority for construction outside the terms of paragraph 1 and 2. He said this authority would be utilized only in the case of a special situation in which both governments agreed that the provisions of paragraphs 1 and 2 would not apply. In response to query by Mr. Whang, he said that no such construction is contemplated at the present time. In the future, any such construction could be carried out only by mutual agreement. Mr. Whang stated that since the terms of the paragraph would apply only after mutual agreement of the two governments, the Korean side agreed to the text of paragraph 3 of the U.S. draft.

24. Mr. Whang stated that the Korean side proposed that paragraph 14 of the Korean draft be inserted between the present paragraphs 1 and 2 of the U.S. draft. Lt. Colonel Miller then stated that the U.S. side

한·미국 간의 상호방위조약 제4조에 의한 시설과 구역 및 한국에서의 미국군대의 지위에 관한 협정(SOFA)
전59권. 1966.7.9 서울에서 서명 : 1967.2.9 발효(조약 232호) (V.50 실무교섭회의 합의의사록, 제10-37차, 1963) (2/2)

0246 ⑪

wished to suggest alternative language to paragraph
14. He tabled the following proposed paragraph: 0518

"The Republic of Korea is not obligated
to compensate the United States for improvements
made in United States facilities and areas or
for the buildings or structures remaining
thereon upon the return of the facilities and
areas".
Mr. Whang stated that the Korean side would take this
proposal under consideration.

25. Before adjourning the meeting, Mr. Whang
introduced Mr. Park Bong Jin, Chief of the Customs Duties
Section of the Ministry of Finance, who attended the
meeting on behalf of Mr. Shin Kwan Sup.

26. It was agreed to hold the next meeting on
April 11 at 2.p.m.

0248

0220

April 11, 1963

1. Time and Place: 2:00 to 4:20 p.m. April 11, 1963
   at the Foreign Minister's
   Conference Room

II. Attendants:

ROK Side:

Mr. Whang, Ho Eul	Director Bureau of Political Affairs Ministry of Foreign Affairs
Mr. Koo, Choong Whay	Chief, America Section Ministry of Foreign Affairs
Col. Lee, Nam Koo	Chief, Military Affairs Section Ministry of National Defense
Mr. Chu, Mun Ki	Chief, Legal Affairs Section Ministry of Justice
Mr. Park, Bong Jin	Chief of Customs Section Ministry of Finance
Mr. Lee, Kyung Hoon	2nd Secretary Ministry of Foreign Affairs
Mr. Kang Suk Jae	3rd Secretrary Ministry of Foreign Affairs
Mr. Kim, Yoon Taik	3rd Secretary Ministry of Foreign Affairs

U.S. Side:

Mr. Philip C. Habib	Counselor of the Embassy for Political Affairs
Brig. Gen. J. D. Lawlor	Deputy Chief of Staff 8th Army
Mr. William J. Ford	First Secretary of the Embassy
Col. G. G. O'Connor	Deputy Chief of Staff 8th Army
Capt. R. M. Brownlie	Assistant Chief of Staff USN/K
Col. W. A. Solf	Staff Judge Advocate 8th Army

0249

0250

Mr. Benjamin A. Fleck (Rapporteur and Press Officer)	First Secretary of the Embassy
Mr. Robert A. Lewis	Second Secretary and Consul of the Embassy
Lt. Col. R. E. Miller	Staff Officer, JAG 8th Army
Lt. Col. W. A. Burt	J-5

Military Post Offices

1. Mr. Whang opened the discussion by pointing out that there was no difference in the draft texts of paragraph 1 of the MPO Article, except for the reference in the Korean draft to the "Republic of Korea", whereas the U.S. draft referred only to "Korea". Mr. Habib stated that the U.S. side accepted the ROK wording in principle and suggested that editorial differences of this sort could be worked out at a later date.

2. Mr. Whang said the ROK side wished to place the text of paragraph 2 of the U.S. draft in an Agreed Minute rather than as paragraph 2 of the article, since this paragraph stipulated the exceptional provisions on the use of MPO's. He said the content of the paragraph was closely related to the Customs Article, which was still under discussion. He suggested, therefore, that discussion of paragraph 2 be suspended until agreement had been reached on the relevant portions of the Customs Article. Mr. Habib replied that the U. S. side wished to limit the number of Agreed Minutes. For that reason, and for the sake of clarity, the U.S. side believed it preferable to include it in the text of the Agreement rather than as an Agreed Minute. Therefore, it was hoped that the ROK side would reconsider the matter. However, if the ROK

0251

side insisted, the U. S. side would not object to making the paragraph an Agreed Minute.

3. Mr. Habib stated that the U.S. side had no fundamental objection to deferring further discussion of paragraph 2 until after the discussion of the Customs Article. He pointed out that the paragraph, by itself, had no more relevance to the customs article than did any other article of the SOFA. Mr. Whang replied that paragraph 2 was relevant to paragraphs 3 and 5 of the customs article. He said these latter paragraphs define the exemptions from customs duty and examination. He said it appeared that persons covered by paragraph 2 of the MPO article would not necessarily be entitled to the exemptions set forth in customs article. Therefore, the Korean side wished to defer further discussion and final agreement on the substance of paragraph 2 until after the relevant paragraphs in the customs article had been agreed upon. However, the ROK side wished to reach agreement now to convert paragraph 2 into an Agreed Minute. Mr. Habib expressed agreement.

Customs

4. Turning to the Customs Article, Mr. Whang reminded the negotiators that full agreement had previously been reached on the text of paragraph 1. He said that discussion of paragraph 2 had been held on the original U.S. draft rather than on the revised draft tabled by the U.S. side at the 7th meeting. Mr. Ford stated that the U.S. side was willing to continue to negotiate on the basis of the original U.S. draft of paragraph 2. The U.S. side wished to have the record show, however, that the U.S.

0253

side interprets this paragraph as providing exemption from customs duties and other such charges for articles imported by others than the U.S. armed forces and/or forces logistically supported by the U.S. armed forces, such as contractors, which articles are to be used exclusively by those Forces or are ultimately to be incorporated into articles or facilities to be used by such forces. Mr. Whang said that the Korean side would give its comments and views on Mr. Ford's remarks att the next meeting.

5. Mr. Whang noted that the ROK side had previously proposed the addition of the words "under the Unified Command" following the words "in Korea" in the final sentence of paragraph 2. Mr. Ford stated that the U.S. side agreed to this change.

6. Mr. Whang then recalled that there was some question about the use of the word "organizations" or the word "activities". Mr. Habib said the U.S. side had requested the ROK side to agree to delete the word "organizations" and to insert in its place the word "activities" and further to place the phrase "including their authorized procurement agencies and their non-appropriated fund activities provided for in Article _____" in parentheses. He pointed out that these changes were desired in paragraph 2 (twice), paragraph 5 (c), and Agreed Minute #3.

7. Mr. Whang said the ROK side believed the word "activities" to be ambiguous and therefore preferred to stick to "organizations". He asked the U.S. side to give some examples of what was meant by "activities". Mr. Habib replied that the word was a more practical definiton

한·미국 간의 상호방위조약 제4조에 의한 시설과 구역 및 한국에서의 미국군대의 지위에 관한 협정(SOFA)
전59권. 1966.7.9 서울에서 서명 : 1967.2.9 발효(조약 232호) (V.50 실무교섭회의 합의의사록, 제10-37차, 1963) (2/2) 101

of the entities to which it applied than was the word "organizations". He said that "activities" included 0528 organized sports and officers clubs, to name but two, neither of which was an "organization" in the strict sense of the word. Nevertheless, the U.S. armed forces imported supplies for their use. Mr. Habib pointed out that the phrase "activities provided for in Article ___" obviously would include the activities covered by that article. Inasmuch as the U.S. armed forces import supplies for the use of these various activities, the use of the word "organizations" would be innaccurate. Mr. Whang replied that the explanation given by the U.S. side would be of assistance to the ROK side in its consideration of this question. He said the ROK would be prepared to discuss this point at a later meeting, after further study.

8. Turning to paragraph 3, Mr. Whang reminded the negotiators that the introductory section and sub-paragraphs (a) and (c) had already been agreed upon. He recalled that the ROK side had proposed to introduce into subparagraph (b) a time limit of three months for the importation of vehicles and parts free from customs duties and charges. He asked if the Korean proposal was acceptable to the U.S. side. Mr. Ford replied that this point had already been thoroughly discussed and that the U.S. side had stated all of the reasons why it would not agree to a time limitation. Mr. Whang said that the ROK side realized that certain difficulties might arise from the imposition of a time limitation. However, the purpose of such a limitation was to limit the number of automobiles imported duty free into

한·미국 간의 상호방위조약 제4조에 의한 시설과 구역 및 한국에서의 미국군대의 지위에 관한 협정(SOFA)
전59권. 1966.7.9 서울에서 서명 : 1967.2.9 발효(조약 232호) (V.50 실무교섭회의 합의의사록, 제10-37차, 1963) (2/2) 103

the Republic of Korea in the future. He asked if
the U.S. side had any alternative suggestions.

9. Mr. Ford reiterated the objections of the U.S.
side to a time limitation. He cited the delays involved
in ordering a new car from the factory, in shipment
of the car from the factory to the port, the possibility
of strikes, and the vagaries of the weather (during the
past winter Inchon harbor had completely forzen, as a
result of which transportation schedules had been
disrupted and incoming shipments delayed). He pointed
out that many people might wish to wait until after
their arrival in Korea to order a vehicle. He referred
to the problem of obtaining replacement parts, required
because of normal wear and tear or because of accident.
If necessary parts could not be imported, the automobile
would be useless. For many of the persons involved,
he said, the personally owned automobile was their sole
means of transportation to and from their places of
employment. In short, he said, the possession of an
automobile and the ability to maintain it in proper
running condition was an important morale factor.

10. Mr. Habib added that the fundamental question
at isse was not the entry of vehicles but their
disposal. He said this was something which was well
within the power of the ROK Government to control
through its existing tax laws and regulations. This
paragraph in the SOFA would not affect the ability of
the ROK Government to protect itself against the
indiscriminate importation of vehicles. The imposition
or lack of imposition of a time limitation on importation would not affect this ability in any way.

11. Mr. Whang stated that the explanation given by the U.S. side showed the difficulties which would arise from the imposition of a time limitation. However, unlimited importation would also cause difficulties. He pointed out that Embassy personnel not included on the Diplomatic List were limited to a six-month period for duty-free importation of vehicles. Mr. Whang proposed a limitation of six months on the importation of duty free vehicles, no time limitation on the importation of spare parts as may be required for repair, or replacement, and the establishment of procedures whereby a vehicle unserviceably demolished through accidents or cllision while in Korea could be replaced without payment of customs duty.

12. Mr. Habib said that there was also the problem of allowing for reasonable replacement, since many of the persons involved, aprticularly members of the civilain compoenent, remained in the Republic of Korea for a relatively lengthy period. He again urged that this problem could be solved through use of the laws and regulations governing disposal of vehicles. He suggested that if the ROK side took the preceding discussion into account, it would understand why the U.S. side was reluctant to agree to a time limitation. Mr. Whang replied that the ROK side would take the explanation of the U.S. side under consideration.

13. Mr. Whang noted that the text of paragraph 4 had already been agreed upon. Mr. Habib then suggested that discussion of paragraph 5 be deferred until a later meeting, since the U.S. side was still considering certain portions. Mr. Whang pointed out that paragraph

한·미국 간의 상호방위조약 제4조에 의한 시설과 구역 및 한국에서의 미국군대의 지위에 관한 협정(SOFA)
전59권. 1966.7.9 서울에서 서명 : 1967.2.9 발효(조약 232호) (V.50 실무교섭회의 합의의사록, 제10-37차, 1963) (2/2) 107

5(b) was relevant to the second paragraph of the U.S. draft of the Military Post Offices Article. He asked whether the U.S. side was prepared to discuss paragraph 5(b). Mr. Habib replied that the U.S. side wished to reserve its position and postpone discussion of the entire paragraph.

14. Mr. Whang noted that paragraphs 6,7, and 8 had already been agreed upon. He then recalled that the ROK side had proposed the insertion of paragraph 7(e) of the Korean draft immediately following paragraph 9(c) of the U.S. draft. Paragraph 7(e) would thus become paragraph 9(d) of the U.S. draft and the original paragraph 9(d) would become 9(e). Mr. Habib replied that the U.S. side had no objection to this change. The full text of paragraph 9 of the U.S. draft, as amended by the insertion of paragraph 7(e) of the Korean draft, was thereupon agreed upon.

15. Turning to the Agreed Minutes, Mr. Whang stated that the ROK side agreed to the text of Agreed Minute #1 of the U.S. draft. Mr. Habib pointed out that the U.S. side wished to substitute the word "activities" in place of the word "organizations", as previously pointed out with regard to paragraph 2. Mr. Whang said the ROK side would consider this proposed change on the basis of the foregoing discussion. When final agreement was reached with regard to the proposed change in paragraph 2, agreement on the wording of Agreed Minute #1 in conformity with the agreed wording for paragraph 2 would be automatic. The U.S. side agreed.

16. With regard to Agreed Minute #2, Mr. Whang recalled that the ROK side had previously suggested the insertion of the phrase "reasonable quantities of". If the U.S. side agreed to this addition, he said, 0263

complete agreement on the text of Agreed Minute #2 was
possible. Mr. Ford replied that in the view of the
U.S. side, this phrase would add nothing to the substance of the Minute and would have no real meaning in
this context. Mr. Habib pointed out that the subject
of the Minute was personal effects. He said there is
no definition of what constitutes a reasonable amount
of personal effects. For that reason, this phrase
does not appear in this context in any other Status of
Forces Agreement. Mr. Ford added that one of the
factors involved was the great variation in the type of
quarters occupied by persons falling under this provision and in the adequacy with which those quarters are
furnished. Thus, what is a reasonable amount in one
case might not be reasonable in another. Here again,
Mr. Ford continued, the solution to the problem envisioned by the ROK side lay in the effective implementation
of the ROK Government's disposal regulations.

17. Mr. Whang replied that the ROK side did not
agree that the phrase had no meaning. He pointed out
that the negotiators had already agreed on the inclusion
of this language in another paragraph of the article
He said the Korean side did not think it reasonable
that one individual should be albe to import 10 tele-
vision sets or 5 refrigerators, regardless of the size
of his family. Mr. Habib replied that paragraph 3(c),
to which Mr. Whang had alluded, deals with goods mailed
through postal channels. The subject currently under
disucssion, however, was the personal effects of
individuals; not articles ordered for initial delivery
in the ROK. He reiterated that there is no definition

0265

0266

of what constitutes a "reasonable" amount of household
effects. Such a definition could never be applied;
therefore why insert it in this Minute? Mr. Whang
assured the U.S. side that the Korean side did not
intend to create difficulties or inconvenience. He
suggested that both sides consider this question and be
prepared for further discussion at a subsequent meeting.
Mr. Habib agreed.

18. Turning to Agreed Minute #3, Mr. Whang said the
ROK side proposed that the text be changed to read:
"... including their authorized procurement agencies,
but excluding their non-appropriated fund organizations
provided for in Article _____". Mr. Habib remarked
that the U.S. side did not understand the desire of
the Korean side to impose customs examination for goods
imported for non-appropriated fund activities and not
for goods imported for other purposes. He said this
would be inconsistent with exemptions granted elsewhere
in the customs article. He pointed out that in fact
the non-appropriated fund activities are part of the
U.S. armed forces and that they were referred to as a
separate entity only for organizational reasons.
He further pointed out that paragraph 2 of the article
defined the scope of "military cargo", which includes
goods imported by the U.S. armed forces and their non-
appropriated fund activities. The U.S. draft of
Agreed Minute #3, he continued, was consistent with
that definition.

19. Mr. Whang said that Agreed Minute #3 was
relevant to paragraph 5(c) of the article, on which

agreement had not yet been reached. He suggested, therefore, that further discussion on Agreed Minute #3 be deferred until paragraph 5(c) had been discussed more fully. Mr. Habib agreed.

20. Mr. Habib recalled that Agreed Minutes #4 and #5 had already been agreed upon. He said the U.S. side agreed to the ROK side's previous proposal to delete from Agreed Minute #6 the phrase "authorized by United States law and service regulations". Complete agreement was then reached on the text of the U.S. draft of Agreed Minute #6, as amended.

Facilities and Areas

21. Turning to the Facilities and Areas articles, Mr. Habib recalled that at the previous meeting, the U.S. side had proposed alternate language to the text of paragraph 14 of the ROK draft. He asked if the Korean side had a chance to consider the U.S. proposal. Mr. Whang replied that the Korean side had considered the U.S. proposal. He continued that removable property brought into Korea by the U.S. armed forces remains the property of the United States and may be removed from Korea by the U.S. armed forces. However the ROK side would like to ensure that no obligation is placed on the ROK Government to protect U.S.-owned supplies remaining on facilities which have been returned by the U.S. armed forces to the ROK Government. He suggested that the U.S. proposed language be revised by removing the word "or" before the word "structures", inserting commas before and after the word "structures", and inserting the phrase "supplies or any other materials" in front of the word "remaining". Mr. Whang said that

0269

once facilities were turned over to the ROK Government,
no obligation would fall on the ROK Government for the
protection of those supplies or materials left thereon.

22. Mr. Whang then suggested deletion from paragraph 2 of Article "C" of the U.S. draft of the phrase
"will remain the property of the United States Government" and, taking into consideration the additional
phrase "supplies or any other materials" proposed by the
Korean side. Mr. Habib replied that the U.S. side
could not agree to the deletion of this phrase since
the text of the Agreement must indicate U.S. ownership.
With regard to the ROK side's proposal to amend the U.S.
proposed language (see preceding paragraph), Mr. Habib
pointed out that there is in operation at the present
time a Surplus Property Disposal Agreement. Supplies
and other materials which the U.S. armed forces did not
wish to remove from Korea would be disposed of under the
terms of that agreement or would be moved to facilities
still in use by the U.S. Armed forces. He said the
ROK proposal would merely delay the return of facilities
to the ROK Government by the U.S. armed forces since
those forces would not return a facility until all the
movable supplies located thereon had been transferred
to some other facility. Obviously, he continued, the
supplies and materials which were not required by the
U.S. armed forces would not be turned over to the ROK
Government free of charge. If the supplies remained
the property of the U.S. Government, the ROK Government
would be under no obligation to protect them unless a
special agreement to that effect were made by the two
governments. He pointed out that the ROK Government

0271

incurred no obligation to compensate the U.S. government
if such an obligation were not specifically mentioned
in the SOFA. He expressed the opinion that the ROK
side was creating a problem where none actually exists.
Mr. Whang stated that the ROK side would study the views
expressed by the U.S. side and be prepared for further
discussion of this question at a later date.

23. Mr. Whang pointed out that the agreement
reached at the previous meeting on the text of paragraph 3
of the U.S. draft was conditional upon final agreement
to the text of paragraphs 1 and 2 of the U.S. draft and
the text of paragraph 14 of the Korean draft. Mr. Habib
remarked that there was no clear relationship between
the substance of paragraph 2 and that of paragraph 14 of
the ROK draft.

24. Turning to article "D" of the U.S. draft, Mr.
Whang stated that each side had fully discussed paragraphs 1 and 2. He said the ROK side was not prepared
to discuss paragraphs 3 and 4, covering utilities and
services, at that time. Mr. Habib agreed to defer
discussion of utilities and services until the next
meeting. Mr. Habib then expressed his confidence that,
although paragraphs 1 and 2 had been thoroughly discussed
with neither side changing its position, the negotiators
would eventually be able to reach agreement.
Mr. Whang expressed his personal opinion tthat since
neither side had anything to add, some other method
of discussing the substance of these two paragraphs
would have to be found. Mr. Habib replied that
although the U.S. side had nothing to add at the moment,
he did not rule out the possibility of further discussion

at a later date. 05.

25. The closing minutes of the meeting were given
over to expressions of appreciation for the splendid
contribution to the negotiations which had been made by
Colonel Solf, who was attending his last negotiating
meeting.

26. It was agreed to hold the next meeting on
April 24 at 2:00 p.m.

April 24, 1963

1. Time and Place: 2:00 to 3:40 p.m. April 24, 1963
                at the Foreign Minister's
                Conference Room

II. Attendants:

ROK Side:

Mr. Whang, Ho Eul	Director Bureau of Political Affairs Ministry of Foreign Affairs
Mr. Shin, Kwan Sup	Director Bureau of Costums Duty Ministry of Finance
Mr. Yoon, Ha Jong	1st Secretary Ministry of Foreign Affairs
Mr. Koo, Chong Whay	Chief, America Section Ministry of Foreign Affairs
Mr. Lee, Nam Koo	Chief, Military Affairs Section Ministry of National Defense
Mr. Chu, Mun Ki	Chief, Legal Affairs Section Ministry of Justice
Mr. Lee, Kyung Hoon	2nd Secretary Ministry of Foreign Affairs
Mr. Cho, Kwang Je	2nd Secretary Ministry of Foreign Affairs
Mr. Kim, Yoon Taik	3rd Secretary Ministry of Foreign Affairs

U. S. Side:

Mr. Philip C. Habib	Counselor of the Embassy for Political Affairs
Brig. Gen. J. D. Lawlor	Deputy Chief of Staff 8th Army
Mr. William J. Ford	First Secretary of the Embassy
Col. G. G. O'Connor	Deputy Chief of Staff 8th Army
Capt. R. M. Brownlie	Assistant Chief of Staff USN/K

0277

Mr. L. J. Fuller	Staff Judge Advocate United Nations Command
Mr. Benjamin A. Fleck (Rapporteur and Press Officer)	First Secretary of the Embassy
Lt. Col. R. E. Miller	Staff Officer, JAG 8th Army
Lt. Col. W. A. Burt	J-5
Kenneth Camper	Interpreter

1. Mr. Whang opened the meeting by introducing First Secretary Yoon Ha Jong, Assistant Director of the Bureau of Economic Affairs in the Foreign Ministry and Second Secretary Cho Kwang Je, of the same Bureau. Mr. Whang also announced that Mr. Kim Yoon Taik would act as interpreter for the Korean side at this meeting in place of Mr. Kang, who was on his honeymoon. Mr. Habib welcomed Mr. Yoon and Mr. Cho and then introduced Colonel Lawrence J. Fuller, Staff Judge Advocate of the United Nations Command, who assumed Colonel Solf's place on the U.S. negotiating team. Mr. Whang welcomed Colonel Fuller.

Utilities and Services

". Mr. Whang began discussion of the utilities and services drafts by referring to the desire of the U.S. side to incorporate these provisions into the facilities and areas article. He said the Korean side believed that it would be better to have a separate utilities and services article in view of the great length of the facilities and areas article. He recalled that in the initial discussion of the scope of the SOFA, a list of 28 articles to be included in the Agreement had been drawn up and utilities and services had been included on the list.

0279

3. Mr. Habib replied that the U.S. side had no objection in priciple to placing utilities and services in a separate article, subject, of course, to the approval of U.S. Government authorities in Washington. He pointed out that the list of 28 subjects was not intended to be an all-inclusive list. The U.S. side had included utilities and services in its facilities and areas drafts. He suggested that the negotiators proceed on the basis that utilities and services would constitute a separate article, with final disposition and arrangement within the SOFA to be decided upon at a later date. Mr. Whang agreed and it was decided to proceed with discussion of the utilities and services drafts on a paragraph by paragraph basis.

4. Mr. Whang recalled that at the 14th meeting, the Korean side had proposed the deletion from the first sentence of paragraph 3(a) of the U.S. draft of the phrase "whether publicly or privately owned". Mr. Habib stated that the U.S. side had considered that proposal and was willing to agree to deletion of the phrase, provided that Korean side would agree to the insertion of "owned", following the words "which are". He said the U.S. side also wished to substitute the words "local administrative subdivisions" in place of the words "political subdivisions" in the latter portion of the same sentence. Mr. Whang said that had no objection in principle to the insertion of "owned", but it would be necessary to obtain the concurrence of other Ministries. Therefore, the Korean side would reply to this proposal at a later date.

5. With regard to the suggested insertion of "local administrative subdivisions", Mr. Whang remarked that such subdivisions are included in the Government of the Republic of Korea and there is, therefore, no need to spell out the term. However, if the U. S. side believed it important, he suggested that this phraseology be placed in an Agreed Minute. Mr. Habib replied that the U.S. side did not want to proliferate Agreed Minutes. Indeed, both sides had consistently been trying to hold the number of Agreed Minutes to a minimum. He said it was clear that certain utilities are owned, controlled, or regulated by such subdivisions and not by the Government of the Republic of Korea. Mr. Whang stated that the Korean side would consider this point.

6. Mr. Whang then referred to the proposal of the Korean side that the phrase "however produced" be deleted from the second sentence of paragraph 3(a) of the U.S. draft. Mr. Habib stated that retention of the phrase does not complicate the sentence and is consistent with the language of the Utilities and Claims Settlement Agreement, which will remain in effect after the SOFA becomes effective. He said the phrase was a clarifying phrase and reminded the Korean side that the phrase had appeared in the original Korean draft as well as the U.S. draft.

7. Mr. Whang stated that the purpose of this paragraph was to enumerate the types of utilities and services to be furnished and that no reference should be made to the means of production. Mr. Habib pointed out that utilities and services can be produced by various means. The purpose of the paragraph is to clearly state that the U.S. armed forces shall have the

미든 87→20 ④

0583

0281 ④

use of certain types of utilities and services, regardless of how they are produced. He pointed out that if
this clarifying phrase is not included, disagreement
might later occur over the availability of utilities or
services produced by certain means. The purpose of the
article is to provide for the provision of utilities and
services to the U.S. armed forces; it should not be subject to later misinterpretation over the furnishing of
specific utilities or services. He suggested, therefore,
that the Korean side reconsider its position, Pointing
out that the phrase imposes no obligation on the Korean
authorities not already agreed to by the Korean side,
he asked what was the specific objection of the Korean
side to this phrase.

8. Mr. Whang replied that if the qualification
"however produced" were included, then similar qualifications such as "by whomsoever produced" or whenever
produced" should also be added. He said there was no
need to include any of these phrases. The purpose of
the presence of the U.S. forces in the Republic of
Korea was to contribute to the common defense of the
Free World. The Government of the Republic of Korea,
therefore, considered the U.S. forces to be guests and
treated them accordingly. The U.S. side should rest
assured, he continued, that the ROK Government would
furnish utilities and services to the U.S. forces.

9. Mr. Habib replied that the U.S. side was not
worried about the provision of utilities and services
by the ROK Government to the U.S. armed forces. He
reiterated that if the phrase were not included, arguments
could arise later over the provision of utilities and

0285

services produced in certain ways. He pointed out that 0588 one of the arguments being advanced by the Korean side was the fact that the manner of production was irrelevant to the provisions of this article. He said this was precisely why the U.S. side wished to include the phrase, which made the irrelevancy clear. Otherwise, the question of means of production would be left unclear. Mr. Whang suggested that inclusion of the phrase was made unnecessary by the presence in the sentence of the phrase "shall include, but not be limited to". He also suggested that if any misunderstanding arose in the furture concerning the meaning of the sentence, the negotiating record would clearly indicate the positions of the negotiators on this point. Mr. Habib suggested that both sides consider this matter further and stated that the U.S. side would study the arguments put forward by the Korean side.

10. Mr. Whang then requested an explantion of the third sentence in the U.S. draft and asked whether the U.S. side wished to comment on the alternative language suggested by the Korean side at the 14th meeting. Mr. Habib replied that the U.S. side was prepared to agree in principle to the Korean side's proposal but wished to suggest new language. The U.S. side thereupon tabled the following suggested new third and fourth sentence of paragraph 3(a):

> "The use of utilities and services as provided herein shall not prejudice the right of the United States to operate military transportation, commun- cation, power and such other utilities and services deemed necessary for the operations of the United States armed forces. This right shall not be exercised in a manner inconsistent with the operation by the Government of the Republic of Korea of its utilities and services."

0287

Mr. Habib stated that the use of the words "not....
inconsistent" means that the U.S. armed forces, in
operating such facilities as military trains on the
Korean railway system and military bus lines, will do so
in conformance with existing Korean laws and regulations.
Mr. Whang stated that he, personally, had no objection
to the proposed language. He said the Korean side would
consider the U.S. proposal and give its response at a
later date.

11. Turning to subparagraph (b) of paragraph 3 of
the U.S. draft, Mr. Whang stated that the most favorable
rates are those which are provided to agencies of the ROK
Government. Mr. Habib said that if that is the case,
the Korean side should have no objection to the first
sentence of the U.S. draft, with the phrase "governmental
or private" deleted. He said this deletion would be
acceptable to the U.S. side and should satisfy the Korean
side. He pointed out that this deletion did not constitute
any substantive change in the intent of the subparagraph
but was a word change designed to satisfy the desires of
the Korean side. He assured the Korean side that all
the U.S. side desired was the assurance that the U.S.
armed forces would be charged rates no less favorable
than those accorded any other user.

12. Mr. Whang replied that the term "any other user"
requires specification. He said the language of the
third sentence of paragraph 1 of the Korean draft was more
appropriate. Mr. Habib stated that the purpose of this
subparagraph was not to identify the various users of
utilities and services but to establish the principle that
the U.S. armed forces will not be charged discriminatory

0289

0290

rates. He said the U.S. side was prepared to agree to deletion of the second sentence of paragraph 3(b) of the U.S. draft, to which the Korean side had previously objected, provided that the Korean side was willing to accept the first sentence with the deletion of the phrase "governmental or private". He suggested that placing a period after the word "user" in the first sentences and deleting the second sentence would be the simplest way of meeting the desires of both sides. Mr. Whang replied that the Korean side would consider this proposal.

13. Regarding the third sentence of paragraph 3(b) of the U.S. draft, Mr. Habib recalled that the Korean side had previously indicated that it had under consideration a separate article dealing with emergency situations. He said the U.S. side was prepared to defer discussion of the third sentence until it had heard the views of the Korean side on possible alternatives. Mr. Whang reminded the negotiators that the previous chief negotiator had said that a separate article, to be discussed later, would define steps to be taken in the event of the most serious emergency which could arise, and that even if it were not spelled out in this article, the treatment accorded to the U.S. armed forces in the event of emergency would be equivalent to that accorded to the ROK armed forces in such event. He said the Korean side agreed to defer discussion of this sentence until it reached a decision on this matter.

14. Turning to the next paragraph, Mr. Whang stated that paragraph 2(a) of the Korean draft was more appropriate to the itent of the article than was paragraph 4 of the U.S. draft. Mr. Habib replied that the

0291

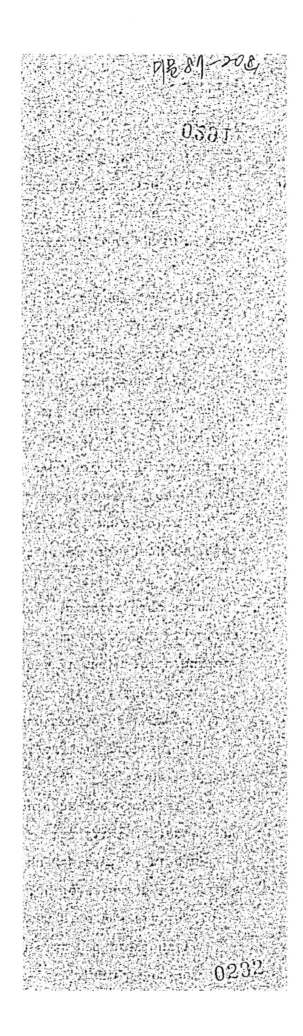

U.S. side could not accept paragraph 2(a) and (b) of the
Korean draft because the language was too braod and
indefinite. He said paragraph 4 was intended to cover
one factor only, i.e. accounting arrangements, whereas
paragraph 2(a) refers to arrangements regarding use of
utilities and services. He pointed out that paragraph
3(a) of the U.S. draft states that "the United States armed
forces shall have the use of all utilities and services".
He said the U.S. side saw no reason to expand paragraph 4,
which refers only to accounting procedures, into a paragraph which is indecisive and ill-defined. He added
that the substance of paragraph 2(b) of the Korean draft
was covered in Agreed Minute #2 of the U.S. draft.

15. Mr. Whang said that paragraph 2(a) of the
Korean draft provides for the concrete use of utilities
and also arrangements necessary for payment forsuch use.
Mr. Habib replied that payment is provided for in
paragraph 3(b) of the U.S. draft, which states that "the
use of utilities and services by the United States shall
be in accordance with **priorities**, conditions, and rates
or tariffs no less favorable than those accorded any
other user". Arrangements for payment are provided for
in paragraph 4 of the U.S. draft. He pointed out that
the language of the entire U.S. draft article, including
the Agreed Minutes, covers everything that the Korean
side has in mind. Mr. Whang replied that the Korean
side would give further consideration to this matter.

16. Turning to the Agreed Minutes of the U.S. draft,
Mr. Whang remarked that they corresponded with paragraph
2(b) of the Korean draft. He then proposed that paragraph
2(b) be reworded as follows:

주한미군지위협정(SOFA) 서명 및 발효 20

"The existing arrangements (including the utilities and claims Settlement Agreement of December 18, 1958) concerning the use of such public utilities and services by the United States armed forces and the payment therefor at the effective date of this Agreement may be regarded as the arrangements referred to in the foregoing paragraph".

17. Mr. Habib asked the Korean side to identify the "existing arrangements" referred to. He said if the Korean side was fererring to the ordinary day-to-day arrangements entered into by various units, these should not be involved. So far as the U.S. side was concerned, he continued, the existing arrangements are those existing under the Utilities and Claims Settlement Agreement. The U.S. side wished to make it clear that this Agreement will continue in full force after the SOFA goes into effect. For this purpose, he stated, the language of the U.S. draft is clearer. Mr. Whang replied that "existing arrangements" include the Utilities and Claims Settlement Agreement and other arrangements entered into between the U.S. armed forces and the authorities operating various utilities and services.

18. Mr. Habib replied that day-to-day arrangements will always exist. He said any existing arrangement presumably would continue unless specifically modified or exempted from modification by the SOFA, as in the case of the Utilities and Claims Settlement Agreement. He said the U.S. draft meets the needs of the Korean side. He remarked that there was no need to change the language of paragraph 2(b) and suggested that the Korean side give further study to the U.S. draft paragraph 4 and Agreed Minute #2.

0295

With regard to Agreed Minute #1, Mr. Habib
stated that at the 14th meeting, the Korean side 0508
indicated reluctance to accept a specific stipulation in
the Minute, providing for changes in rates. He said
the U.S. side had considered the Korean side's objections
and was not prepared to agree to deletion of the phrase
"increase in utility or service" from Agreed Minute #1.
He pointed out that the U.S. side was trying to protect
the U.S. armed forces from discriminatory or unwarranted
changes in rates or priorities. Unless some other means
of protection could be found, he said, the U.S. side was
not prepared to drop the requirement for prior consultation.

20. Reverting to paragraph 4 of the U.S. draft,
Mr. Whang asked for an explanation of the word "accounting".
Mr. Habib replied that the purpose of the paragraph was
to provide for the establishment of systematic methods
for keeping the accounts of payments made for the use of
utilities and services by the U.S. armed forces. He
stated that at the next session devoted to this article,
the U.S. side would give a brief description of the
current procedures.

Meteorological Services

21. Turning to the meteorological services article,
Mr. Whang stated that the Korean side had studied the
U.S. draft. He stated that at present, the ROK
meteorological organizations were providing data to the
U.S. meteorological services. He said that in view of
the close cooperation which has existed between them in
the past and which the Korean side is confident will

0297

continue to exist in the furture, the Korean side accepted
the U.S. draft of this article, provided the words
"Government of Korea" were changed to read "Government
of the Republic of Korea". Mr. Habib agreed to the
changed and complete agreement was reached on the text
of this article.

Contractors & Non-Appropriated Fund Activities

22. Drafts of the articles regarding contractors
and non-appropriated fund activities were then exchanged
and it was agreed to defer discussion of them until the
negotiators had a chance to study them.

23. It was agreed to hold the next meeting on May
3 at 2:00 p.m.

한·미국 간의 상호방위조약 제4조에 의한 시설과 구역 및 한국에서의 미국군대의 지위에 관한 협정(SOFA)
전59권. 1966.7.9 서울에서 서명 : 1967.2.9 발효(조약 232호) (V.50 실무교섭회의 합의의사록, 제10-37차, 1963) (2/2)　145

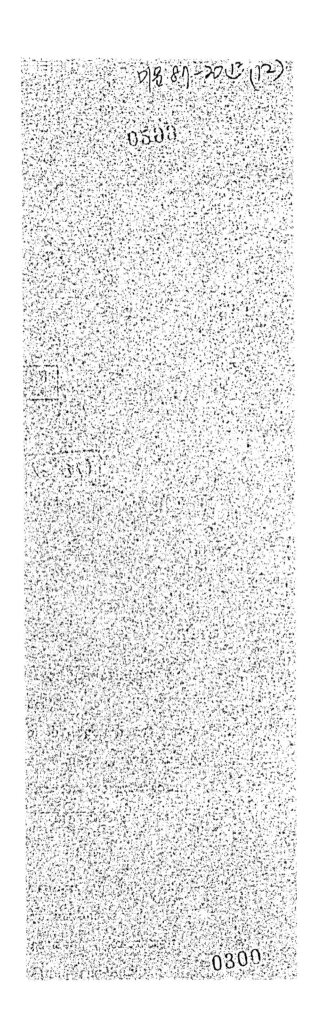

주한미군지위협정(SOFA) 서명 및 발효 20

0303

May 3, 1963

I. Time and Place : 2:00 to 4:10 p.m. May 3, 1963
at the Foreign Minister's
Conference Room

II. Attendants:

ROK Side:

Mr. Whang, Ho Eul	Director Bureau of Political Affairs Ministry of Foreign Affairs
Mr. Shin, Kwan Sup	Director Bureau of Costums Duty Ministry of Finance
Mr. Yoon, Ha Jong	1st Secretary Ministry of Foreign Affairs
Mr. Koo, Choong Whay	Chief, America Section Ministry of Foreign Affairs
Mr. Shin, Jung Sup	Chief, Treaty Section Ministry of Foreign Affairs
Mr. Lee, Nam Koo	Chief, Military Affairs Section Ministry of National Defense
Mr. Chu, Mun Ki	Chief, Legal Affairs Section Ministry of Justice
Mr. Roh Jae Won	2nd Secretary Ministry of Foreign Affairs
Mr. Lee, Kyung Hoon	2nd Secretary Ministry of Foreign Affairs
Mr. Cho, Kwang Je	2nd Secretary Ministry of Foreign Affairs
Mr. Kang, Suk Jae	3rd Secretary Ministry of Foreign Affairs

U.S Side:

Mr. Philip C. Habib	Counselor of the Embassy for Political Affairs
Mr. William J. Ford	First Secretary of the Embassy
Col. G.G. O'Connor	Deputy Chief of Staff 8th Army

0301

Capt. R.M. Brownlie	Assistant Chief of Staff USN/K
Mr. L.J. Fuller	Staff Judge Advocate United Nations Command
Mr. Benjamin A. Fleck (Rapporteur and Press Officer)	First Secretary of the Embassy
Mr. Robert A. Lewis	Second Secretary and Consul of the Embassy
Lt. Col. R.E. Miller	Staff Officer, JAG 8th Army
Lt. Col. W.A. Burt	J-5
Kenneth Campen	Interpreter

1. Mr. Whang opened the meeting by welcoming back to the negotiating table Mr. Shin Chung Sup, who had just returned from a diplomatic mission abroad, and Mr. Kang Suk Jae, who had just returned from his honeymoon. On behalf of the U.S. side, Mr. Habib extended congratulations to both gentlemen upon the successful completion of their assignments and welcomed them back to the SOFA negotiations. Mr. Whang then introduced Mr. Roh Jae Won, Second Secretary in the America Section of the Ministry of Foreign Affairs, as a new member of the Korean negotiating team.

Non-Appropriated Fund Activities/Organizations

2. Turning to the drafts of the article dealing with Non-Appropriated Fund Activities/Organizations, both sides agreed to a paragraph by paragraph discussion in order to clarify the views of each side on the differences of language.

3. Speaking for the Korean side, Mr. Shin Kwan Sup pointed out that the Korean draft used the word

"organizations" throughout whereas the U.S. draft used
the word "activities". He referred to the use in the
first paragraph of the Korean draft of the phrase
"within the facilities and areas in use by the United
States armed forces" and the words "exclusive use".
Referring to that portion of the U.S. draft which provides
that "such activities shall not be subject to Korean regulations", he requested clarification of the word
"regulations". Specifically, he asked whether this would
would include Korean customs regulations. He reminded
the negotiators that the article dealing with Korean
customs regulatinns had not yet been agreed upon.

4. Following Mr. Shin's opening remarks, Mr.
Habib began a review of the first paragraph. He stated
that the words "military exchanges" were used in the
U.S. draft because this was an all-inclusive term which
embraced Navy exchanges, post exchanges, and base
exchanges. Mr. Shin stated that the term "military
exchanges" was acceptable to the Korean side.

5. Continuing his review of paragraph one, Mr.
Habib stated that commissaries had not been mentioned
in the U.S. draft (although included in the Korean draft)
because they are official U.S. Government agencies
financed by appropriated funds. Therefore, they do
not fall within the category of non-appropriated fund
activities. The U.S. draft did list newspapers, Mr.
Habib continued, because they are non-appropriated fund
activities. Regarding the question of whether to use
the word "activities" of the word "organizations",

Mr. Habib said that the U.S. side had frequently pointed out that the word "activities" was a more accurate description of the entities concerned, since they are not organizations in the real sense of the word. With regard to the phrase in the Korean draft "within the facilities and areas in use by the United States armed forces", Mr. Habib pointed out that it was customary to use temporary or mobile exchanges during maneuvers outside established facilities and areas. He said it might also be desirable to establish exchange facilities in tourist hotels. For these reasons, the phrase had not been included in the U.S. draft. *With regard to the phrase "exclusive use" in the Korean draft, Mr. Habib said that this term* would not permit the extension of the use of non-appropriated fund activities to invited contractors. It also would not be consistent with paragraph 5 of the U.S. draft, which extends the use of these activities to certain designated groups of persons. In response to Mr. Shin's question whether the last sentence of the 1st paragraph of the U.S. draft included Korean customs regulations, Mr. Habib pointed out that the phrase "except as otherwise provided in this Agreement" was a key phrase in that sentence. The answer to Mr. Shin's question, therefore, was that Korean customs regulations would be included among those regulations to which non-appropriated fund activities would not be subject, except as this exemption might be modified by the provisions of the customs article.

6.   Turning to paragraph 1(b) of the Korean draft, regarding the regulation of newspapers on sale to the

0307

general public, Mr. Habib remarked that the U.S. side
considered this question to be relatively unimportant.
The public sale of "The Pacific Stars and Stripes"
was carried on at hotels as a service to troops who
might be there as transients. He said the U.S. side
would like to exempt such sales from taxation but
would not strongly object to the inclusion of the Korean
paragraph 1(b) in the article. He pointed out that
the result of any such taxation would probably be that
all sales of the newspaper outside of established
facilities and areas would cease. In reply, Mr. Whang
stated that the Korean side believed that the SOFA
should establish the principle that when newspapers
regulated by the U.S. armed forces are sold to the
general public, they should be subject to the same
regulations and procedures as other publicly sold
newspapers. He said the manner in which such a SOFA
provision would be implemented was another matter.
What the Korean side wished to do was to establish the
principle. Mr. Habib said that the U.S. side agreed
in principle to the inclusion of the Korean paragraph
1(b); however the U.S. side was not entirely happy with
the wording and punctuation of the Korean draft and
would suggest alternative language at a subsequent
meeting.

7. In response to a question by Mr. Shin, Mr.
Habib stated that the phrase "other non-appropriated
fund activities" in the first sentence of the U.S. draft
included such activities as sports activities, craft

shops, and schools. Mr. Shin stated that the reason
for his question was that the word "activities" was
so indefinite as to make it difficult to know which
activities are meant to be included. To make these
ambiguous points clear and incontrovertible and
in view of U.S. side's original proposal in which
it put forward the word "organizations", the Korean
side preferred the word "organizations" which carries
a conception of structure and duration. Mr. Habib
pointed out that the phrase "authorized and regulated
by the United States military authorities" provides
the assurance of the official nature of activities to
be covered by this article. At this point, to the
further question raised by Mr. Shin as to wether or
not, for instance a baseball team invited by the U.S.
armed forces in Korea would be a non-appropriated fund
activity, Mr. Habib replied in the negative. In this
connection, Mr. Habib read into the record the
definitions of "organization" and "activity" given in
Webster's International Dictionary, as follows:

"Activity - an instance of being active, as
in an occupation, recreation, or the like; as
business or social activities. Education:
an extracurricular activity.

"Organization - Any systematic whole, as the
organization of an army or a government."

8.   Mr. Habib stated that the procedure for
authorization of a non-appropriated fund activity is
specifically laid out in the military regulations.
He said such an activity was just as much a part of
the U.S. armed forces as any supply room which issues
equipment to the troops. Mr. Shin said that if the

0311

word "activities" were adopted, it would impose difficulties on the Korean side. Therefore, he suggested that in case the word "activities" was used in the text of the Articles, every specific non-appropriated fund activity falling under the phrase "other non-appropriated fund activities" in paragraph 1 of the U.S. draft should be designated and listed by agreement between the two Governments through the Joint Committee. Mr. Habib replied that the question could properly be a subject of discussion by the Joint Committee.

9. Mr. Shin remarked that the Korean side believed that the provisions of paragraph 5 of the U.S. draft were outside the scope of the SOFA. He further stated that the phrase "exclusive use" in the Korean draft, conflicted with the proposed provisions of paragraph 5 of the U.S. draft. Mr. Habib agreed and pointed out that by excluding contractors it also conflicted with both the U.S. and Korean drafts of the article dealing with contractors (para. 3(d), U.S. draft and para. 3(c), Korean draft). It was agreed to discuss this question more thoroughly in connection with subsequent discussion of paragraph 5 of the U.S. draft.

10. Regarding the phrase "within the facilities and areas in use by the United States armed forces", Mr. Shin remarked that activities conducted outside such areas, as proposed by the U.S. side, would be difficult to control. If restrictions were not provided for, confusion might result. Mr. Habib replied that this need not be the case. He said it

한·미국 간의 상호방위조약 제4조에 의한 시설과 구역 및 한국에서의 미국군대의 지위에 관한 협정(SOFA)
전59권. 1966.7.9 서울에서 서명 : 1967.2.9 발효(조약 232호) (V.50 실무교섭회의 합의의사록, 제10-37차, 1963) (2/2) 159

is normal procedure to provide mobile exchanges during field maneuvers. Such exchanges provide cigarettes, candy, tobacco and similar items and are a major factor in maintaining the morale of the troops. He pointed out that although they are not located within a facility or established area, they are regulated in the normal fashion. Mr. Shin suggested that whenever it is necessary to operate such a temporary exchange outside the facilities and areas such an exchange should be established at the place agreed upon between the two governments through the Joint Committee. Mr. Habib stated that the U.S. side would consider this suggestion but believed that it would create an unnecessary set of consultations for members of the Joint Committee.

11. Turning to paragraph 2 of the U.S. draft, Mr. Shin stated that the paragraph was generally acceptable to the Korean side. However, the Korean side wondered if the words "other purchasers" referred to general purchasers. Mr. Habib replied that this was a correct interpretation and that the draft was intended to avoid the imposition of discriminatory taxes on the non-appropriated fund activities. Mr. Whang suggested that the phrase "except as provided in paragraph 1(b)" be added to the first sentence. Mr. Habib said the U.S. side agreed in substance to this addition, with the final wording to be worked out later.

12. Mr. Shin stated that the Korean side accepted paragraph 3 of the U.S. draft. He then asked whether the word "goods" included newspapers. Mr. Habib replied

that paragraph 1(b), which had just been agreed upon
in substance, established an exception to the provisions
of paragraph 3 by providing for the sale of newspapers
to the general public. Paragraph 1(b), therefore, came
within the scope of the phrase "except as such
disposal may be permitted by the United States and
Korean authorities in accordance with mutually agreed
conditions". Therefore, the term "goods" does include
newspapers, which are not to be sold to unauthorized
purchasers except under the provisions of paragraph 1(b).

13. Turning to paragraph 4 of the Korean draft
(which has no counterpart in the U.S. draft), Mr. Shin
noted that the paragraph provided for a limitation on
the quantity of goods to be imported "to the extent
reasonably required". Mr. Habib stated that this would
be very difficult to define and for that reason such
a limitation was not to be found in any other Status
of Forces Agreement. The goods imported were for the
consumption and use of the people utilizing the
particular activity; the amount required for such use
at any one time would not be subject to any reasonable
definition. Previous paragraphs in this article
specify that these activities are for the use of authorized
persons and that there shall be no disposal of goods
to unauthorized persons, except as mutually agreed upon.
Mr. Habib pointed out that one man's consumption is
not necessarily the same as that of other men. We
cannot define, he continued, the limits of individual
consumption. He pointed out that abuses were taken

0317

care of in other articles, which define the measures
to be taken. There is no need, he concluded, for a
vague redefinition, such as that proposed for
inclusion in this paragraph.

14. Mr. Shin stated that the reasonable amount
of consumption by a group of 3,000 men or 20,000 men
could be calculated through common sense. Mr. Habib
replied that this was the basis on which buyers for
these activities place their orders. He said it was
quite clearly a question of rational ordering, purchase,
and import. What is reasonalby required is what is
used within the limits imposed. He pointed out that if
the Korean side's proposal were accepted, there would
be no change in present procedures, nor any improvement
in the methods currently used to prevent abuse, such
as the rationing system in the exchanges regarding
purchases of cigarettes, cosmetics and similar items.

15. Mr. Shin stated that Korean law prohibits the
use by Korean nationals of goods imported through
military channels. He stated that the Government of
the Republic of Korea was endeavoring to restrict
consumption and was receiving much aid from the United
States. He asked the U.S. side to consider the Korean
draft in the light of aiding the growth of the Korean
economy. Mr. Habib replied that the U.S. side was
fully aware of the Korean efforts to develop the
national economy. He said that the only effect on
the economy of goods imported by non-appropriated fund
activities occurred as a result of abuse or black

0319

0310

0320

market operations. He said that the U.S. armed forces maintained full cooperation with the Korean police and there existed a remarkably good measure of prevention against such abuses. He said the black market has nothing to do with the quantity of goods imported but was the result of the breaking of Korean and U.S. laws and regulations. He pointed out that the latter was an entirely different subject. It was agreed to defer further discussion on this question.

16. Turning to paragraph 4 in the U.S. draft and its counterpart, paragraph 5 in the Korean draft, Mr. Shin noted that the U.S. draft provided for the passing of information to the Korean tax authorities after consultation ... in the Joint Committee". He said discussion by the Joint Committee would be unnecessary, inasmuch as this was a matter involving customs. Mr. Habib replied that the purpose of the U.S. language is to forestall unreasonable requests upon the authorities administering the activities. He said such requests could become an excessive administrative burden and the Joint Committee could serve a useful function by screening out the more unreasonable ones. He pointed out that consultation does not necessarily mean agreement. In the absence of this provision, he said any agency of the ROK Government could make a request, which the U.S. armed forces would feel obliged to answer. He pointed out that the armed forces are obviously prepared to provide that information which is necessary and the U.S. draft so states. Mr. Shin stated that the Korean side was willing to accept the U.S. draft

0321

미등하→1⑪
0354

0322→1⑪

of paragraph 4, except for the phrase "after consultation between the representatives of the two governments in the Joint Committee".

17. Mr. Habib pointed out that paragraph 5 of the U.S. draft had no counterpart in the Korean draft. He said this paragraph had appeared as an Agreed Minute in the SOFA with Japan. He said the U.S. side preferred to include it in the body of the Agreement in order to keep the number of Agreed Minutes to a minimum. He said the paragraph was intended to regularize the normal practice, wherever non-appropriated fund activities exist. He said it would not provide privileges which the persons covered by the paragraph would not normally have. The U.S. side believed it to be necessary to spell out specifically and with clarity the categories of persons who will be entitled to use the activities. He pointed out that the binding phrase was "ordinarily accorded such privileges". He said persons covered under this phrase included U.S. Government personnel, retired military personnel, and contract personnel. He pointed out that the latter group was also provided for in the article dealing with contractors.

18. Mr. Shin stated that the sale of certain prohibited foreign goods was forbidden in the Republic of Korea. However, for the convenience of foreigners, special shops had been established where foreigners could purchase such articles. These could be expanded, if necessary. He said the Korean side believed that contractors and USO personnel were not qualified for the privileges extended to the U.S. armed forces.

Mr. Habib replied that USO personnel are present in
Korea "primarily for the benefit and service of the
United States armed forces personnel". They are not
in the same position as U.S. businessmen. As a part
of their normal perquisites, they usually enjoy the
use of non-appropriated fund activities. They are part
of the armed services in a practical sense, although
not legally. The same applies to contractors, he
continued.

19. Mr. Shin replied that if such a line of r
reasoning were adopted, the number of persons entitled
to use these activities would be too large. The persons
such as contractors and USO personnel etc were not
qualified. Maintenance of control over the contractors
by either the U.S. armed forces or the ROK Government
and preventin of abuses, would be difficult. Mr. Habib stated that
contractors are subject to the same regulations as any
other user of these activities. Therefore, it is not
correct to say that they are not under control of the
U.S. armed forces. Mr. Shin asked what action could be
taken on the part of the U.S. side if contractors sold
goods on the black market. Mr. Habib replied that
their privileges would be removed and the guilty party
could be shipped out of Korea. He pointed out that
contractors are not exempt from the administrative
provisions or from any other relevant article of the
SOFA. In effect, he continued, they are a support
arm of the U.S. armed forces. If they are not permitted
to use the facilities of the non-appropriated fund
activities, it would become much more difficult to
get them to come to Korea.

20. It was agreed to hold the next meeting on
May 17 at 2 p.m.

0325

0326

JOINT SUMMARY RECORD OF THE 22ND SESSION
STATUS FORCES NEGOTIATIONS

May 17, 1963

I. Time and Place : 2:00 to 4:10 p.m. May 17, 1963
at the Foreign Minister's
Conference Room

II. Attendants:

ROK Side:

Mr. Whang, Ho Eul   Director
Bureau of Political Affairs
Ministry of Foreign Affairs

Mr. Shin, Kwan Sup   Director
Bureau of Costums Duty
Ministry of Finance

Mr. Koo, Choong Hay   Chief, America Section
Ministry of Foreign Affairs

Mr. Shin, Jung Sup   Chief, Treaty Section
Ministry of Foreign Affairs

Mr. Pak, Do Joon   Lt. Col.
Ministry of National Defense

Mr. Roh, Jae Won   2nd Secretary
Ministry of Foreign Affairs

Mr. Lee, Kyung Hoon   2nd Secretary
Ministry of Foreign Affairs

Mr. Cho, Kwang Je   2nd Secretary
Ministry of Foreign Affairs

Mr. Kang, Suk Jae   3rd Secretary
Ministry of Foreign Affairs

US Side:

Brig. Gen. J. P. Rawlor   *Deputy Chief B Staff, 8th Army*

Mr. William J. Ford   First Secretary of the
Embassy

Capt. R.M. Brownlie   Assistant Chief of Staff
USN/K

Mr. L.J. Fuller   Staff Judge Advocate
United Nations Command

0327

Mr. Benjamin A. Fleck (Rapporteur and Press Officer)	First Secretary of the Embassy
Mr. Robert A. Lewis	Second Secretary and Consul of the Embassy
Lt. Col. R.E. Miller	Staff Officer, JAG 8th Army
Lt. Col. W.A. Burt	J-5

1. Before beginning substantive discussion, Mr. Whang introduced Lt. Col. Pak Do Joon, attending in place of Colonel Lee. Lt. Col. Pak was welcomed by the U.S. side.

Non-Appropriated Fund Activities/Organizations

2. Opening substantive discussion, Mr. Whang recalled that at the previous meeting, the U.S. side had said that it would submit alternative language for subparagraph 1(b) of the draft article dealing with non-appropriated fund activities. General Lawlor replied that the U.S. side wished to submit such alternative language and tabled the following suggested sub-paragraph:

> "When a newspaper authorized and regulated by the United States military authorities is sold to the general public, it shall be subject to Korean regulations, licenses, fees, taxes or similar controls so far as such circulation is concerned."

Mr. Whang stated that the Korean side accepted the language proposed by the U.S. side.

Contractors

3. The negotiators then turned their attention to the drafts of the article dealing with contractors. General Lawlor stated that Lt. Colonel Miller would negotiate this article for the U.S. side. Lt. Colonel Miller suggested that the article be taken up paragraph by paragraph. Mr. Whang agreed.

0329

한·미국 간의 상호방위조약 제4조에 의한 시설과 구역 및 한국에서의 미국군대의 지위에 관한 협정(SOFA) 전59권. 1966.7.9 서울에서 서명 : 1967.2.9 발효(조약 232호) (V.50 실무교섭회의 합의의사록, 제10-37차, 1963) (2/2) 175

Paragraph 1

4.   Mr. Whang remarked that the two drafts of paragraph
1 more or less differed both in expression and in substance.
He said it was the view of the Korean side that the
contractors working for the armed forces differed in
nature from the civilian component of the armed forces.
Since the contractors were in business to make profits,
they should be accorded treatment with regard to
privileges and immunities which was different than the
treatment accorded to the civilian component. He said
the Korean side was prepared to agree to favorable
treatment of corporations, organized under the laws of
the United States, contractors and their employees
ordinarily resident in the United States.

5.   Lt. Colonel Miller replied that the contractors
working for the U.S. armed forces were contributing to
the successful completion of the mission of the armed
forces just as much as were the civilian component.
contributing in a different manner. There are times when it is more economical for
However, the contractors were the armed forces to deal
with contractors rather than hiring civilian employees.
He added that it is not always possible to secure
contractors in the United States.   Therefore, the U.S.
draft of this article makes provision for contracting
with third-country corporations and personnel. Lt.
Colonel Miller pointed out that there is little difference
between a corporation operating in order to make a profit
and an individual working for wages. He said that the
contractors should receive the same treatment as the
civilian component of the armed forces. He pointed out
that both drafts applied only to those corporations and
persons who are present in Korea "solely for the purpose

주한미군지위협정(SOFA) 서명 및 발효 20

of executing contracts with the United States for the benefit of the United States armed forces". He said that the word "solely" was a key word and that the only exception to this provision was to be found in the proposed Agreed Minute of the U.S. draft.

6. Mr. Whang said that the U.S. side might be laboring under the misapprehension that the terms of the Korean draft would rule out the possibility of entering into contracts with third-country corporations or personnel. He said the Korean draft did not prevent this from being done when necessary. However, the privileges and immunities conferred by the SOFA would be given only to United States corporations and residents of the United States. Third-country nationals not resident in the United States would be treated by the Government of the Republic of Korea as ordinary aliens.

7. Lt. Colonel Miller pointed out that the U.S. armed forces had to pay for the services of the contractors. If the U.S. armed forces could accomplish their mission in Korea most economically by hiring third-country contractors, they wanted the SOFA to confer on them the right to do so. He pointed out that the third-country national employees of the contractors were in Korea solely to perform services for the accomplishment of the mission of the U.S. armed forces. If they were present in Korea for any other purpose, they would not be subject to the provisions of this article. He pointed out that if they were declared ineligible for the benefits of this article, they would be most reluctant to come to Korea.

0333

8. Mr. Whang said that the Korean draft was similar to the corresponding article of the Status of Forces Agreement between the United States Government and the Government of Japan. Lt. Colonel Miller replied that the SOFA currently under negotiation was intended to fit the needs of the situation in Korea. He said that both sides had been negotiating consistently on that basis and had been seeking an agreement that would meet the unique circumstances existing in Korea. He reiterated the belief of the U.S. side that in order to accomplish their mission most economically, the U.S. armed forces from time to time would need to use third-country contractors.

9. Mr. Whang reiterated the view of the Korean side that inasmuch as the SOFA would be an agreement between the United States Government and the ROK Government, this article should cover only United States corporations and residents of the United States. Although quite willing to extend the suggested privileges and immunities to such corporations and residents, the ROK Government would find it difficult to extend the same treatment to third-country nationals. He said if the U.S. side would agree to the ROK position, the Korean side was prepared to consider favorably the inclusion of dependents of residents of the United States under the provisions of this article.

10. Lt. Colonel Miller replied that agreement had been reached previously with regard to the Definitions Article, which provides for the direct hire by the U.S. armed forces of third-country nationals. The U.S. side

0335

비등87→22토]

0332

0336

주한미군지위협정(SOFA) 서명 및 발효 20

believed that the same principle should apply to 0338
contractors. He said the U.S. side appreciated the
statement of the Korean side with regard to dependents.
Mr. Whang remarked that the ROK draft was similar to the
provisions of the SOFA with Japan, which made no mention
of third-country nationals. He said if the U.S. side
would accept the Korean side's language regarding this
point, the Korean side would accept the U.S. side's
language regarding dependents and "other armed forces
in Korea under the Unified Command". Lt. Colonel Miller
remarked that the latter phrase was almost identical to
language already agreed upon in the Customs Article.

<u>Paragraph 2</u>

11. Turning to paragraph 2, Lt. Colonel Miller
called the attention of the Korean side to an apparent
typographical error in the first sentence of the Korean
draft. He said the word "contracts" apparently should
be "contractors". Mr. Whang agreed and the correction
was made. Lt. Colonel Miller also suggested that the
word "or" immediately following the word "involved" in
the Korean draft could be omitted in order to make a
smoother sentence. Mr. Whang agreed. Lt. Colonel Miller
then stated that the word "consultation" in both drafts
should not be interpreted as meaning agreement. He pointed
out that there would be instances in which decisions
would have to be made concerning the technical qualifications
which would have to be met by the contractor in order to
carry out a specific task. Only the U.S. armed forces
would be able to make such decisions, he said. Mr. Whang
stated that the Korean side would give further consideration

0337

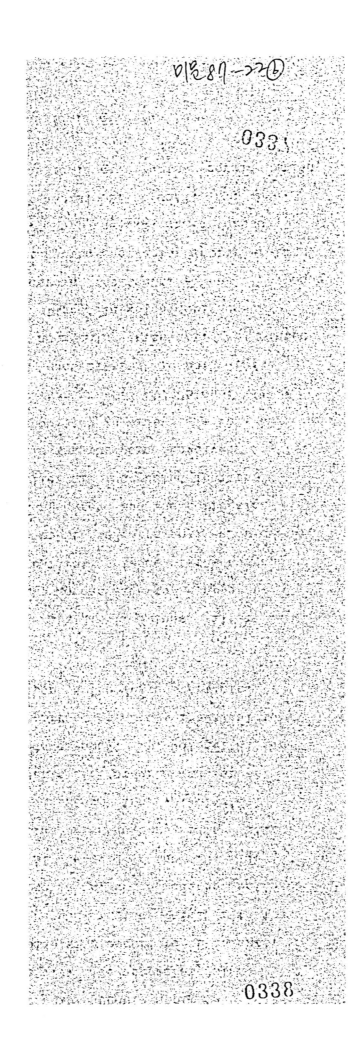

to this point. Lt. Colonel Miller then suggested that
the introductory portion of paragraph 2 of the U.S. draft
be agreed to, subject to further study by the Korean
side of the implications of the word "consultation".
Mr. Whang pointed out that the U.S. draft read "Korea"
instead of "Republic of Korea". Lt. Colonel Miller
replied that this was the type of stylistic question
which it had been agreed would be settled at the close
of the negotiations during final review of the entire
Agreement.

12. Mr. Whang stated that the Korean side accepted
subparagraphs (a) and (b) of the U.S. draft of paragraph 2.

13. Mr. Whang stated that the wording of the two
drafts of subparagraph (c) was different, although the
substance was the same. Lt. Colonel Miller replied that
the U.S. draft, in using the phrase "upon proof that",
states a definite point in time at which the requisite
action can be taken. The details could be worked out
by the Joint Committee. He said the U.S. draft, while
not differing in substance, was more precise than the
Korean draft. Mr. Whang then asked for clarification
of the phrase "upon proof that". Did it mean only after
a court verdict of guilty had been handed down, or did
it mean simply after the presentation of material
evidence of guilt? Lt. Colonel Miller replied that the
U.S. draft did not contemplate the necessity for a court
material evidence of guilt
conviction but only the presentation of such as may be
agreed upon by the two governments through the Joint
Committee. ~~material evidence of guilt~~ General Lawlor
confirmed this interpretation and Mr. Whang said the
Korean side accepted the U.S. draft of subparagraph (c)
with that understanding.

0339

Paragraph 3

14. Turning to paragraph 3, Mr. Whang stated that the U.S. draft omitted mention of employees. He requested an explanation of this omission. Lt. Colonel Miller replied that the phrase "such persons" referred to the contractors, their employees, and their dependents, as identified in paragraph 1 of the U.S. draft. Mr. Whang then stated that the problem here was the same as that with paragraph 1. If the U.S. side would agree to limiting the provision to corporations organized under the laws of the United States and to residents of the United States, the Korean side would agree to the inclusion of dependents throughout the article with regard to such definitions of contractors.

15. Mr. Whang pointed out that subparagraph (a) of paragraph 3 of the U.S. draft had no counterpart in the Korean draft. He said the Korean side had no objection in principle to the inclusion of this subparagraph. However, in view of the use of the word "benefits" which appeared in the introductory part of Paragraph 3, he suggested the deletion from subparagraph (a) of the phrase "rights of". Lt. Colonel Miller replied that the U.S. side did not understand the objection to the use of the word "rights" in this sub-paragraph, particularly in view of the fact that both sides had used the word in other sections of this paragraph — the Korean side in subparagraphs (c) and (e) and the U.S. side in subparagraph (d), (e), (f), (h), and (i). In reply, Mr. Whang pointed out that the "rights" referred to in subparagraphs (c) and (e) of the Korean draft and subparagraphs (d) and (f)

한·미국 간의 상호방위조약 제4조에 의한 시설과 구역 및 한국에서의 미국군대의 지위에 관한 협정(SOFA)
전59권. 1966.7.9 서울에서 서명 : 1967.2.9 발효(조약 232호) (V.50 실무교섭회의 합의의사록, 제10-37차, 1963) (2/2) 187

미문 87-22 ⑧

1480

0342

of the U.S. draft were rights conferred by the U.S. armed forces on the contractors, whereas the other rights referred to in the U.S. draft were benefits conferred on the U.S. armed forces. Lt. Colonel Miller said the U.S. side would consider this question.

16. Mr. Whang stated that the Korean side accepted subparagraph (b) of the U.S. draft.

17. Mr. Whang stated that subparagraph (c) of the U.S. draft and subparagraph (b) of the Korean draft were almost identical. He said the Korean side accepted the U.S. draft, with the understanding that no agreement had yet been reached on paragraph 3 of the Customs Article, to which this subparagraph refers.

18. Mr. Whang stated that the Korean side accepted subparagraph (d) of the U.S. draft, with the understanding that the unresolved question of using the word "activities" or the word "organizations" would be settled at a later date and subject to agreement on the non-appropriated fund organization article.

19. With regard to subparagraph (e) of the U.S. draft and its counterpart, subparagraph (d) of the Korean draft, Mr. Whang suggested acceptance of the Korean language, for the sake of consistency with the introductory language of the paragraph and the other subparagraphs. Lt. Colonel Miller stated that this was the same question that had been raised in connection with subparagraph (a) of the U.S. draft. He said the U.S. side would consider it.

20. Mr. Whang stated that the Korean side accepted subparagraph (f) of the U.S. draft, subject to subsequent agreement on the MPC Article.

한·미국 간의 상호방위조약 제4조에 의한 시설과 구역 및 한국에서의 미국군대의 지위에 관한 협정(SOFA)
전59권. 1966.7.9 서울에서 서명 : 1967.2.9 발효(조약 232호) (V.50 실무교섭회의 합의의사록, 제10-37차, 1963) (2/2) 189

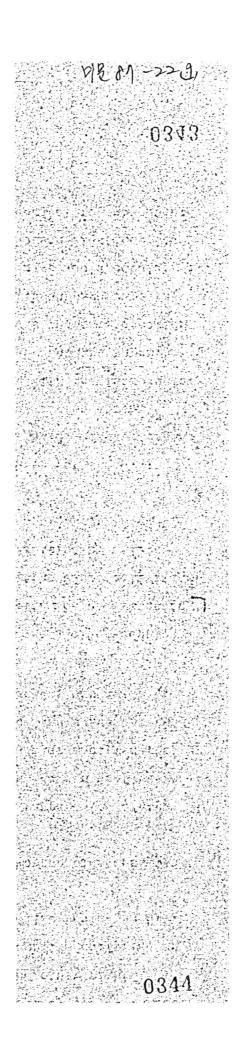

21. Mr. Whang stated that the Korean side accepted subparagraph (g) of the U.S. draft, subject to subsequent agreement on the Military Post Offices Article.

22. Mr. Whang suggested deletion from the U.S. draft of subparagraph (h), which had no counterpart in the Korean draft. He said that contractors working for the U.S. armed forces would be given the use of utilities and services to the fullest extent within the capability of the ROK Government. Lt. Colonel Miller pointed out that this subparagraph was intended to guarantee the contractors the same rates and treatment as those accorded the U.S. armed forces. Mr. Whang then suggested the deletion of the subparagraph with the understand that the right to use the utilities and services which were accorded to the U.S. armed forces would be granted to the contractors. He explained that the draft Utilities and Services Article includes not only the right to use utilities and services but also the right to operate them. He said the Korean side was unwilling to agree to giving the contractors the right to operate utilities involving electric supply, water supply or transportation facilities. He said the Korean side had no objection to the U.S. armed forces being given the right of operation but the Korean side did not believe the SOFA should give the same right directly to the contractors. The contractors could be permitted by the U.S. armed forces to operate some of these utilities on behalf of the armed forces, but the right to do so would be the right of the armed forces and not the right of the contractors. In sum, the SOFA should not give the contractors the right to operate utilities and services in their own name.

0345

Lt. Colonel Miller replied that the U.S. side would
study the Korean position.

23. Mr. Whang stated that subparagraph (i) of the
U.S. draft also had no counterpart in the Korean draft.
He said that the Korean side anticipated that contractors
would follow the same procedure with regard to registration of vehicles and procurement of driving permits as
other aliens and Korean nationals. Lt. Colonel Miller
replied that the contractors would be in Korea for the
purpose of contributing to the accomplishment of the
mission of the U.S. armed forces. Therefore, the U.S.
side believed that they should be treated in the same
manner as members of the armed forces, the civilian
component, and their dependents. Mr. Whang replied that
the importation of vehicles free of duty is one thing
but the registration of those vehicles is quite another
matter. He said there was no objection to the importation
of vehicles by the contractors but the Korean side
believed that the registration procedures covering those
vehicles should be the same as those which applied to
the vehicles of other aliens and Korean nationals. The
Korean side believed this should also be the case with
regard to the vehicles imported by the members of the
civilian component and dependents. Lt. Colonel Miller
suggested that further discussion of this subject be
deferred until after the draft article dealing with the
registration of vehicles was tabled. The Korean side agreed.

24. Mr. Whang stated that the Korean side accepted
subparagraph (j) of the U.S. draft.

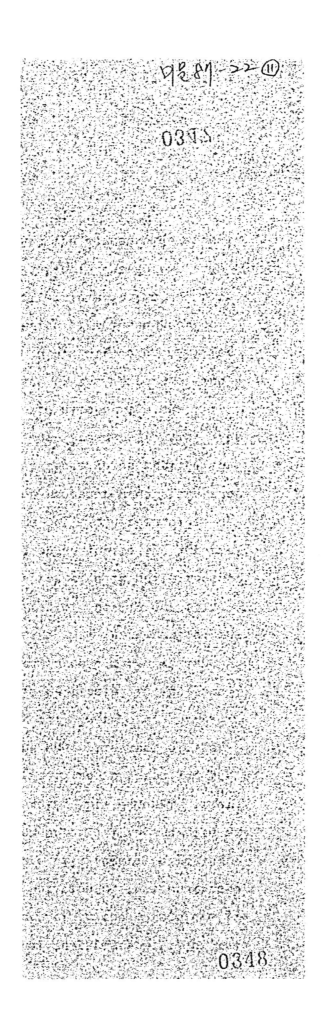

Paragraph 4

25. Turning to the two drafts of paragraph 4, Mr. ○○ Whang stated that this paragraph was relevant to the Entry and Exit Article. He said the Korean side believed the contractors should possess passports which would enable the ROK authorities verify their status. Lt. Colonel Miller pointed out that the Korean side had just agreed to paragraph 3(b), which stated that entry of contractors into Korea should be effected in accordance with the provisions of the Entry and Exit Article. Turning to paragraph 4 of the latter article, Lt. Colonel Miller reminded the negotiators that it called for the issuance of "appropriate documentation" by the United States authorities to permit verification of the status of the bearers. He said it thus appeared that paragraph 3(b) of the Contractors Article covered the points raised in the Korean draft of paragraph 4 of the latter article. Mr. Whang replied that contractors are different from civilian employees because the former are in business to make profits. They should be subject to Korean entry and exit regulations and their status should be verified by the Korean authorities upon entry or exit. Therefore, they should possess passports in which their status is clearly described. Lt. Colonel Miller remarked that paragraph 3(b) and the Korean draft of paragraph 4 appeared to be contradictory.

26. Mr. Whang stated that the Korean side had agreed to paragraph 3(b). However, in paragraph 4, the Korean side wished to define clearly the fact that contractors should be subject to Korean passport and visa regulations. Paragraph 3(b), therefore, was within the scope of the proposed paragraph 4. Mr. Whang added that

0349

when the Korean side had agreed to the Entry and Exit
Article, it had agreed to appropriate documentation in
addition to passports. Members of the U.S. side objected
to this interpretation of the Entry and Exit Article.
Mr. Fleck was asked to read paragraph 7 of the Agreed
Joint Summary Record of the 6th meeting, which records
that Mr. Habib had stated that "persons of U.S. nationality falling under the provisions of paragraph 4, (of
the Entry and Exit Article) would ordinarily carry
documentation including passports and other identify-
ing papers", sufficiently detailed to permit verification of their status. The record shows that the
Korean side then agreed to the use of "appropriate
documentation" with the understanding that it would
include sufficient information to permit verification.

27. Mr. Whang stated that the Korean side desired
the contractors to have passports and additional iden-
tifying documents. He pointed out that paragraph
2 of the Entry and Exit Article specifically exempts
members of the U.S. armed forces from Korean passport
and visa laws and regulations but does not so exempt
the civilian component and dependents, except for the
Korean laws and regulations on the registration and
control of aliens. At this point, it was decided to
adjourn the meeting and continue discussion of this
article at the next meeting.

28. The next meeting was scheduled for May 31
at 2:00 p.m.

0351

May 31, 1963

I. Time and Place: 2:00 to 4:00 p.m. May 31, 1963 at
    the Foreign Minister's Conference
    Room

II. Attendants:

ROK Side:

Mr. Whang, Ho Eul	Director Bureau of Political Affairs Ministry of Foreign Affairs
Mr. Shin, Kwan Sup	Director Bureau of Customs Duty Ministry of Finance
Mr. Koo, Choong Whay	Chief, America Section Ministry of Foreign Affairs
Mr. Shin, Jung Sup	Chief, Treaty Section Ministry of Foreign Affairs
Col. Nam Koo Lee	Chief, Military Affairs Section Ministry of National Defense
Mr. Kee, Kyung Hoon	2nd Secretary Ministry of Foreign Affairs
Mr. Cho, Kwang Je	2nd Secretary Ministry of Foreign Affairs
Mr. Kang, Suk Jae	2nd Secretary Ministry of Foreign Affairs

U.S. Side:

Mr. Philip C. Habib	Counselor of the Embassy for Political Affairs
Brig. Gen. J. D. Lawlor	Deputy Chief of Staff 8th Army
Mr. William J. Ford	First Secretary of the Embassy
Capt. R. M. Brownlie	Assistant Chief of Staff USN/K
Col. G. G. O'Connor	Deputy Chief of Staff 8th Army
Col. L. J. Fuller	Staff Judge Advocate United Nations Command

0353

Mr. Robert A. Lewis	Second Secretary and Consul of the Embassy
Lt. Col. R. B. Miller	Staff Officer, JAG 8th Army
Robert A. Kinney	J-5 United Nations Command
Major Robert D. Peckham	Staff Officer, JAG 8th Army

1. Mr. Habib opened the meeting by announcing regretfully that this would be the last meeting attended by General Lawlor and Lt. Col. Miller, who were both being reassigned. He then intorduced Mr. Robert A. Kinney, a civilian employee of the Department of the Army, working in the J-5 section of the UNC, who was taking Lt. Col. Burt's place on the negotiating team, and Major Robert D. Peckham, who would be replacing Lt. Col. Miller. Mr. Whang welcomed Mr. Kinney and Major Peckham, expressed great regret at the imminent departure of General Lawlor and Lt. Col. Miller, and wished them good fortune in their next assignments.

<u>Contractors Article</u>

2. Turning to substantive matters, Mr. Whang reminded the negotiators that at the previous meeting, discussion of the contractors article had been interrrupted at paragraph 4. He inquired whether the U.S. side wished to resume discussion at that point or to begin discussion again at the beginning of the article. Lt. Col. Miller replied that the U.S. side wished to resume the discussion at the point at which it had been broken off at the last meeting.

3. Lt. Col. Miller then read the following statement:

"Just prior to adjournment of our last meeting we were discussing paragraphs 4 of our respective draft Invited Contractor articles. We had considered the effect of your draft first sentence of your paragraph 4

0355

on paragraph 3(b) of our draft and 3(a) of your draft. The first sentence of paragraph 4 of your draft provides that invited contractors and their dependents shall be subject to Korean passport and visa regulations and shall possess passports with their status described therein.

"In the course of this discussion, we also referred to paragraph 4 of the exit and entry article which provides for appropriate documentation. I believe that there was some misunderstanding at that point. I would like to clarify our views at this time.

"It is our understanding that civilian employees of our armed forces and the dependents of our armed forces personnel and civilian employees will possess passports. In addition, they will possess 'Appropriate documentation' issued by U.S. authorities, so that their status may be varified by Korean officials.

"We also expect that our invited contractors, their employees, and their dependents, will be in possesstion of passports. However, our passport regulations do not provide for all of the other data which may be required to show their status. This is no different than in the case of armed forces civilian employees and dependents. We believe that the additional requirement for "appropriate documentation' which supplements passports, meets your requirements. Inasmuch as we would expect the 'appropriate documentation' provisions to apply to invited contractors, their employees, and dependents, we suggest that the first sentence of paragraph 4 of your draft article is not sufficient. I suggest that you consider accepting our draft in view of the above explanation."

4. Mr. Whang thanked the U.S. side for the explanation given Lt. Colonel Miller. He said that according to paragraph 2 of the Entry and Exit Article, members of the armed forces would be exempt for Korean visa and passport laws and regulations, whereas the civilian component and dependents would only be exempt from Korean laws and regulations on the registration and control of aliens. In addition, Mr. Whang continued, the Entry and Exit article calls for "appropriate documentation" in addition to passports. If invited contractors also carry passports and appropriate documentation, they would be subject to the same control as the civilian component and dependents. Mr. Habib remarked that this was exactly what the U.S. side had in mind.

5. Mr. Whang said that the Korean side was willing to delete the first sentence from the Korean draft of paragraph

한·미국 간의 상호방위조약 제4조에 의한 시설과 구역 및 한국에서의 미국군대의 지위에 관한 협정(SOFA)
전59권. 1966.7.9 서울에서 서명 : 1967.2.9 발효(조약 232호) (V.50 실무교섭회의 합의의사록, 제10-37차, 1963) (2/2) 203

with the understanding that the contractors should carry
passports and appropriate documentation in the same
manner as the dependents of members of the U. S. armed
forces, the civilian component and their dependents in
accordance with paragraphs 2 and 4 of the Entry and Exit
article. He noted that the U.S. draft contained the phrase
"from time to time". He requested clarification of this
phrase. Lt. Colonel Miller replied that the interpretation
of this phrase would be mutually agreed upon by the two
governments through the Joint Committee. He pointed out
that the ROK Government officials would know of the arrival
of contractors almost immediately because of the requirements
involving the possession of passports and appropriate documentation. Mr. Habib added that the phrase in question
referred to lists of arrivals, which lists presumably would
be compiled on other than a daily basis.

6. Mr. Whang commented that the ROKG authorities
would issue visas beforehand to contractors intending to
come to Korea. He asked, however, about departure procedures. Mr. Habib replied that the U.S. side considered
the issuance of visas to be insufficient notification of
arrival. He pointed out that the date of arrival and
temporary residence address would be notified to the ROK
Government by the U.S. armed forces. With regard to departure, he said departure rosters would be kept up to date
and passed to the ROK Government through the Joint Committee.

7. Mr. Whang stated that he presumed there would be
cases in which the ROKG authorities might feel it necessary
to get in touch with a contractor before his departure from
Korea. He asked if this would be possible. Mr. Habib said

0359

0300

this could be done through the Joint Committee. He said that

that any inquiry of this nature would be accepted at face value. Mr. Whang then stated that, with that understanding, the Korean side accepted paragraph 4 of the U.S. draft including the words "from time to time".

8. Mr. Whang pointed out that there was no paragraph in the Korean draft comparable with paragraph 5 of the U.S. draft. He asked what was meant by the phrase "depreciable assest". Lt. Col. Miller replied that paragraphs 5 and 6 of the U.S. draft go together. Paragraph 5 is concerned with land, whereas paragraph 6 is concerned with private and personal property. As an example of depreciable assests, he mentioned a contractor excavating a gravel pit, with the value of the gravel remaining in the pit steadily depreciating. Another example would be a lease held on a building. As the period of the lease is gradually used up, the value of the lease declines proportionately. He pointed out that the only property referred to in paragraph 5 is property held exclusively for the execution of the contract held by the contractor. Mr. Whang stated that the Korean side would consider paragraph 5, making reference to Lt. Colonel Miller's explanation.

9. Mr. Whang stated that there did not appear to be much difference between paragraph 6 of the U.S. draft and paragraph 5 of the Korean draft. Referring to phrases in the U.S. draft such as "tangible or intangible" and "other business in Korea", he said that the Korean draft spelled out the substance of the paragraph more clearly and left no room for misunderstanding. Lt. Col. Miller stated that the U.S. side would consider the proposal but that the extra wording did not appear to be necessary.

10. Mr. Whang noted that the first sentence of paragraph 5 in the U.S. draft provided for certification by

an "authorized representative" while the Korean draft provided for certification by an "authorized officer". Mr. Whang stated that the number of persons authorized to certify should be small and that the Korean draft used "officer" to mean a high ranking official. Mr. Whang then asked what the meaning of "representative". He suggested that the individual should be designated through the Joint Committee. Mr. Habib replied that the designation would be made through the Joint Committee and that the "representative" would be notified through the Joint Committee. Mr. Habib further explained that it would be an appropriate person or persons. Mr. Whang stated that he accepted the word "representative" in view of Mr. Habib's explanation.

11.   Turning to paragraph 7 of the U.S. draft and its counterpart, paragraph 6 of the Korean draft, Mr. Whang stated that the Korean draft did not include corporation taxes but that the Korean side agreed that they shoud be included. Mr. Whang stated that the U.S. paragraph 7 was somewhat redundant and for that reason the Korean side was submitting a revised paragraph 6. Mr. Whang said that the Korean side had no difficulty with the first sentence of the U.S. draft but some with the second sentence. Mr. Habib noted that the second sentence of U.S. draft paragraph 7 provided a specific exemption for income of contractors from sources outside Korea, whereas the Korean draft did not provide this exemption. Mr. Whang stated that the Korean draft was meant to provide the exemption. Mr. Habib replied that the exemption was somewhat obscure in the Korean draft but that the U.S. side would consider the draft. Mr. Habib stated that he thought the Korean

0363

side would find the U.S. wording a little clearer. Mr. Whang stated that the exemption was provided by implication, but if the U.S. side insisted on a specific exemption the Korean side would study the matter further and give their views at a subsequent meeting. Mr. Whang asked if it was the intention of the U.S. side to allow the exemption only during the term of the contract. Mr. Habib stated that the U.S. side would consider the matter.

12. Mr. Whang asked if the U.S. side had a paragraph eight (criminal jurisdiction) for consideration. Mr. Habib stated that ~~we~~ would like to defer on this paragraph. Mr. Whang then asked if the U.S. side had considered paragraph seven of the Korean draft. Mr. Habib replied that we would reserve our opinion. Mr. Whang stated that as contractors were mentioned in the article on Respect for Local Law, consideration of the paragraph on jurisdiction in the contractors article might well ~~preclude~~ discussion of the Respect for Local Law article. Mr. Habib stated that the Respect for Local Law article was not dependent on the contractors article and that the article stood on its own merits. Mr. Whang stated that the article includes persons covered in other articles and without agreement on articles covering these persons the Respect for Local Law article would have little meaning. Mr. Habib stated the obligation to respect local law is imposed on these people regardless of the exact terms of other articles on jurisdiction which are to be negotiated covering these people, but if the Korean side preferred to postpone discussion on this article, that would be agreeable, although the

0365

U.S. side did not see the necessity. Mr. Whang said that he was not insisting on postponing discussion until the jurisdiction article was presented but that there was a relationship with the contractors article as contractors are named in the Respect for Local Law article. Mr. Habib agreed to postponement of further discussion

Agreed Minute to Contractors Article

13. Mr. Habib then asked if the Korean side had any comment to make on the agreed minute. Mr. Whang asked what was the meaning of this agreed minute. Lt. Col. Miller replied that the purpose of this minute was to provide coverage under the SOFA to contractors who might also have a contract with another U.S. Government agency as well as the U.S. armed forces in Korea. The U.S. side did not wish to exclude contractors from coverage by reason of their having a contract with another U.S. Government agency. Mr. Habib suggested that the Korean side examine the principle that the U.S. side is trying to establish. Mr. Whang agreed to examine the principle.

Jurisdiction Article

14. Mr. Whang stated that he was not insisting on postponing discussion of the Respect for Local Law article but that he was suggesting that the jurisdiction article should be tabled as soon as possible to give sufficient time for detailed consideration. Mr. Habib replied that at the opening of these negotiations it was agreed to discuss less complex matters first and that in due time the negotiators would come to the jurisdiction article. He further stated that the U.S. side is not prepared to table a jurisdiction article at this time but that we will

take the Korean request under consideration. Mr. Habib reminded the Korean negotiators that there is still () much work to be done on less complex articles. Mr. Whang said that his understanding was the same but that he hoped that each side would have as much time as possible to study proposals on jurisdiction. Mr. Habib replied that there would be sufficient time to study the proposals. Mr. Whang stated that with that understanding, the Korean side would like to discuss the Respect for Local Law article.

Respect for Local Law

15.   Turning to the Respect for Local Law article, Mr. Whang noted that contractors were included in the U.S. draft. Mr. Habib stated that it was appropriate to include contractors. Mr. Whang stated that the Korean side did not object, but asked if it were appropriate to include contractors in the Respect for Local Law article in view of the fact that there are separate articles on civilian component and contractors. Mr. Habib replied that there was no conflict and that for the sake of completeness contractors were included. Mr. Habib pointed out that contractors are not named in the Japanese SOFA, but that they should be to make the article complete. Mr. Whang stated that he was seeking assurance that contractors and the civilian component are different. Mr. Habib replied that the Korean side could be assured that there is a difference and that reference to the definitions article would show the difference. Mr. Whang thanked Mr. Habib and stated that the Korean side would consider the article further and give its views at a later meeting.

Mortor Vehicles

16.   Drafts of the article on Licensing and Regis-

0369

tration of Motor Vehicles were then tabled by each side. Mr. Habib noted that there were substantial differences in the two drafts and suggested that detailed discussion be delayed. Mr. Whang agreed.

17. The next meeting was scheduled for June 12, 1963 at 2:00 p.m.

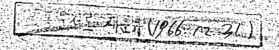

0371

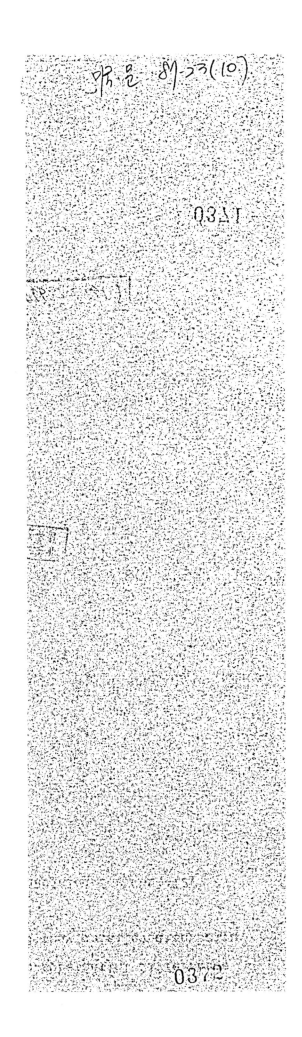

JOINT SUMMARY RECORD OF THE 24TH SESSION
STATUS OF FORCE NEGOTIATIONS

0327

June 12, 1963

I. Time and Place : 2:00 to 4:20 p.m. June 12, 1963
at the Foreign Minister's
Conference Room

II. Attendants:

ROK Side:

Mr. Whang, Ho Eul   Director
                                  Bureau of Political Affairs
                                  Ministry of Foreign Affairs

Mr. Shin, Kwan Sup   Director
                                  Bureau of Customs Duty
                                  Ministry of Finance

Mr. Koo, Choong Whay   Chief, America Section
                                  Ministry of Foreign Affairs

Mr. Shin, Jung Sup   Chief, Treaty Section
                                  Ministry of Foreign Affairs

Col. Nam Koo Lee   Chief, Military Affairs Section
                                  Ministry of National Defense

Mr. Lee, Kyung Hoon   2nd Secretary
                                  Ministry of Foreign Affairs

Mr. Kang, Suk Jae   2nd Secretary
                                  Ministry of Foreign Affairs

Mr. Cho, Kwang Je   2nd Secretary
                                  Ministry of Foreign Affairs

U.S. Side:

Mr. Philip C. Habib   Counselor of the Embassy
                                  for Political Affairs

Mr. William J. Ford   First Secretary of the
                                  Embassy

Col. G.G. O'Connor   Deputy Chief of Staff
                                  8th Army

Col. Howard Snigelow   Deputy Chief of Staff UNC

Capt. R.H. Brownlie   Assistant Chief of Staff
                                  USN/K

0373

2

Col. L.J. Fuller   Staff Judge Advocate   0348
                         United Nations Command

Mr. Benjamin A. Fleck   First Secretary Embassy
   (Rapporteur and
    Press Officer)

Mr. Robert A. Lewis   Second Secretary and
                     Consul of the Embassy

Robert A. Kinney   J-5

Major Robert D. Peckham   Staff Officer, JAG
                       8th Army

1. Mr. Habib opened the meeting by introducing Colonel Howard Smigelow, Colonel O'Connor's replacement as Deputy Chief of Staff, United Nations Command. Mr. Habib reminded the negotiators that Colonel O'Connor had succeeded Brigadier General Lawlor as Deputy Chief of Staff, Eighth United States Army and would henceforth be the principal military member of the U.S. negotiating team. Mr. Whang congratulated Colonel O'Connor and welcomed Colonel Smigelow to the negotiations.

Respect for Local Law

2. Turning to substantive matters, Mr. Whang stated that at the previous meeting the U.S. side had given assurances that the status of contractors was different than the status of the civilian component, even though contractors were mentioned in the Respect for Local Law article. With that understanding, he said, the Korean side accepted the U.S. draft of the Respect for Local Law article. Mr. Habib replied that Mr. Whang's statement was correct and that any exception would be specifically stated in the relevant article.

0375

3

Licensing and Registration of Motor Vehicles

0378

3. Mr. Whang began discussion of the Motor Vehicle article by pointing out a few minor differences in the two drafts of paragraph 1. He said the U.S. draft mentioned "Korea" where the Korean draft read "Republic of Korea"; he assumed that this divergence could be adjusted in the final stage of negotiation. He also pointed out that the U.S. draft spoke of "political subdivision thereof" whereas in the article on Utilities and Services the U.S. side had previously proposed changing the term "political subdivisions" to "local administrative subdivisions". He suggested that, for the sake of consistency, "local administrative subdivisions" be made the language in both articles.

4. Mr. Habib replied that the entities referred to in the two articles were different. Whereas in the Utilities and Services article, the "local administrative subdivisions" referred to in the Motor Vehicles article were the individual states in the United States. He reminded the Korean side that because it had said that there were no political subdivisions in the Republic of Korea, the U.S. side had proposed to subsitute the phrase "local administrative subdivisions". "Political subdivision", however, was the only term which would accurately describe the states under the existing federal system in the United States. Furthermore, automobile licenses and registrations were handled by the individual states and not, as in Korea, by the national government.

0377

미등87-24⑨

0311

0378

4

He said the U.S. side had suggested changing the 0380
language in the Utilities and Services article to
suit the internal situation described by the ROK side;
therefore, he requested the ROK side to accept the
terminology used by the U.S. side to describe the internal situation in the United States. Mr. Whang
thanked Mr. Habib for the explanation and said that the
Korean side accepted the phrase "political subdivision
thereof".

5. Mr. Whang noted that the only difference between
the U.S. draft of paragraph 2 and paragraph 2(a) of the
Korean draft was that the U.S. draft used the plural
whereas the ROK draft used the singular. He said the
ROK side accepted the U.S. draft. Mr. Habib remarked
that the U.S. side believed the plural usage to be more
accurate and more appropriate.

6. Mr. Whang noted that there were substantial
differences between the U.S. draft paragraph 3 and its
counterpart, paragraph 2(b) of the Korean draft,
particularly with regard to privately-owned vehicles.
He noted that the U.S. draft called for licensing by the
U.S. armed forces, whereas the Korean draft would provide
for licensing and registration under the same conditions
as those applicable to nationals of the Republic of Korea.
Mr. Whang pointed out that a separate provision for the
importation of privately owned vehicles free of customs
duty was included in the Customs Article. He reminded
the negotiators that there are ROK regulations setting
forth certain requirements for the registration of vehicles.

0379

5

In order to permit the ROK Government to keep accurate
account of the inflow of vehicles, registration should
be the responsibility of the ROK Government under the
existing regulations.   Mr. Whang added that the ROK
side did not wish to cause the U.S. armed forces any
inconvenience. He stated that applications for registration would be handled as speedily as possible. He
stated further that the members of the U.S. armed forces,
civilian component, and their dependents would not be
asked to pay to taxes which Korean nationals are required
to pay in connection with licensing and registration.
On the contrary, they would be asked to pay only the
actual costs of issuing licenses.

7.   Mr. Habib replied that the U.S. negotiators
were not trying to cause the ROK Government any difficulty
but were endeavoring to establish an administrative
system that would be simple and easy to operate. He
said that certain portions of the existing Korean
regulations regarding licensing and registration,
particularly those requiring the payment of taxes, were
inappropriate for application to members of the U.S.
armed forces. Although Mr. Whang had stated that the
ROKG had no intention to tax members of the armed forces,
the civilian component, or their dependents, nevertheless one of the existing requirements under the Korean
regulations is the submission of a certificate to the
appropriate authority stating that all taxes have been
paid. This, of course, would be a useless exercise if,
in fact, the taxes were not collected. Moreover, Mr.
Habib continued, applicants for licenses and registration

0381

0382

are required to purchase a minimum number of national
savings bonds. This also is an inappropriate requirement, insofar as the U.S. armed forces are concerned.

8. Mr. Habib stated that under the provisions of
the Automobile Tax Law (Law No. 511), the current
annual cost of a license for a U.S. made passenger automobile for non-business use is 100,000 Won (or about
$769 at the current official exchange rate). In addition,
he continued, for the purpose of limiting the number of
automobiles as well as providing for tax revenue, a
surtax of 60% is imposed in the Seoul area, which would
make the total annual cost of a license approximately
$1230.00 for a standard size privately owned automobile.
Mr. Habib stated that the U.S. draft reflects the Status
of Forces Agreements with the NATO countries, particularly
paragraph 3, Article IX of the Agreement of August 3,
1959 to supplement the Agreement between the Parties to
the North Atlantic Treaty regarding the Status of their
Forces with respect to Foreign Forces stationed in the
Federal Republic of Germany. Through experience throughout the world, he said, the U.S. Government has reached
the conclusion that the problem under disucssion is best
handled by allowing the U.S. armed forces to do the
actual licensing, with adequate safety measures and
technical supervision of the vehicles, with the names
and addresses of the owners furnished to the host government. He said this system has worked very well in other
parts of the world. He asked if the Korean side had any
further suggestions to put forward as ways of expediting

the issuance of licenses, meeting the problems faced
by both sides, and avoiding the inappropriate aspects
of the existing ROKG regulations.

9. Mr. Whang replied that the U.S. side appeared to
have given very careful study to the problems under
consideration. He assured the U.S. side that taxes,
certificates, purchase of national savings bonds, and
similar requirements levied on Korean nationals would
not be applied to the U.S. armed forces, members of the
civilian component, or their dependents. In response to
Mr. Habib's statement that such exemption was not spelled
out in the Korean draft, Mr. Whang said that the Korean
side had no intention to impose upon the U.S. armed
forces any taxes in connection with licensing and registration of motor vehicles with the same spirit as
envisaged in the Taxation and customs certicles.
He said the total cost to each applicant would come only
to about $1.10 or $1.20 for the license plates. He said
it would be sufficient if the Joint Committee informed
the ROK Government of the type of car, make, year, engine
number and name and address of the owner. He said the
ROK Government would make the procedure simple as possible.
In reply to a further query by Mr. Habib, Mr. Whang said
that a system similar to that now in force with regard to
automobiles imported by diplomatic personnel would be
satisfactory.

10. Mr. Habib said that Mr. Whang's explanation had
made the position of the Korean side much clearer. He
asked whether the Korean side envisaged any limitation

0385

이용하기 귀@

0387

0386

on the number of licenses to be issued. Mr. Whang
replied that if a five-member family applied for 0388
registration of five vehicles, the request would not be
considered reasonable. The Korean side was thinking
in terms of the average needs of the average family
in the U.S.. He said the ROK Government was concerned
with the traffic problem which would result from an
increasing number automobiles. He inquired about the
number of privately owned automobiles currently in use
by the U.S. armed forces. Mr. Habib replied that at
present there were about 400 automobiles which were owned
by members of the Military Advisory Group, and that
about 50 additional care are authorized for other
personnel on two year tours in the ROK.

Utilities and Services

11. Turning to the drafts relating to utilities
and services, Mr. Whang summarized the changes proposed
by each side at the 20th meeting regarding paragraph 3(a)
of the U.S. draft and paragraph 1 of the Korean draft.
He said the Korean side was prepared to accept the U.S.
proposals to delete "whether publicly or privately owned",
to insert "owned" following the words "which are", to
substitute the phrase "local administrative subdivisions"
for "political subdivisions", as well as to accept the
new 3rd and 4th sentences proposed by the U.S. side,
provided the U.S. side was willing to delete the phrase
"however produced".

12. In reply, Mr. Habib stated that the U.S. side
continued to favor the retention of the phrase "however

0387

produced" and did not understand the objection to it of
the Korean side. He said that this article should not
differentiate the sources of production of utilities.
Furthermore, the U.S. armed forces did not want to be
placed in the position of being refused use of a
particular type of utility on the basis of the manner
in which it was produced. He said that Mr. Whang's
previous arguments that if "however produced" were retained,
the phrases "by whomever produced" and "wherever produced"
should also be used were already taken care of in the
paragraph. "By whomever produced" was covered by the
phrase "owned, controlled or regulated by the Governmrnt
of Korea" and "wherever produced" was covered by the
obvious fact that any such utilities would be produced
in Korea. He said the U.S. side appreciated and accepted
Mr. Whang's assurances that the U.S. armed forces would
be furnished with utilities and services. That being
the case, the Korean side should have no objection to
inclusion of the phrase. He pointed out that the phrase
is included in the text of the Utilities and Claims
Settlement Agreement, which will remain in force, and
was also included in the first Korean draft of the
Utilities and Services Article. Therefore, he urged the
Korean side to reconsider its position.

13. Mr. Whang replied that the paragraph under
discussion applied only to the scope of the utilities and
services to be furnished and not to the manner of their
production. Pointing out the phrase "but not be limited
to", he continued that the phrase "however produced" was
not necessary. He said that the ROK Government intended

0281

0330

to provide such utilities and services to the U.S. armed
forces, since Far Eastern ethics required the host to
treat his guest well.   In reply, Mr. Habib pointed out
that the phrase "however produced" applied only to
electricity, gas, water, steam, heat, light, and power
and did not modify all of the items covered by the phrase
"shall include, but not be limited to".   He said if
ethics were to determine the content of the SOFA, there
was no need for an Agreement at all, since each party
would feel itself bound to deal with the other party
in an ethical manner.   He said the U.S. side appreciated
the willingness of the ROK Government ot furnish
utilities.   The U.S. side believed that the phrase
"however produced" added clarity to the paragraph and
therefore should cause the Korean side no difficulty.
Mr. Whang stated that the Korean side would be prepared
to discuss the matter further at the next meeting.

14.   Turning to paragraph 3(b) of the U.S. draft,
Mr. Whang asked the U.S. side to specify whom it meant
by the phrase "any other user". Mr. Habib replied that
the phrase was meant to include any other user, public
or private, in Korea of the utilities in question.
He pointed out that Agreed Minute #1 of the U.S. draft
was related and would require consultation in the Joint
Committee prior to any change in priority or rates.
He said the U.S. side was trying to avoid the possibility
of discriminatory rates being levied against the U.S.
armed forces.

15.   Mr. Whang replied that the Korean side fully
understood the concern of the U.S. side.   However, the

rates charged the U.S. armed forces are better than those
charged to other users. Mr. Habib remarked that all the
U.S. side asked was that the rates be no less favorable
than those charged to other users. He said that large
users like the U.S. armed forces might justifiably be
charged more favorable rates on economic grounds. Mr.
Whang said that the U.S. armed forces were receiving
discrimination of a favorable nature. He said the
Korean side agreed to the deletion of "governmental or
private" from the first sentence of paragraph 3(b) of
the U.S. draft and the deletion of the entire second
sentence.

16. Turning to Agreed Minute #1 of the U.S. draft,
which is related to paragraph 3(b), Mr. Habib said the
U.S. side agreed to the deletion of the phrase "increase
in utility or service". Mr. Whang stated that the Korean
side desired the deletion of the entire Agreed Minute.
Mr. Habib pointed out that all the U.S. side was asking
was that the ROK Government consult with the U.S. armed
forces in advance of any changes. He said the U.S. draft
would not require the ROK Government ot seek agreement
of the U.S. armed forces for any such changes. He said
the requirement for consultation was not unreasonable in
view of the magnitude of the operations involved.

17. Mr. Whang replied that the ROK Government would
not drastically change the rates because to do so would
cause a great strain on the national economy. Therefore,
any change in rates would require the exercise of utmost
prudence. Prior consultation under these circumstances
would not be convenient. He suggested insertion of the

phrase "shall, at the Joint Committee, be notified 0300
within 15 days after the effective date of such a change"
in substitution for the phrase "shall be the subject of
prior consultation in the Joint Committee". He said
that in view of the close friendly relations existing
between the ROK Government and the U.S. Government, this
matter would normally be discussed in advance with the
armed forces. He asked the U.S. side to consider his
proposal. Mr. Habib agreed to take the proposal under
consideration.

18. Referring to the third sentence of paragraph
3(b) of the U.S. draft, Mr. Whang asked how the existence
of emergency operating needs would be determined. He
asked whether the reopening of hostilities would be a
criterion. Mr. Habib replied that a state of hostilities
would be a primary determinant but that the occurance
of natural disasters should also be considered as a
source of evergency operating needs. It was then agreed
to defer further discussion of this sentence until the
tabling of a separate article dealing with hostility
situations.

19. Turning to paragraph 4 of the U.S. draft, Mr.
Habib reminded the negotiators that at the previous
meeting, the U.S. side had promised to give a short
explanation of current accounting procedures in use by
the U.S. armed forces. He then asked Captain Brownlie
to present such an explanation.

20. Captain Brownlie stated that the purpose of
paragraph 4 of the U.S. draft is to provide for the
establishment of systematic methods of keeping accounts

한·미국 간의 상호방위조약 제4조에 의한 시설과 구역 및 한국에서의 미국군대의 지위에 관한 협정(SOFA)
전59권. 1966.7.9 서울에서 서명 : 1967.2.9 발효(조약 232호) (V.50 실무교섭회의 합의의사록, 제10-37차, 1963) (2/2)　241

of financial transactions arising out of the Status of
Forces Agreement, for the mutual benefit of both the
ROK Government and the U.S. Government. He pointed out
that such a paragraph is normally included in Status
of Forces agreements. For example, the wording of
paragraph 4 is identical with that of paragraph 3, Article
XXIV of the U.S.-Japan SOFA. In general, he continued,
the U.S. side is not concerned with the details of how
ROK Government agencies or private contractors keep
their books. However, it is in the interest of both
governments to insure systematic accounting in the
financial transactions between the U.S. armed forces
and the Korean contractors and/or ROK Government agencies.
the present procedures used by the U.S. armed forces in
executing contracts and in providing for accounting,
proper billings, and appropriate payments, Captain
Brownlie continued, were outlined in a paper, copies of
which he then distributed to the Korean side.

21. The paper handed to the Korean side reads as
follows:

"Method of Accounting Currently Used by USFK

"1. The appropriate Technical Service has
specifications prepared for the type of services
or purchases desired and processes these specifications along with fund citations to the U.S. Army
Korea Procurement Agency.

"2. The U.S. Army Korea Procurement Agency
analyses the specifications, determines the type of
action required, and then either advertises for
bids from private Korean contractors or arranges
for contract negotiations with Korean government
agencies, as in the case of nationalized utility
systems. Bids or negotiations are usually on the
basis of unit price for the utility or service
furnished. Contracts normally specify what is to
be shown on billings so that a proper basis of

미문회-24 ㉠

0398

making payments can be established.

"3. Upon completion of successful bidding or negotiations the U.S. Army Korea Procurement Agency awards the contract for the specified services or purchases. Normally service contracts run for one year and indicate that the contractor or Korean government agency will present a bill for the services every 30 days or at least once each quarter. A Contracting Officer Representative from the Technicial Service concerned accomplishes inspection duties for the U.S. armed forces and insures that the services rendered are of the quality and amount required by specifications. The appropriate Technical Service certifies to the correctness of the billing received and forwards the certified billing to the U.S. Army Korea Procurement Agency.

4. "4. The Army Procurement Agency process the billing and prepares appropriate payment documents and processes these to the U.S. Army Finance and Accounting Office.

"5. U.S. Army Finance and Accounting Office makes payment by check to the contractor or Korean agency involved."

22. Mr. Whang thanked Captain Brownlie but stated that paragraph 2(a) of the Korean draft was more comprehensive, since it provided for specific arrangements to be made by the appropriate authorities of the two governments. He pointed out that these arrangements were to include not only payment but also means of requesting the use of additional utilities and services by the U.S. armed forces.

23. Mr. Habib remarked that the intent of the language of the Korean draft appeared to relate to the "supply" of utilities and services, rather their "use", inasmuch as the U.S. armed forces after receiving the supply of utilities and services, would determine their use. He said that the problem which the Korean side was raising was outside the scope of this article. In effect, the two drafts dealt with two different subjects, since

미문위 -24 내

0331

0100

the U.S. draft was intended to establish a mutually
acceptable system of accounting for financial transactions
arising out of the Agreement. It was decided to devote
further study to this question and to defer further
discussion of this paragraph.

24. The negotiators then turned their attention
to Agreed Minute #2 of the U.S. draft. Mr. Whang remarked
that this Agreed Minute was similar in intent to paragraph
2(b) of the Korean draft. Mr. Habib demurred, saying
that the intent of the Agreed Minute was to specifically
establish that the right of the U.S. armed forces to use
utilities and services shall not be construed as
abrogating the Utilities and Claims Settlement Agreement
of December 18, 1958. Pointing out that the 1958
agreement is not duplicated by the SOFA and that the
SOFA would not abrogate any of the provisions of the
earlier agreement, Mr. Habib stated that unless this was
specifically stated in the SOFA, there was a possibility
that arguments might arise in the future. He suggested
that both sides review the question and defer further
discussion until a later meeting. Mr. Whang agreed.

Taxation

25. Each side tabled a draft article on taxation
and it was agreed that these should be discussed at the
next meeting.

Procedural Question - Tabling of Additional Articles

26. Mr. Habib stated that he would like to discuss
a subject which had arisen in informal conversation

0401

outside the negotiating room. He said the U.S. side wished to have clearly and firmly established the principle that either side could table for discussion any subject or article which it believed pertinent to the negotiations. This would include articles or subjects not included in the list of subjects discussed at the second and third negotiating meetings. Mr. Habib emphasized that list had never been intended to be all-inclusive. He said that either side should feel free to table any pertinent document after appropriate notification to the other side. He stated that the U.S. side was under instructions to table an article on health and sanitation. If the Korean side was in agreement with the general principle he had just mentioned, the U.S. side would table and explain the draft article at the next meeting. Mr. Whang replied that the Korean side in principle and no objection to the principle referred to by Mr. Habib, nor to the tabling of the article in question by the U.S. side at the next meeting.

27. It was then decided to hold the next meeting on June 26 at 2 p.m.

한·미국 간의 상호방위조약 제4조에 의한 시설과 구역 및 한국에서의 미국군대의 지위에 관한 협정(SOFA)
전59권. 1966.7.9 서울에서 서명 : 1967.2.9 발효(조약 232호) (V.50 실무교섭회의 합의의사록, 제10-37차, 1963) (2/2) 249

0400

June 26, 1963

I. Time and Place : 2:00 to 3:10 p.m. June 26, 1963
at the Foreign Minister's
Conference Room

II. Attendants:

ROK Side:

Mr. Whang, Ho Eul	Director Bureau of Political Affairs Ministry of Foreign Affairs
Mr. Shin, Kwan Sup	Director Bureau of Customs Duty Ministry of Finance
Mr. Koo, Choong Whay	Chief, America Section Ministry of Foreign Affairs
Mr. Shin, Jung Sup	Chief, Treaty Section Ministry of Foreign Affairs
Col. Lee, Nam Koo	Chief, Military Affairs Section Ministry of National Defense
Mr. Chu, Mun Ki	Chief, Legal Affairs Section Ministry of Justice
Mr. Lee, Kyung Hoon	2nd Secretary Ministry of Foreign Affairs
Mr. Kang, Suk Jae	2nd Secretary Ministry of Foreign Affairs
Mr. Kim, Yu Taik	3rd Secretary Ministry of Foreign Affairs

U.S. Side:

Col. G.G. O'Connor	Deputy Chief of Staff 8th Army
Col. Howard Smigelow	Deputy Chief of Staff UNC
Capt. R.M. Brownlie	Assistant Chief of Staff USN/K
Col. L.J. Fuller	Staff Judge Advocate United Nations Command

0405

미중 B 87-25상(10)

0402

0406

Mr. Benjamin A. Fleck   First Secretary Embassy
(Rapporteur and
Press Officer)

Robert A. Kinney   J-5

Major Robert D. Peckham   Staff Officer, JAG
8th Army

1. Mr. Whang opened the meeting by welcoming Colonel
O'Connor, who was heading the U.S. side for the first
time, and Mr. Rodney Armstrong, an Economic Officer of
the Embassy, who was sitting in for Mr. William Ford.

Taxation

2. In taking up the draft articles dealing with
taxation, Colonel O'Connor announced that Colonel Fuller
would be the U.S. spokesman on this subject and Mr. Whang
stated that Mr. Shin Kwan Sup would be the spokesman for
the Korean side. In introducing the U.S. draft, Colonel
Fuller made the following opening statement:

"The taxation articles of our various status
of forces agreements provide generally that the
visiting armed forces are not subject to host-
country taxes on property which they hold or use or
transfer. They also provide generally that the
members and civilian employees and dependents of
the visiting forces are not subject to host-
country income taxes or property taxes except on
such private business income and investment type
property they may have in the host country apart
from their official presence there.

"The reasons for such exemptions are first that
the visiting forces themselves should not be taxed
on the property which they must use or hold for
mutual defense purposes and second, the members,
civilian employees, and dependents, being fully
taxed on their income and property by their own
country should not be taxed a second time by the
host country to which they are involuntarily ordered.

"In the United States the income and property
of a service member, civilian employee, and dependents are already fully taxed by the federal
government, state government, county government,
and city government. These taxes continue and must
be paid even when the serviceman, employee, or

0407

0408

dependent is serving overseas, in Korea or elsewhere. It would not be proper to subject him to additional taxes because of such overseas service."

Colonel Fuller noted that the U.S. and Korean drafts are generally similar and that they both are based on other existing status of forces agreements. He proposed that they be discussed paragraph by paragraph. The Korean side agreed.

3. Colonel Fuller noted that the two drafts of paragraph 1 are identical except for the variation between "Korea" and "the Republic of Korea". He proposed that the paragraph be agreed to, with the adjustment of this difference in language to be made during the final editing of the agreement. Mr. Shin agreed.

4. Turning to paragraph 2, Colonel Fuller pointed out that in the first sentence of the U.S. draft the word "any" appears before the words "Korean taxes". Although it does not appear in the Korean draft, he pointed out that it is included in the taxation articles of other status of forces agreements. He stated that its presence or absence would not appear to make any substantive difference. He proposed that it be included in the sentence. He pointed to two more instances in the first sentence of the variation between "Korea" and "the Republic of Korea", which he proposed should be handled in the manner already proposed. He also referred to a recurrence in the first sentence of the previously discussed usage of the word "activities" in the U.S. draft and "organizations" in the Korean draft. He proposed that the basic decision in regard to this difference of usage be made in relation

한·미국 간의 상호방위조약 제4조에 의한 시설과 구역 및 한국에서의 미국군대의 지위에 관한 협정(SOFA)
전59권. 1966.7.9 서울에서 서명 : 1967.2.9 발효(조약 232호) (V.50 실무교섭회의 합의의사록, 제10-37차, 1963) (2/2)   255

to the article on Non-Appropriated Fund Activities/
Organizations and that this sentence then be made to
conform to that decision. Whichever word is decided upon,
he stated that the word "including" in the U.S. draft is
more appropriate than the words "or by" in the Korean
draft, inasmuch as the nonappropriated fund activities or
organizations referred to are official agencies of the
United States armed forces.

5. Mr. Shin replied that the first sentence of the
U.S. draft was acceptable to the Korean side, with the
understanding that the question of "activities" or
"organizations" would be settled later.

6. Colonel Fuller pointed out that the second
sentence of paragraph 2 of the U.S. draft has two clauses.
The first clause, he said, is intended to provide tax
exemption on income derived from sources outside Korea.
Although this provision does not appear in the Korean
draft, Colonel Fuller stated that it should be included
here inasmuch as it is not covered elsewhere in the SOFA.
The second clause of the second sentence, he continued,
is substantially the same as paragraph 4 of the Korean
draft. The U.S. side, he said, believes that since it
relates to the other provisions of paragraph 2 it should
form a part of that paragraph, as it does in other status
of forces agreements.

7. Mr. Shin stated that the second sentence of
paragraph 2 of the U.S. draft appeared to be similar in
construction to the second sentence of paragraph 7 of the
U.S. draft of the contractors article. The Korean side

wondered, therefore, whether the sentence in the taxation article might not be redundant. If not, was there any particular reason for including it? Colonel Fuller replied that the Korea draft of paragraph 2 and the first and third sentences of the U.S. draft refer only to income derived from sources inside Korea. Therefore, the inclusion of the second sentence was not redundant, since there should be some mention in the article of income from sources outside of Korea.

8. Mr. Shin stated that the third sentence of the U.S. draft of paragraph 2 does not exempt members of the U.S. armed forces from payment of taxes on income derived from sources within Korea other than those sources refferred to in the first sentence of the paragraph 2. Therefore, it could be taken for granted that no tax would be imposed on income derived from sources outside Korea. He suggested that it would be more appropriate to place the substance of the second sentence of the U.S. draft in an Agreed Minute.

9. Colonel Fuller pointed out that if this sentence were not included, the SOFA would contain no explicit provisions regarding taxation on income derived from outside sources. The U.S. side, he said, preferred to have an explicit statement in the agreement. Mr. Shin replied that the Korean side interpreted this sentence also to be related to the question of prevention of double taxation, a question which was currently of concern to the authorities of both governments. He suggested that this question be left for settlement outside of the SOFA. To avoid misunderstanding, he reiterated his

0413

미등해 →5비

0413

0414

suggestion that the substance of the second sentence be placed in an Agreed Minute.

10. Colonel Fuller referred to the frequently expressed desire of both sides to hold the number of Agreed Minutes to a minimum. He also referred to Mr. Shin's previous statement that the ROK Government had no intention to tax income derived from sources outside of Korea. If that is so, he inquired, why was the Korean side so reluctant to spell it out in the SOFA? Mr. Shin replied that the Korean side desired this provision to be placed in an Agreed Minute because the first and third sentences of the U.S. draft refer to income from sources within Korea. It was then agreed to defer further discussion of this point until after both sides had the opportunity to give it further study.

11. Mr. Whang reiterated the position of the Korean side that the first clause of the second sentence of the U.S. draft of paragraph 2 should be placed in an agreed minute. He asked whether the second clause of that sentence was relevant to the prevention of double taxation. Colonel Fuller replied that the entire article relates to the prevention of double taxation as well as to escape from all taxation. Mr. Whang stated that the Korean side believed the second clause should appear as a separate sentence, as in paragraph 4 of the ROK draft. It was agreed to give further study to this question.

12. Colonel Fuller then stated that the third sentence of paragraph 2 of the U.S. draft is similar to the last sentence of paragraph 2 of the Korean draft,

0415

with three exceptions. First, the U.S. draft, in
accordance with the example of other agreements, uses the
word "Korean" before the word "sources", whereas the word
"Korean" has been omitted from the Korean draft.
Inasmuch as the U.S. side presumes that the ROK Government
does not intend to tax income derived from non-Korean
sources, Colonel Fuller continued, there should be no
objection to the inclusion of the word "Korean" before
the word "sources". Secondly, he pointed out, the U.S.
draft uses the words "other than those sources referred
to in the first sentence of this paragraph" while the
corresponding words in the Korean draft are "other than
those provided for in this paragraph ". He said the U.S.
side believed the wording of the U.S. draft stated more
precisely the substance intended by both sides. Thirdly,
Colonel Fuller continued, the U.S. draft ends with the
following words not included in the Korean draft:
"nor do they exempt United States citizens who claim
Korean residence for United States income tax purposes
from payment of Korean taxes on income". These words,
he said, are designed to prevent a person from escaping
from both U.S. and Korean taxes by providing that if a
U.S. citizen covered by this agreement seeks to avoid
or reduce his U.S. taxes because he claims residence in
Korea, then he loses his exemption from paying Korean
taxes. Colonel Fuller pointed out that this wording
has precedents in other status of forces agreements and
the U.S. side proposed its adoption as beneficial to both
governments. Mr. Shin stated that the Korean side

appreciated the additional language at the end of the sentence and that the entire final sentence of the U.S. draft of paragraph 2 was acceptable to the Korean side.

13. Turning to paragraph 3 of both drafts, Colonel Fuller stated that they were similar, with three exceptions. First, the U.S. draft includes the words "tangible or intangible" to clarify the intent of the words "movable property". They are not included in the Korean draft, although they are found in other status of forces agreements. Secondly, there was another occurrence of the difference between "Korea" and "the Republic of Korea", which he proposed should be handled in the previously agreed upon manner. Thirdly, the U.S. draft contains the following words not found in the Korean draft: "or to any intangible property registered in Korea". He said these words had been included in the U.S. draft to make it clear that the ROK Government may tax intangible property if it is registered in Korea. These words also are found in other status of forces agreements, he pointed out. Mr. Shin stated that the third paragraph of the U.S. draft was acceptable to the Korean negotiators.

14. Colonel Fuller stated that paragraph 4 of the Korean draft had already been discussed in connection with paragraph 2 of the U.S. draft and that both paragraphs would be given further study.

Health and Sanitation

15. Mr. Whang reminded the negotiators that at the previous meeting, it had been agreed that either side might table whatever draft articles or documents it considered appropriate. He inquired whether the U.S. side

0419

한·미국 간의 상호방위조약 제4조에 의한 시설과 구역 및 한국에서의 미국군대의 지위에 관한 협정(SOFA)
전59권. 1966.7.9 서울에서 서명 : 1967.2.9 발효(조약 232호) (V.50 실무교섭회의 합의의사록, 제10-37차, 1963) (2/2) 265

had a draft article to table. Colonel O'Connor replied affirmatively and made the following statement:

"The United States Government proposes that an article on Health and Sanitation be included in the ROK-U.S. Status of Forces Agreement in order to regularize the current U.S. medical services to the Republic of Korea. We believe that such an article in the SOFA will provide a sound basis for continued cooperation and coordination in these fields between our respective governments. The United States armed forces have endeavored to work closely with the ROK armed forces and other agencies of the Korean Government in the fields of public health and sanitation. Most of the joint ROK-U.S. cooperation in these fields occurs in the front lines areas in the environs of the forward U.S. military installations, in such fields as preventive medicine and the treatment of Korean personnel in need of emergency medical treatment because of injries or other causes. Incidental to their performance of their normal services to U.S. personnel, the Medical Services of the United States armed forces have been ready and willing to respond to ROK Government requests for assistance to meet urgent needs in times of natural disasters and other emergencies. Of course this Article does not obligate the U.S. to continue to supply medical services to Korean nationals, but we feel it does provide the basis for continued mutually beneficial joint ROK-U.S. cooperation in these fields."

16. Colonel O'Connor then tabled the U.S. draft of an article dealing with Health and Sanitation. He said the Korean side could see from reading the draft that the U.S. side believed the article should be stated in general terms. He suggested that detailed implementation of matters of mutual concern to the two governments in the fields of health and sanitation could be handled as required through the Joint Committee. He offered to answer any questions by members of the Korean side, either immediately or after they had a chance to study the draft article.

17. Mr. Whang stated that the Korean side was quite aware of the excellent cooperation and coordination which has existed and continues to exist in this field. He

미문협증 ⑨

0422

said the Korean side hoped that the U.S. armed forces
would continue to provide such aid in times of emergency
or disaster. He said the Korean side would study the
U.S. draft.

18. Each side then tabled a draft of the article
dealing with Local Procurement.

19. Each side then tabled a draft of the article
dealing with security measures.

20. The next meeting was scheduled for July 10 at
2:00 p.m.

마ㅎ·문 87-25(18)

0424

July 18 , 1963

I. Time and Place : 2:00 to 4:00 p.m. July 10 , 1963
at the Foreign Minister's
Conference Room

II. Attendants:

ROK Side:

Mr. Shin, Kwan Sup	Director Bureau of Customs Duty Ministry of Finance
Mr. Koo, Choong Whay	Chief, America Section Ministry of Foreign Affairs
Mr. Shin, Jung Sup	Chief, Treaty Section Ministry of Foreign Affairs
Col. Lee, Ham Koo	Chief, Military Affairs Section Ministry of National Defense
Mr. Chu, Mun Ki	Chief, Legal Affairs Section Ministry of Justice
Mr. Lee, Kyung Hoon	2nd Secretary Ministry of Foreign Affairs
Mr. Kang, Suk Jae	2nd Secretary Ministry of Foreign Affairs
Mr. Cho, Kwang Je	2nd Secretary Ministry of Foreign Affairs

U.S. Side:

Mr. Philip C. Habib	Counselor of the Embassy for Political Affairs
Col. G.G. O'Connor	Deputy Chief of Staff 8th Army
Col. Howard Smigelow	Deputy Chief of Staff UNC
Capt. R.M. Brownlie	Assistant Chief of Staff USN/K
Col. L.J. Fuller	Staff Judge Advocate United Nations Command

0426

Mr. Benjamin A. Fleck   First Secretary
    (Rapporteur and
     Press Officer)

Mr. Rodney Armstrong   Economic Officer,
                            American Embassy

Mr. Robert A. Kinney   J-5

Major Robert D. Peckham   Staff Officer, JAG
                            8th Army

Mr. Kenneth Campen   Interpreter

1. Mr. Shin Kwan Sup opened the meeting by announcing
that in the absence of Mr. Whang Ho Eul on an official trip
abroad, Mr. Shin would act as Chief Negotiator for the Korean
side. Mr. Habib welcomed Mr. Shin on behalf of the U.S. side.

Health and Sanitation

2. Taking up the Health and Sanitation Article tabled by
the U.S. side at the previous meeting, Mr. Shin requested the
U.S. side to explain its draft.

3. Mr. Habib stated that it is a fact that the U.S. medical services, incidental to their normal duties of looking after
the health of the U.S. armed forces, civilian component, and
dependents, render extensive medical services to Korean personnel
and to the Korean community in general, particularly in the
areas immediately adjacent to U.S. military installations. He
pointed out that in these endeavors, the U.S. medical services
enjoy a great deal of cooperation from ROK personnel. Medical
facilities and treatment are provided to members of the Korean
Service Corps. Efforts are undertaken in the field of preventive
medicine in order to control communicable diseases in the areas
near U.S. installations. Koreans injured as a result of activities of the U.S. armed forces are given treatment. Instruction
and advice are given on public health, sanitation, and other
preventive medicine measures. Also, Mr. Habib continued, U.S.
military medical authorities are members of the ROK Ministry
of Health and Social Welfare's Public Health Coordinating Committee.

0427

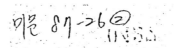

미은 87-26㉣

0428

4. In effect, Mr. Habib stated, the purpose of this article is to recognize and regularize within the SOFA those activities and services which are currently being carried out, establish a sound basis for their continuance, and place in the hands of the Joint Committee the responsibility for working out details. The article speaks of matters of mutual concern, coordination, and the role of the Joint Committee. There is nothing in the draft, he continued, which would obligate the U.S. armed forces to extend medical services to the Korean people, nor would the ROK side wish to include such a provision. The article is intended to regularize and authorize the continuance of the medical services which are being provided, particularly in the vicinity of U.S. military camps.

5. Mr. Shin thanked Mr. Habib for his explanation and stated that the ROK side realized the friendly intent of the U.S. side. However, the ROK side did not completely understand the intent of the introductory language and would appreciate a further explanation of the first three lines of the draft.

6. Mr. Habib replied that the primary function of the U.S. medical services is to take care of the members of the U.S. armed forces, the civilian component, and their dependents. Consistent with that primary responsibility, he continued, the U.S. side is prepared to agree that other functions of the medical services will be carried out through mutual agreement in the Joint Committee. He said the U.S. side realizes that the SOFA with the Government of Japan does not contain such an article. However, there are provisions similar to those contained in this draft article in Article 59 of the German Supplementary Agreement, Article VIII of the Philippine SOFA, and Article V of the 1953 Ethiopian Base Agreement. He pointed out that these provisions are more or less standard and that experience has shown that it is well to regularize medical activities by means of a SOFA article.

0429

7. Mr. Shin stated that each government should be responsible for furnishing medical services to its own people. The
U.S. side had asserted that matters of mutual concern pertaining
to medical services would be carried out through mutual agreement
in the Joint Committee. Therefore, the ROK side suggested the
deletion of the introductory clause. Mr. Habib replied by pointing out that the language in no way commits the U.S. armed forces
to providing medical services to the Korean people nor does it
involve ROK medical services to U.S. forces. He presumed that
the ROK side was not questioning the right of the U.S. Government to provide medical support to the U.S. armed forces. Mr.
Shin asked what was meant by the phrase "furnish medical support".
Mr. Habib replied that it meant the provision of medical services,
doctors, hospitals, and other facilities for members of the U.S.
armed forces.

8. Mr. Shin remarked that there were two principal methods
which could be used in "the prevention of diseases". One was
to treat patients who appeared for treatment; the other was to
practice preventive medicine. He asked whether the language
of the U.S. draft covered both methods. Mr. Habib replied that
the operative phrase in this conneciton was "mutual concern".
These matters were to be worked out mutually by the authorities
of both governments. He said it was the understanding of the
U.S. side that the ROK Government welcomed the various medical
services which are now being provided for Koreans by the U.S.
armed forces. He referred to the provision of vaccines during
epidemics and the spraying of insecticides to eliminate noxious
insects. Was the ROK side implying, he asked, that such services
were not wanted? If they are to be continued, he added, they
should be recognized and regularized in this SOFA, as has been
done in other similar agreements. Mr. Shin replied that the ROK
side believed that such services should be continued. He said
the ROK side would consider the explanation of the draft article

0431

given by the U.S. side and would give its views at the next
meeting.

Local Procurement

9. Turning to the Local Procurement Article, Mr. Shin
remarked that paragraphs 1 and 2 in both drafts were identical
in language and substance. They were thereupon accepted by both
sides.

10. Turning to paragraph 3, Mr. Shin stated that the U.S.
draft contained the phrase "including their authorized procurement agencies" and Agreed Minute 3(b) proposed by the U.S. side
contained the phrase "an authorized agent of the United States
armed forces". He asked for an explanation of these phrases.
Mr. Habib replied that the first phrase referred to by Mr. Shin
was consistent with the phraseology used in the Customs Article,
which had already been discussed. He said this language was
more appropriate than the phrase "or by authorized procurement
agencies of the United States armed forces" used in the Korean
draft, inasmuch as these procurement agencies are actually a
part of the armed forces. They are the machinery of the armed
forces by which procurement is effected. With regard to the
use of the term " agent" rather than "officer", Mr. Habib pointed
out that the former term is a broader one which would include
a member of the civilian component or a non-commissioned officer.
The term "officer", he explained, has a very specific meaning
which is too narrow for the purposes of this provision.

11. Mr. Shin then referred to the tax exemptions provided
for in the two drafts of paragraph 3. He said the Korean side
had included only commodity, gasoline, and electricity and gas
taxes because of the ambiguity which would result from the inclusion of any others. He said that the Korean draft did not
exempt goods and services procured for ultimate use from the
payment of electricity and gas taxes because of the great difficulty in distinguishing those amounts of electricity and gas

0433

생등 87 -26.(인)○○

0434

used for official purposes from those procured for ultimate use.

12. Mr. Habib replied that one of the purposes of the Agreed Minute #3 proposed by the U.S. side was to establish procedures for certification. He said that the ROK side accepted the principle of exemption from payment of taxes. He said the negotiators were now engaged in trying to define the taxes and to establish appropriate procedures for claiming exemptions. He said that the proposed Agreed Minute #3 would establish the exemption procedures and would specify the amounts of materials and/or services used. He said that the U.S. draft had placed items procured for ultimate use in the first sentence of paragraph 3 since the U.S. side believed that these items should also be exempted from taxation. He said paragraph 3 and Agreed Minute 3 should be read together.

13. Mr. Shin stated that there should be a clear distinction in paragraph 3 between items procured for official purposes by the U.S. armed forces and items procured for ultimate use. With particular reference to the electricity tax, he said that it would be difficult and impractical to try to identify electricity procured by the U.S. armed forces for ultimate use because of the difficulty of differentiating between electricity used for the manufacture of goods to be ultimately used by the armed forces and goods intended for immediate sale on the Korean market. Mr. Habib stated that the U.S. side would consider the Korean position.

14. Mr. Shin stated that the ROK side agreed to the inclusion of business tax in the list of exemptions but suggested that the term should be "Business Activities Tax". Mr. Habib replied that the terminology in the SOFA should correspond with the terminology of the ROK laws. Mr. Shin agreed and stated that the relevant laws were the Business Tax Law and the Petroleum Tax Law. It was agreed to use the terms "Business Tax" and "Petroleum Tax" in the article.

0435

15. With regard to the desire of the U.S. side include

traffic taxes in the list of exemptions, Mr. Shin remarked that the tax was levied on persons, not on goods. It would be diffi- cult, therefore, to identify how much of an individual bus fare, for instance, would be tax. The amount would be trifling and the difficulty of providing exemption would be great. In reply, Colonel Fuller pointed out that paragraph 3 relates only to bulk procurement by the U.S. armed forces, including their procurement agencies, but not to purchases by individuals. He said that currently the armed forces were making bulk purchases of transportation on an annual basis. He said this system was obviously practical since it is currently in effect. Mr. Habib pointed out that paragraph 4 covers individual purchases and provides that such purchases shall not be exempt from payment of the relevant taxes. Mr. Shin stated that the ROK side had thought that paragraph 3 included individual purchases. He said the ROK side would consider the explanation given by the U.S. side.

16. Mr. Shin pointed out that paragraphs 4 and 5 in both drafts are identical with the exception of the omission of the word "the" before the word "taxes" in the third line of paragraph 5 in the U.S. draft. It was agreed to leave this difference in wording until the final editing of the agreement and both paragraphs were agreed upon.

Agreed Minute #1

17. Mr. Habib stated that inasmuch as major changes in the procurement program of the U.S. armed forces in the Republic of Korea would have definite effects on the Korean economy, it was only right that the Korean authorities should be notified as far in advance as practicable of any such changes. Such notification is provided for in Agreed Minute #1, which places on the U.S. armed forces the obligation to make such notifica- tion. Mr. Shin inquired whether the U.S. armed forces were

0437

0438

prepared to provide information also on the current procurement
program. In reply, Mr. Armstrong pointed out the existence of
the ROK-U.S. Joint Meeting for Military Supply Promotion, a body
established for that very purpose which has been meeting on a
monthly basis for a little more than a year.

Agreed Minute #2

18. Referring to Agreed Minute #2, Mr. Habib stated that
this proposed Minute recognizes that there are differences between the laws and business practices of Korea, where the
procurement occures, and the laws and business practices of the
United States, which governs the internal procurement activities
of the U.S. armed forces. The Minute provides for the resolution
in the Joint Committee of any conflict between the two sets of
law or business practices.

19. Mr. Shin stated that the ROK side did not believe that
"other appropriate persons" should be concerned with questions
of law. Mr. Habib said this phrase in the U.S. draft referred
to groups as well as individuals. He said there might be in
existence bodies more appropriate than the Joint Committee to
consider legal questions. Mr. Shin said the ROK side was not
suggesting deletion of thephrase. Perhaps "representatives" would
be a better word than "persons". Mr. Habib said the U.S. side
agreed in principle to the proposed change but, of course, would
have to seek approval from Washington. He pointed out that the
key operative word in the phrase was "appropriate".

20. Mr. Shin referred to the use in subparagraph (a) of
Agreed Minute #3 of the word "representative" and the use in
subparagraph (b) of the word "agent". He suggested that for
the sake of uniformity, the wording in both cases should be
"representative". Colonel Fuller replied that in each case,
the operative word was "authorized". Mr. Habib said the U.S.
side accepted the suggestion of the ROK side in principle, subject

0439

to approval from Washington.

21. Mr. Shin asked for clarification of the phrase "in subparagraph (d) of Agreed Minute #3 "out of funds contributed by the Government of the Republic of Korea for disbursement by the United States". Mr. Habib explained that this wording referred to percentage of certain counterpart funds which is turned over by the ROK Government to the U.S. Government under the provisions of the Commodity Sales Agreement.

Security Measures

22. Mr. Shin referred to the reference in the first sentence of the U.S. draft to invited contractors and stated that if the ROK government provided the same treatment for invited contractors as that provided for the civilian component, it would bring about discrimination against third country nationals. The ROK side believed that the ROK Government should not be obligated to take security measures on behalf of invited contractors. Therefore, he suggested the deleting of invited contractors from the draft article. Mr. Habib replied that to exclude the invited contractors from the provisions of this article would be discriminatory to the contractors. He pointed out that the contractors would be in the Republic of Korea solely for the purpose of providing services to the U.S. armed forces. He reminded the negotiators that they had previously agreed that if a particular benefit were not specifically mentioned in the Invited Contractors Article, it should be included in the relevant article. Since security measures are not mentioned in the Invited Contractors Article, this benefit should be extended to the contractors in the Security Measures Article.

23. Mr. Shin replied that the invited contractors are in the Republic of Korea for the purpose of making a profit and therefore they should be treated differently from the other groups covered by the provisions of this article.

0441

Mr. Habib said that the status of the contractors was in no way comparable to that of foreign businessmen operating in the Republic of Korea, or to that of other third country nationals. These contractors are here solely for the purpose of providing services to the U.S. armed forces. He suggested that inasmuch as the two sides appeared to have differing ideas of the role and functions of the invited contractors, it would be well to defer further discussion on this provision until after agreement was reached on the Invited Contractors Article. Mr. Shin agreed.

24. Mr. Shin proposed that discussion of the remainder of the article be deferred until after the Criminal Jurisdiction Article had been tabled. Mr. Habib agreed.

25. The next meeting was scheduled for July 25 at 2:00 p.m.

한·미국 간의 상호방위조약 제4조에 의한 시설과 구역 및 한국에서의 미국군대의 지위에 관한 협정(SOFA)
전59권. 1966.7.9 서울에서 서명 : 1967.2.9 발효(조약 232호) (V.50 실무교섭회의 합의의사록, 제10-37차, 1963) (2/2) 289

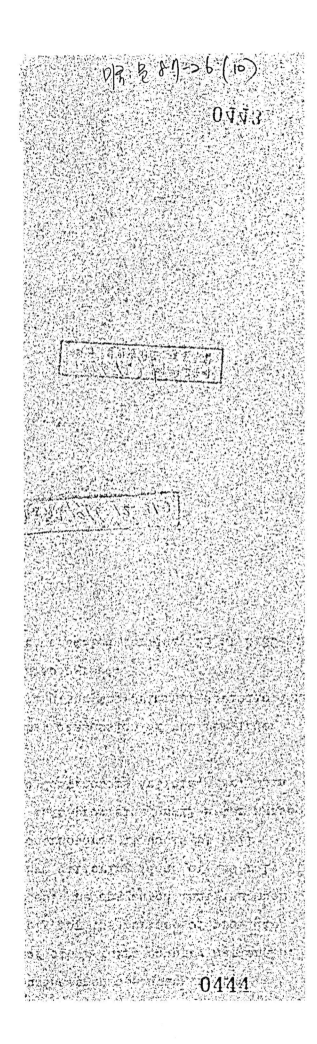

JOINT SUMMARY RECORD OF THE 27TH SESSION

August 2, 1963

I. Time and Place : 2:00 to 3:30 p.m. July 25, 1963
at the Foreign Minister's
Conference Room

II. Attendants :

ROK Side:

Mr. Shin, Kwan Sup	Director Bureau of Customs Duty Ministry of Finance
Mr. Koo, Choong Whay	Chief, America Section Ministry of Foreign Affairs
Mr. Shin, Jung Sup	Chief, Treaty Section Ministry of Foreign Affairs
Col. Lee, Nam Koo	Chief, Military Affairs Section Ministry of National Defense
Mr. Chu, Mun Ki	Chief, Legal Affairs Section Ministry of Justice
Mr. Lee, Kyung Hoon	2nd Secretary Ministry of Foreign Affairs
Mr. Kang, Suk Jae	2nd Secretary Ministry of Foreign Affairs
Mr. Cho, Kwang Je	2nd Secretary Ministry of Foreign Affairs
Mr. Chung, In Young	Observer Ministry of Finance

U.S. Side :

Mr. Philip C. Habib	Counselor of the Embassy for Political Affairs
Col. G.G. O'Connor	Deputy Chief of Staff 8th Army
Col. Howard Smigelow	Deputy Chief of Staff UNC
Mr. William J. Ford	First Secretary of the Embassy
Capt. R.M. Brownlie	Assistant Chief of Staff USN/K

0445

291

Col. L.J. Fuller	Staff Judge Advocate, United Nations Command
Mr. Rodney Armstrong	Economic Officer, American Embassy
Lt. Col. W.A. Burt	J-5
Major Robert D. Peckham	Staff Officer, JAG 8th Army

1. Mr. Shin Kwan Sup opened the meeting by introducing Mr. CHUNG In-young, of the Foreign Exchange Division of the Ministry of Finance, who was to be present of the Korean side as an observer of the discussion on the subject of foreign exchange controls. Mr. Habib noted that Mr. Rodney Armstrong would replace Mr. Benjamin Fleck as repporteur and press officer for the U.S. negotiating team during the latter's absence from Korea on home leave.

Health and Sanitation

2. Opening substantive discussion, Mr. Shin turned to the subject of health and sanitation. Mr. Shin said that there had been extensive and detailed discussion of the U.S. draft article on the subject of health and sanitation at the last negotiating session, and the Korean side believed that they now understood the U.S. position on the subject. Mr. Shin said that he wished to emphasize the provision of the draft U.S. article which provides that the two parties to the agreement will consult on matters in the fields of health and sanitation in the Joint Committee, where due consideration and respect would be given to the medical laws and regulations of the Republic of Korea. Mr. Shin said that he wished to emphasize that in all matters in this area the laws and regulations of the Republic of Korea should be taken into account and duly respected. Mr. Shin said

0447

that, with this preliminary statement, he wished to agree to the U.S. draft article on behalf of the Korean side.

3. Mr. Habib said that it was his understanding that Mr. Shin had just offered an interpretation of the U.S. draft article to the effect that the Joint Committee, during the course of its consulatations on the subjects of health and sanitation, would take into account Korean laws and regulations. Mr. Habib said that it was obvious that this would happen. He wished to reiterate that the U.S. draft article on health and sanitation merely sets forth broad principles for mutual coordination and cooperation between the U.S. and Korean authorities concerned with these matters, and leaves the detailed implementation of these principles to the Joint Committee. It is the intention of the U.S. that the Joint Committee take into account the laws and regulations of the Republic of Korea relevant to medical matters in the course of consulatations on the subjects of health and sanitation. Mr. Habib said that the negotiating record would now show the above exchange between Mr. Shin and himself and thus set forth the principles which should guide the Joint Committee in its consultations on the subjects of health and sanitation.

4. Mr. Shin said that Mr. Habib's statement that the record of the meeting would provide guidance to the Joint Committee with respect to its consultations on the subject of health and sanitation was significant and welcome.

5. Mr. Habib said that he wished to point out again that nothing in the U.S. draft article on health and sanitation obligated the U.S. medical authorities to provide any particular medical services. The article merely provides that the past history of mutual ROK-US cooperation in these matters is recognized and will be regularized. Mr. Habib said that one of the early topics for consultation in the Joint Committee should be the relationship of Republic of Korea Law No.1035, promulgated March 20,1962,

to the services currently being provided to Koreans by U.S. medical authorities. Under that Law, which deals with the licensing of medical practitioners in Korea, U.S. personnel are not licensed to provide medical services in Korea. One of the tasks of the Joint Committee would be to regularize the provision of medical services to Koreans by U.S. medical authorities, taking into account the provisions of the law he had just cited.

6. Mr. Shin said that matters concerning the provision of medical services to Koreans by U.S. medical authorities had been coordinated with the Korean Government in the past, and that the work of the Joint Committee would be to carry forward this coordination into the future with due respect for Korean Laws and regulations pertaining to medical services.

7. Mr. Habib agreed with Mr. Shin's statement, and stated that the article could now be regarded as agreed.

Local Procurement

8. Turning to the draft article and agreed minutes concerning local procurement, Mr. Shin said that the Korean side desired to continue the discussion of the previous meeting with respect to the exemption from taxation of materials, supplies, equipment and services procured for the "ultimate use" of the U.S. armed forces. Mr. Shin said that at the previous discussion of this subject the Korean side had noted its objections to granting exemption from electricity and gas tax to items procured for the "ultimate use" of the U.S. forces. He said that at the present meeting the Korean side wished to mention also its objections to the granting of exemptions from the traffic and business taxes to items procured for "ultimate use", and to outline the arguments in favor of separating the exemptions for items procured directly and for items procured for "ultimate use", as is done in the Korean draft

한·미국 간의 상호방위조약 제4조에 의한 시설과 구역 및 한국에서의 미국군대의 지위에 관한 협정(SOFA)
전59권. 1966.7.9 서울에서 서명 : 1967.2.9 발효(조약 232호) (V.50 실무교섭회의 합의의사록, 제10-37차, 1963) (2/2) 297

of the local procurement article.

9. Mr. Habib said that it was not the U.S. side's intention, in providing for the same exemptions for items procured directly and for those procured for "ultimate use", to seek the exemption of taxes which did not constitute a readily identifiable portion of the cost of the article. He said that the U.S. side's contention was simply that there taxes constituted a readily identifiable portion of the cost of an item, as they often did in the case of items procured in bulk for the ultimate use of the U.S. forces, they should be exempted. The U.S. draft article should be read in close correlation with the U.S. draft agreed minute 3 (a), which was then read aloud. Mr. Habib said that this agreed minute provided a detailed explanation of the certification process by which items for "ultimate use" would be exempted from taxation, and that certification process depended upon the taxes involved being readily identifiable.

10. Mr. Habib said that it was not the intention of the U.S. side to create any of the problems for the Korean taxation authorities which seemed to figure in the Korean side's thinking upon these matters. Mr. Habib cited the example a contractor serving exclusively for the U.S. forces builds a structure of a U.S. facility under the terms of a contract with the U.S. forces. Obviously, Mr. Habib said, the electricity and gas being utilized on such a project can be metered, and should be exempted from Korean taxes. Mr. Habib said that, on the other hand, there would be cases where the amounts of electricity and gas going into the manufacture of a product for the "ultimate use" of the U.S. forces would not be readily identifiable and the U.S. would not request a waver; such would be the case with the brewing of beer by a brewer who sold only part of his output to the U.S. Forces. Mr. Habib said that the effect of the Korean draft article on local procurement would

0453

be to negate the principle of exemption from Korean taxes, of materials purchased locally and to penalize the U.S. Forces for their local procurement.

11. Mr. Shin said that implementation of the procedure provided for in agreed minute 3 (a) may be feasible on the U.S. side, but that it seemed to be difficult from the point of view of Korean tax administration. Mr. Shin said that, for example, according to Korean law, business tax should be levied at all stages of production and manufacture, whenever a sale of intermediate products was involved. Thus, in the case of the brewing of beer, the farmer grows hops; sells the hops to a wholesaler who in turn sells them to the brewer, business tax would be levied on the sale of the hops by the farmer to the wholesaler and on the sale of the hops to the brewer. Likewise, the tax would be imposed on the sale of each component part of the beer from the original producers to the brewer. Mr. Shin said that, according to the U.S. draft of the article under discussion, the taxes at all of these levels should be exempted if the beer went for the "ultimate use" of the U.S. forces.

12. Mr. Habib said the U.S. side recognized these problems, and that it was not the intention of the U.S. side to seek exemption of taxes which did not constitute a readily identifiable element of the cost of an item procured for "ultimate use".

13. Mr. Shin said that, where it was demonstrable that an item had been procured for the "ultimate use" of the U.S. forces, the Korean authorities would be forced, under the terms of the U.S. draft of the local procurement article, to exempt taxes levied at as many stages of the production of that article as the U.S. authorities wished to identify. Mr. Shin said that problems of the sort which he had been discussing did not arise in the case

한·미국 간의 상호방위조약 제4조에 의한 시설과 구역 및 한국에서의 미국군대의 지위에 관한 협정(SOFA)
전59권. 1966.7.9 서울에서 서명 : 1967.2.9 발효(조약 232호) (V.50 실무교섭회의 합의의사록, 제10-37차, 1963) (2/2) 301

of the exemption of commodity and petroleum taxes, and that these
taxes were readily identifiable at the point of "ultimate use".

14. Mr. Habib asked if the Korean side would agree that,
in the case of the contractor which he had outlined earlier, the
contractor should be exempt from the payment of electricity and
gas tax.

15. Mr. Shin said that, in the case cited there would,
in the case of business tax, be three stages at which the tax
would be levied: (a) when the manufacturer of materials for the
project purchased his own raw materials; (b) when the manufacturer
sold his processed materials to the contractor; and (c) when the
contractor sold his finished project to the U.S. forces. Mr. Shin
said that the Korean side would agree that an exemption from
business tax should be granted only at stage (c).

16. Mr. Habib said that it would not be the intention of
the U.S. forces under the terms of the U.S. draft article to trace
back the taxes upon intermediate stages in the production of
articles manufactured for their "ultimate use" and claim exemptions
from these taxes. He urged the Korean side to read the U.S. draft
article in correlation with the U.S. draft agreed minutes, and
to note that agreed minute 3 (a) provided that the U.S. forces
would take delivery of items directly from the manufacturer, and
certify exemptions from Korean taxation only at that point.

17. Mr. Shin asked a hypothetical question: would the U.S.
forces, under the terms of the U.S. draft article, issue a certificate of exemption from business tax to a wholesale dealer in cement
if they purchased cement from such a dealer? Would the U.S. forces
also seek to secure exemption of the business tax levied upon the
sale of the cement in question to the dealer by the Korean
manufacturer of the cement?

0458

8

18. Mr. Habib replied that the U.S. Forces would take delivery of the cement directly from the manufacturer.

19. Mr. Shin said that, in view of the preceding discussion, the U.S. side might find that it could agree with the provisions of the Korean draft article on local procurement, which exempts items procured for "ultimate use" from commodity and petroleum tax.

20. Mr. Habib said that the preceding discussion had clarified for the U.S. the points of the U.S. draft on which the Korean side had reservations, and that the U.S. would see if there might not be ways in which the intent of that draft might be better expressed. He noted that the U.S. draft agreed minutes were the same as those attached to the Status of Forces Agreement with Japan, and that the procedures outlined in these agreed minutes had worked well in Japan. The U.S. side would be able at some future time to explain in detail how problems connected with the implementation of the procedures in the agreed minute had been solved in Japan.

21. It was agreed that, with respect to the other outstanding differences concerning the wording of the agreed minutes to the local procurement article, the U.S. side agreed in principle with the Korean side's suggested changes in wording, subject to later confirmation. The two suggested changes in the U.S. draft agreed minutes are: (a) in agreed minute No. 2, the substitution of "representative" for "persons"; and (b) in agreed minute No.3, the substitution of "representative" for "agent".

Foreign Exchange Control

22. Mr. Shin noted that the article on foreign exchange control had been ~~fully discussed~~ agreed, and that there remained only two differences of view concerning the wording of the agreed minute

한·미국 간의 상호방위조약 제4조에 의한 시설과 구역 및 한국에서의 미국군대의 지위에 관한 협정(SOFA)
전59권. 1966.7.9 서울에서 서명 : 1967.2.9 발효(조약 232호) (V.50 실무교섭회의 합의의사록, 제10-37차, 1963) (2/2)   305

0460

to the article. The first of these differences of view was part
of the general disagreement over the proper term to use for the
description of non-appropriated fund entities. It was agreed
between the U.S. and Korean sides that a resolution of this difficulty would be sought when the article concerning these entities
was again discussed. The second of the differences of view, Mr. Shin
said, had to do with the wording of the last sentence of the
agreed minute and concerned the proper description of the rate
of exchange. Mr. Shin said that the Korean position upon this
point had not changed since the 17th negotiating session on March
19, 1963, and the Korean side still preferred its formulation of
"the highest rate.... not unlawful". Mr. Shin noted that it had
been agreed at the 17th session to attempt to have this difference
of view resolved in an informal working party composed of Mr. Lee
Chae Sul, Chief of the Foreign Exchange Division of the Ministry
of Finance and Mr. William Ford of the U.S. negotiating team, but
that this working party had apparently not met.

23. Mr. Habib asked Mr. Ford to state the U.S. side's
position upon the question of the differing formulations of the
language describing the rate of exchange. Mr. Ford reviewed the
differences in draft language on this point, and said that previous
discussion had shown that the language proposed by the Korean
side is ambiguous and subject to many interpretations. These
differences in interpretation could lead to disputes in the
future which should be avoided by foresight in the present negotiations. Mr. Ford said that he would like to inquire of the Korean
side if the "effective official rate" is at present: won 125, won
130 (won 125 plus the certificate of won 5), won 129.5, or won
130.5 (the current selling rate).

24. Mr. Ford said that under the terms of the U.S. draft

한·미국 간의 상호방위조약 제4조에 의한 시설과 구역 및 한국에서의 미국군대의 지위에 관한 협정(SOFA)
전59권. 1966.7.9 서울에서 서명 : 1967.2.9 발효(조약 232호) (V.50 실무교섭회의 합의의사록, 제10-37차, 1963) (2/2) 307

of the last sentence of the agreed minute no difficulty in interpretation exists. The wording suggested by the U.S. side is already
incorporated in a major agreement between Korea and the United States,
and for nearly two and one-half years has governed transactions
running into many millions of dollars. Mr. Ford said that it would
be a mistake to abandon this clear and unequivocal wording which
has already proved to be satisfactory, in favor of the language
proposed by the Korea side which would be open to many interpretations and give the two governments trouble in the future. Mr. Ford
said that differing terminolgy upon the rate of exchange in the
status of forces agreement and comprehensive aid agreement would
open up the possibility that two agencies of the U.S. Government
might be purchasing won at different rates of exchange. Mr. Ford
said that standard language in the two agreements would preclude
such a situation, the consequences of which would be serious for
both sides.

25. Mr. Shin said that the arguments which Mr. Ford had just
advanced were the same as those made by the U.S. side at the 17th
negotiating session, and that he again proposed that the difference
in wording discussed by a working party made up of Mr. Lee and
Mr. Ford.

26. Mr. Habib agreed with Mr. Shin's suggestion that Mr. Ford
and Mr. Lee meet together, but asked to have Mr. Ford's question
concerning the current "effective official rate of exchange"
answered by the Korean side.

27. Mr. Chung of the Ministry of Finance said that the
present "effective official rate of exchange" for the won is won
129.5 per U.S. dollar. He said that the "basic rate of exchange"
for the won is now won 130 per U.S. dollar.

28. It was agreed that Mr. Ford and Mr. Lee Chae-sul would
meet in an effort to discuss the differences in view concerning

0463

the wording of the last sentence of the Agreed Minute.

29. It was agreed that the next negotiating session
would be held on August 8, at 2:00 P.M.

****

<u>The Text of Health and Sanitation Article as agreed</u>
<u>upon at the 27th session of the SOFA negotiation</u>
<u>held on July 25th, 1963</u>:

<u>Health and Sanitation Article</u>

Consistent with the right of the United States
to furnish medical support for its armed forces,
civilian component and their dependents, matters of
mutual concern pertaining to the control and prevention of diseases and the coordination of other public
health, medical, sanitation, and veterinary services
shall be resolved by the authorities of the two
Governments in the Joint Committee established under
Article _____.

한·미국 간의 상호방위조약 제4조에 의한 시설과 구역 및 한국에서의 미국군대의 지위에 관한 협정(SOFA)
전59권. 1966.7.9 서울에서 서명 : 1967.2.9 발효(조약 232호) (V.50 실무교섭회의 합의의사록, 제10-37차, 1963) (2/2)   313

미등록-개 (II)

0468

JOINT SUMMARY RECORD OF THE 28TH SESSION

0110

August 8, 1963

I. Time and Place : 2:00 to 3:40 p.m. August 8, 1963
at the Foreign Minister's
Conference Room

II. Attendants:

ROK Side:

Mr. Whang, Ho Eul	Director Bureau of Political Affairs Ministry of Foreign Affairs
Mr. Shin, Kwan Sup	Director Bureau of Customs Dupty Ministry of Finance
Mr. Koo, Choong Whay	Chief, America Section Ministry of Foreign Affairs
~~Mr. Shin, Jung Sup~~	Chief, Treaty Section Ministry of Foreign Affairs
Col. Lee, Nam Koo	Chief, Military Affairs Section Ministry of National Defense
Mr. Chu, Mun Ki	Chief, Legal Affairs Section Ministry of Justice
Mr. Lee, Kyung Hoon	2nd Secretary Ministry of Foreign Affairs
Mr. Kang, Suk Jae	2nd Secretary Ministry of Foreign Affairs
Mr. Cho, Kwang Je	2nd Secretary Ministry of Foreign Affairs
~~Mr. Chung, In Young~~	Observer Ministry of Finance

U.S. Side:

Mr. Philip C. Habib	Counselor of the Embassy for Political Affairs
Gen. G.C. O'Connor	Deputy Chief of Staff 8th Army
Mr. William J. Ford	First Secretary of the Embassy

0469

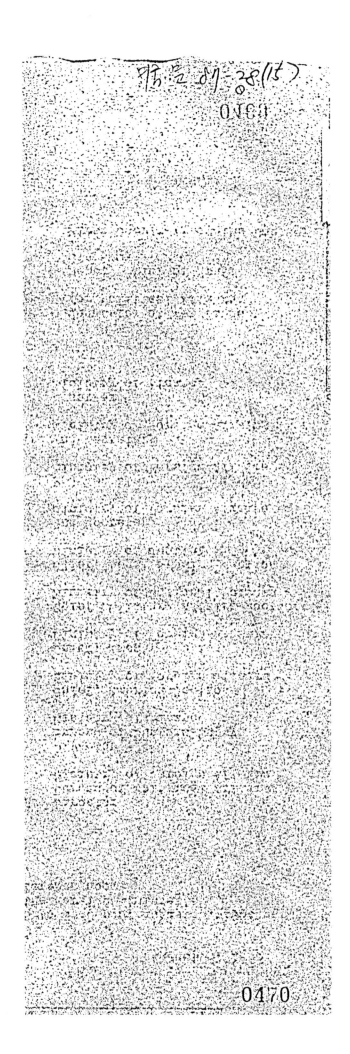

Capt. R.M. Brownlie	Assistant Chief of Staff USN/K
Col. L.J. Fuller	Staff Judge Advocate United Nations Command
Mr. Rodney Armstrong	Economic Officer, American Embassy
Lt. Col. W.A. Burt	J-5
Major Robert D. Peckham	Staff Officer, JAG 8th Army
Kenneth Campen	Interpreter

1. Mr. Hwang Ho-eil noted that he had been absent from the previous two negotiating sessions. He said that he was gratified that good progress had been made in the negotiations during his absence.

2. Mr. Habib said that, since members of the two negotiating teams were now a band of brothers, he knew that members of both teams would take great pleasure in noting the promotion of Colonel G.G. O'Connor to the rank of Brigadier General. Mr. Hwang responded that he had been just about to mention the brilliant new star which was gracing the negotiating table, and to offer the congratulations of the Korean side to its proud possessor. General O'Connor accepted the congratulations of his colleagues on the American and Korean negotiating teams, and offered to stand the house to its traditional round of ginseng tea.

VEHICLE AND DRIVERS LICENSES

3. Opening substantive discussion, Mr. Hwang noted that there had been an exchange of views at the twenty-fourth negotiating session on the subject of the vehicle and drivers licenses article. Mr. Hwang asked if the U.S.

0471

side had any comments in response to the explanations offered by the Korean side at the twenty-fourth negotiating session.

4. Mr. Habib noted that at the twenty-fourth negotiating session there had been complete agreement between the negotiators on paragraph 1 and 2 of the U.S. draft article. The discussion had also revealed to the U.S. negotiators a clearer understanding of the points involved in paragraph 2b of the Korean draft article. Mr. Habib then reviewed in some detail the discussion at the twenty-fourth negotiating session on the subject of vehicle and drivers licenses. He said that the U.S. side had now developed a draft paragraph 3 which it would like to table in replacement for paragraph 3 of its original draft. He said that he was confident that the new U.S. alternative draft for paragraph 3 would meet the requirements of both sides to the negotiations.

5. Mr. Hwang examined the U.S. alternative paragraph 3, and stated that on first inspection he found no difficult points in it. He said that the Korean side accepted the U.S. draft in principle, and would give its definite answer at the next negotiating session.

CONTRACTORS

6. Turning to the next item on the agenda, Mr. Hwang asked if the U.S. side had comments or questions relative to the article on contractors.

7. Colonel Fuller said that in discussing the Invited Contractor Article and references to Invited Contractors in other articles, the Korean negotiators had on several occasions stated that because such persons were making

0473

0474

a""profit" they should receive less favorable treatment
than other elements to be covered by the Status of Forces
Agreement. Colonel Fuller said that under the United
States system of democracy, civilian control, and free
enterprise, the United States Armed Forces, both in the
United States and overseas, obtain a large part of their
required services not by troop labor, or drafting of
local labor, or even by direct-hire, but rather through
contracts with private business. In overseas areas most
of these contracts are with local national businessmen,
but it has been found in many countries that for some few
highly specialized operations no local businessmen existed
who were technically equipped and experienced in such
operations. In these cases the United States Forces had
brought in their own experienced contractors from the
United States. Colonel Fuller said that he wished to
emphasize that procedures he had prescribed were the
American way of using private contractors instead of drafting
people into the direct employment of the U.S. Forces.

8. Colonel Fuller said that the U.S. side had
prepared paper on this subject for distribution to the
Korean side in the hope that the Korean side might see
this question from the same perspective as the U.S. negotiators.
Colonel Fuller said that, as to the question of profit,
the paper points out that any reduction of privileges for
this group, who are mostly employees anyway, would not
affect the contractors carefully calculated profit, but
would instead simply increase the cost to the United States,
a result which would not be beneficial to either side.

5

9. Colonel Fuller said that in order that both sides might see the question of invited contractors from the proper perspective in future discussions, he would distribute the prepared paper. The text of the paper distributed follows:

THE TEXT OF COLONEL FULLER'S PAPER ENTITLED "INVITED CONTRACTORS" SHALL BE REPRODUCED HERE.

10. Mr. Ku Chung-whe thanked Colonel Fuller for his explanation of the role of Invited Contractors. He said that he also has a few general remarks on the subject of contractors to offer. He said that, as Colonel Fuller had explained, it was a well-known general principle that all persons should be treated according to the principles of democracy, as human beings. He continued that the Status of Forces Agreement would be chiefly for the purpose of regulating the status of members of the United States Armed Forces, the civilian component, and their dependents, and that Invited Contractors are an exceptional category of personnel. Therefore, they are to be regulated under a separate article within the scope of the Status of Forces Agreement, and this regulation should not extend to the Invited Contractors the same privileges and immunities as granted to the members of the armed forces and the civilian component.

11. Mr. Habib said that he wished to make clear the feeling of the U.S. side that the status of Invited Contractors is relevant to the conclusion of a Status of Forces Agreement with the Republic of Korea. He said that the distinctions between Invited Contractors and other categories of personnel covered by the Status of Forces

6

Agreement is made clear by the fact that Invited Contractors are treated in a separate article of the draft agreement. Mr. Habib noted that the first Sentence of the U.S. draft article states that "except as otherwise provided in the draft paragraph below", Invited Contractors are subject to the laws and regulations of the Republic of Korea. Mr. Habib said that he hoped that there was no disagreement between the negotiators upon the legitimacy of Invited Contractors as a proper subject to be covered by the Status of Forces Agreement. Colonel Fuller's presentation and the paper he had distributed were efforts to define more clearly the U.S. position with respect to this subject.

12. Mr. Ku said that the Korean negotiators knew the Invited Contractors were in Korea solely for the purpose of serving the United States Forces and that this was the reason for the regulation of their status in the Status of Forces Agreement. Turning to the actual provisions of the Korean draft article on contractors, Mr. Ku noted that the Korean draft defines Invited Contractors as persons, including corporations "organized under the laws of the United States", and their employees "who are ordinarily resident in the United States."

13. Mr. Habib said that, prior to responding to Mr. Ku's statement, he would like Colonel Fuller to sum up the U.S. side's response to the Korean side's presentation at the twenty-second and twenty-third negotiating sessions on the subject of Invited Contractors.

14. Colonel Fuller said that he had one more general remark on the subject of Invited Contractors. He said that the U.S. side was not seeking any privileges or

immunities for Invited Contractors which would be for these individuals' private benefit. He said the intent of the U.S. draft was merely to seek to prevent the imposition of burdens on by Invited Contractors which would be passed on to the United States Government, and which would affect the performance of the mission of the United States Forces in Korea.

15. Colonel Fuller said that, turning to the provisions of the Invited Contractor article itself, the U.S. side had given further consideration to the points raised on both sides in the discussions of paragraph 3 of the draft article at the twenty-second negotiating meeting. He said that the U.S. side had been able to revise their draft of paragraph 3 to accord with the views expressed by the Korean side at the twenty-second meeting. Colonel Fuller said the U.S. side had reproduced a new draft of paragraph 3 and would now table this draft. Colonel Fuller said that the Korean negotiators would notice first that throughout the paragraph the U.S. side had, at the suggestion of the Korean negotiators, removed the word "right" or "rights" from each of the sub-paragraphs (a) through (j), so that they were all now consistent and uniform in not containing such unnecessary words. Colonel Fuller said that, secondly, at the suggestion of the Korean side, the U.S. negotiators had greatly altered sub-paragraph (h) to provide only for the use of utilities and services and had removed language that might have permitted the contractors to operate such public utilities in ways other than under contract with the U.S. Government.

한·미국 간의 상호방위조약 제4조에 의한 시설과 구역 및 한국에서의 미국군대의 지위에 관한 협정(SOFA)
전59권. 1966.7.9 서울에서 서명 : 1967.2.9 발효(조약 232호) (V.50 실무교섭회의 합의의사록, 제10-37차, 1963) (2/2)   327

미문형-780

18/0

0482

8

Colonel Fuller said that, while these changes had resulted in a new draft, it was the hope of the U.S. negotiators that, because all of the changes had been suggested by the Korean side, it would be possible to come to agreement on the draft he had just offered of paragraph 3. Colonel Fuller suggested that the negotiators adopt this paragraph.

16. Mr. Ku, after examination of the new U.S. draft paragraph 3, said he thought it would probably be agreeable to the Korean negotiators. He said the Korean negotiators would study the relationship of sub-paragraph 3(i) to the new U.S. draft of paragraph 3 of the article on vehicle and drivers licenses.

17. Colonel Fuller, turning to paragraph 1 of the draft article on contractors said that the U.S. side felt that the United States should retain the right to bring in whatever contractor would best advance the mission of the United States Forces in Korea. He said that this qualification would not always be possessed solely by "corporations organized under the laws of the United States" (the wording of the Korean draft paragraph 1).

18. Mr. Ku said that the wording of the Korean draft paragraph 1 would not prevent the United States Forces from bringing third country nationals to Korea to perform services for the United States Forces. He said that third country nationals could be used as contractors or employee by contractors provided that they are "ordinarily resident in the United States." He said the Korean negotiators were concerned that, under the wording of the U.S. draft paragraph 1, third country nationals employed as Invited Contractors would be treated differently from ordinary alien visitors to Korea. He said that the Korean

0483

negotiators had studied carefully the U.S.-Japan Status
of Forces Agreement, and that their draft paragraph 1 had
been based on the comparable article in the U.S.-Japan
Agreement. Mr. Ku said that, even though in the Korean
draft the dependents of the employees of Invited
Contractors were not granted privileges and immunities,
the Korean side would consider including these dependents
if the American side would agree to the Korean draft
wording of paragraph 1.

19. Colonel Fuller asked if it was the Korean side's
intention that the dependents of U.S. employees of U.S.
corporations be given or denied the benefits of paragraph 3?

20. Mr. Ku replied that the dependents of those
employees ordinarily resident in the United States would
be given such benefits.

21. Colonel Fuller then asked the intent of the
Korean draft with respect to employees who were not
ordinarily resident in the United States.

22. Mr. Ku replied that, under the terms of the
Korean draft, such individuals would come to Korea, but
they would not be provided for by the Status of Forces
Agreement.

23. Colonel Fuller asked if the the Korean side then
desired that third-country national employees of U.S.
Invited contractors not be paid in military payments
certificates or not be authorized the use of Post Exchanges
Army post offices or Commissaries? Colonel Fuller said
that if the United States Forces could not provide these
services to third-country national employees, it would be
necessary to make up for the lack of these benefits by
additional compensation.

한·미국 간의 상호방위조약 제4조에 의한 시설과 구역 및 한국에서의 미국군대의 지위에 관한 협정(SOFA)
전59권. 1966.7.9 서울에서 서명 : 1967.2.9 발효(조약 232호) (V.50 실무교섭회의 합의의사록, 제10-37차, 1963) (2/2) 331

10

24. Mr. Ku said that it was the position of the 88 Korean side that third-country national contractors and their employees who were not ordinarily resident in the *as accorded U.S Contractor and their* U.S. should not be accorded the benefits employees. He asked the U.S. side would point out those benefits which were deemed most necessary.

25. Mr. Whang said that he would like to supplement Mr. Ku's statement of the Korean position on this subject. He said that the Korean side had no desire to impose upon the U.S. Forces the necessity for providing additional compensation to the Invited Contractors. He said that the principal point of concern which was reflected in the Korean draft wording of paragraph 1 was that grant of the full range of privileges and immunities to third-country nationals would constitute agreement to a less favorable competitive position for its own contractors in respect of contracts with the United States Forces in Korea at the present time? Mr. Whang also inquired in this connection whether the United States Government imposed tax on incomes derived from contracts let by United States Forces within the boundaries of the continental United States?

26. Colonel Fuller said that, with respect to Mr. Hwang's concern about the competitive position of Korean contractors, the United States Forces did not have contracts with Invited Contractors when it was possible to conclude such contracts with local businessmen. He believed, therefore, that there should be no case of conflict if the U.S. wording were adopted. In this connection, Mr. Habib then read aloud to the negotiators the provisions of paragraph 2 of the United States draft, emphasizing those provisions which

한·미국 간의 상호방위조약 제4조에 의한 시설과 구역 및 한국에서의 미국군대의 지위에 관한 협정(SOFA)
전59권. 1966.7.9 서울에서 서명 : 1967.2.9 발효(조약 232호) (V.50 실무교섭회의 합의의사록, 제10-37차, 1963) (2/2) 333

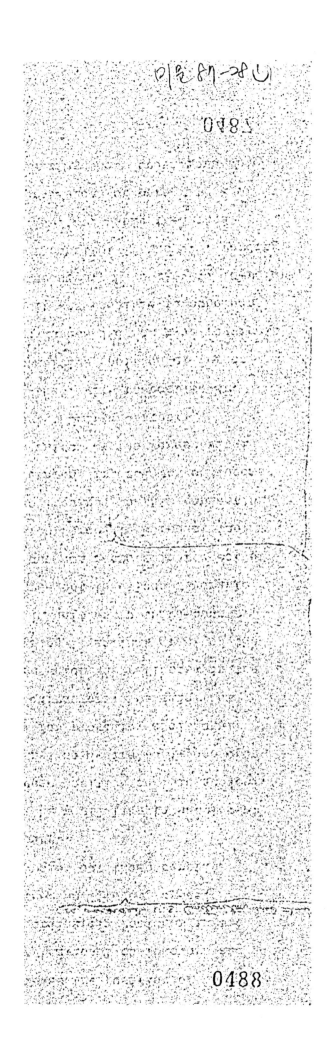

state that services of Invited Contractors are to be utilized only when such services are not obtainable locally.

27.   Colonel Fuller, in replying to Mr. Whang's question about the number of Invited Contractors, said he could offer only rough figures. He said there were some forty Invited Contractors serving the U.S. Forces in Korea, that these contractors have approximately 600 non-Korean employees of which 225 not ordinarily resident in the United States, and that over half of the forty odd Invited Contractors are "technical representatives", that is, one-man contracts for the supply of factory represent-atives of U.S. companies who supervise the maintenance of ~~with~~ advanced weapon systems and other equipment activities. Mr. Ku said that it would be helpful for the Korean side in conducting a review of its position on the article under discussion to have a statement from the U.S. side of those privileges and immunities in paragraph 3 of the draft article which the U.S. side believes are absolutely necessary for its third country national employees of Invited Contractors.

28.   Mr. Habib replied that the U.S. side considered that all of these privileges and immunities were necessary. Colonel Fuller agreed with Mr. Habib's statement that it was the thought of the U.S. negotiators that all of the privileges and immunities were necessary for third country national employees and that U.S. negotiators saw no basis for discrimination between contractors and their employees on the basis of nationality.

29.   Mr. Habib said that it was the U.S. side's feeling that on the basis of equitability all of these privileges should be granted to Invited Contractors and their employees

without distinction on the basis of nationality. He would, however, like to reverse Mr. Ku's question to the U.S. side and aks which of the privileges and immunities granted by paragraph 3 was the Korean side most concerned about?

30. Mr. Ku replied that it had been the general position of the Korean negotiators that no privileges or immunities should be accorded to any third country nationals who are not ordinarily resident in the U.S. in the provisions of paragraph 3 of the Article.

31. Mr. Ku noted that paragraph 2 of the draft article had a slight editorial difference, e.g., "Government of Korea" (U.S. draft) versus "Government of the Republic of Korea" (Korean draft). He stated that the Korean side would accept paragraph 2 of the U.S. draft Article with the understanding that the word "consultation" be interpreted as implying that Korean reviews would be duly considered in the process of consultation. Mr. Habib agreed to this interpretation. He said that the Korean side accepted paragraph 5 of the U.S. draft Article.

32. Mr. Ku noted that the Korean draft of paragraph 6 included a phrase, the purpose of which was to make certain that the exemptions from taxation granted to Invited Contractors would apply only to their business with the United States Forces, and not to any other business they might conduct in the Republic of Korea. He said that the Korean position upon the inclusion of such a phrase had not changed.

33. Colonel Fuller asked if the Korean side had agreed that the phrase "tangible or intangible" should be included in paragraph 6 of the contractors articles as a description of the movable property to be excluded from Korean taxation.

13

34. Mr. Ku said that the Korean side agreed to this inclusion. It was agreed that each side would give further consideration to the remaining points of difference in paragraph 6.

35. Turning to paragraph 7 of the U.S. draft of the article on contractors, Mr. Ku noted that the Korean side had presented an alternative draft at the twenty-third meeting. He inquired as to the U.S. side's position on this draft. Colonel Fuller responded that the U.S. side still considered it necessary to include the exemption specified in the second sentence of the U.S. draft of paragraph 7.

36. Mr. Ku noted that the Korean draft did include as a separate sentence a provision intended to fulfill the same purpose as the second clause of the second sentence of the U.S. draft. In this sentence, the Korean draft states that periods during which Invited Contractors were in Korea solely in connection with the execution of a contract with the United States Forces should not be considered as periods of residence for the purpose of Korean taxation.

37. Mr. Habib inquired why the Korean side did not care to state specifically that contractors were not liable for payment of Korean taxes on income derived from sources outside Korea?

38. It was agreed to suspend discussion upon paragraph 7 of the U.S. draft at this point, and Mr. Ku inquired if the U.S. side was prepared to table its draft of paragraph 8 of the contractors article. Mr. Habib replied that the U.S. side would table its draft of paragraph 8 at the time when it was prepared to discuss the subject of criminal jurisdiction.

0493

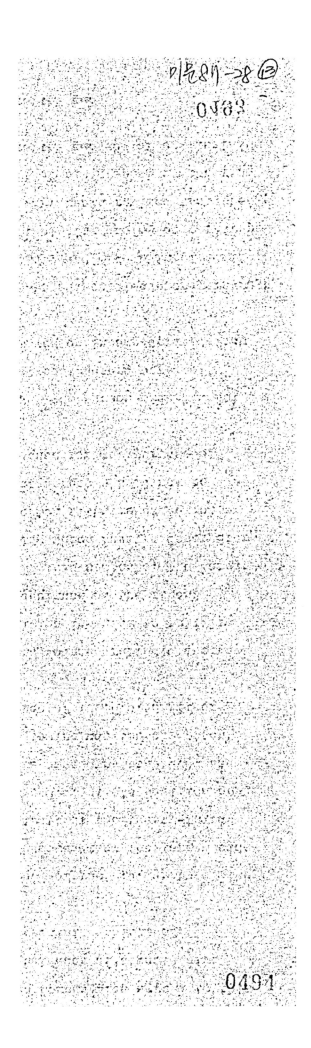

14

39. Colonel Fuller asked if the Korean side had any
comments upon the U.S. draft Agreed Minute to the
Contractors Article.

40. Mr. Ku said that the Korean side had carefully
studied the U.S. draft Agreed Minute. He suggested that
the phrase "except paragraph 7" of the U.S. draft Article be
added at the end of the Agreed Minute.

41. Mr. Habib said that the addition of such a phrase
would permit the leving of Korean income taxes on Invited
Contractors having contracts with non-military U.S. government agencies. He said that the U.S. believed that the
proposed Korean change would negate the entire purpose of
the U.S. draft Agreed Minute.

42. Mr. Ku then asked which non-military agencies of
the United States Government in Korea had contracts with
the Invited Contractors?

43. Colonel Fuller replied that, the Embassy and the
United States Operations Mission were the non-military
agencies contemplated in the proposed agreed minute.

Claims

44. The negotiators exchanged draft articles dealing
with the subject of claims.

Other Business

45. Mr. Habib noted that, in accordance with the
instructions issued to them at the twenty-seventh negotiating session
Mr. Ford of the U.S. negotiating
team and Mr. Yi Chae-sul, Chief of the Foreign Exchange
Division of the Ministry of Finance, had met to discuss the
differences between the U.S. and Korean drafts of the last
sentence of the Agreed Minute to the Foreign Exchange Controls
Article. Mr. Habib said Messrs. Ford and Yi required

0495

15

0498

additional time for further discussion, and that they
were hopeful of presenting a favorable report at the next
negotiating session.

    45. It was agreed that the next negotiating session
would be held on August 22, 1963, at 2:00 p.m.

0200

August 22, 1963

1. Time and Place : 3:00 to 4:40 p.m. August 22, 1963
   at the Foreign Minister's
   Conference Room

II. Attendants:

ROK Side:

Mr. Whang, Ho Eul	Director Bureau of Political Affairs Ministry of Foreign Affairs
Mr. Shin, Kwan Sup	Director Bureau of Customs Dupty Ministry of Finance
Mr. Koo, Choong Whay	Chief, America Section Ministry of Foreign Affairs
Col. Lee, Nam Koo	Chief, Military Affairs Section Ministry of National Defense
Mr. Chu, Mun Ki	Chief, Legal Affairs Section Ministry of Justice
Mr. Shin, Jung Sup	Chief, Treaty Section Ministry of Foreign Affairs
Mr. Lee, Kyung Hoon	2nd Secretary Ministry of Foreign Affairs
Mr. Kang, Suk Jae	2nd Secretary Ministry of Foreign Affairs
Mr. Cho, Kwang Je	2nd Secretary Ministry of Foreign Affairs
Mr. Huh, Sung	Third Secretary Ministry of Foreign Affairs

U.S. Side:

Mr. Philip C. Habib	Counselor of the Embassy for Political Affairs
Gen. G.G. O'Connor	Deputy Chief of Staff 8th Army
Mr. William J. Ford	First Secretary of the Embassy

0499

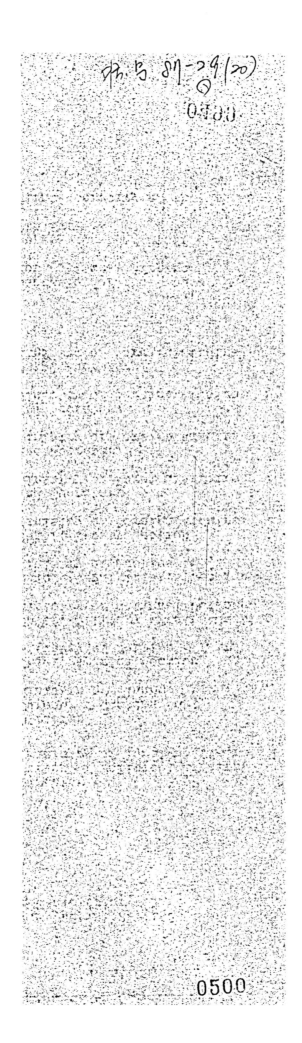

Col. Howard Smigelow, USA	Deputy Chief of Staff UNC
Capt. R.M. Brownlie	Assistant Chief of Staff USN/K
Col. L.J. Fuller	Staff Judge Advocate United Nations Command
Mr. Rodney Armstrong	Economic Officer, American Embassy
Lt. Col. W.A. Burt	J-5
Mr. Robert A. Lewis	Second Secretary and Consul of the Embassy
Major Robert D. Peckham	Staff Officer, JAG 8th Army
Lt. Col. Charles Nye III,	Chief, U.S. Armed Forces Claims Service, 8th Army (Observer)
Kenneth Campen	Interpreter

1. Mr. Whang Ho Eul opened the meeting by introducing in replacement on Mr. KIM Yun-t'aek Mr. Huh, who was joining the Korean Negotiating Team. He announced that Mr. Lee Kyung Hoon was participating in his last negotiating session, having recently received an assignment to the Korean Mission in Japan. Mr. Habib welcomed Mr. Huh and expressed regret at the imminent departure of Mr. Lee & Mr. Kim. He introduced Lieutenant Charles Nye III, Chief of the United States Armed Forces Claims Service, Korea, who would be present as an observer on the U.S. side during the discussions on the subject of claims.

VEHICLE AND DRIVERS LICENSES

2. Opening substantive discussion, Mr. Whang stated that the Korean side accepted the alternative draft of paragraph 3 of the article on vehicle and drivers licenses tabled at the last negotiating session. Mr. Whang noted that the first two paragraphs of the article had been agreed at previous meetings, and stated that he believed that the negotiators had now reached agreement

upon the complete text of this article. Mr. Habib concurred in this statement.

CLAIMS

3. Mr. Chang said that Mr. CHU Mun-ki, of the Ministry of Justice would present an explanation of the Korean side's position upon the subject of claims. Mr. Chu said that it was the Korean side's belief that the claims article, together with the article on criminal jurisdiction, were the most important articles of the prospective Status of Forces Agreement. Mr. Chu said that in studying the draft tabled by the U.S. negotiators at the last negotiating session, the Korean side had come to the conclusion that there are fundamental differences in principle between the two sides' respective drafts on the subject of claims.

4. Mr. Chu then summarized on the provisions of the Korean draft article on the subject of claims as follows: First, the Korean draft provided in the same manner as the U.S. draft, that each Party waives claims against the other Party for damage to any property owned by it and used by its armed forces, if such damage was caused by members or employees of the armed forces or from the use of any vehicle, vessel or aircraft owned by the other Party in the execution of official duties, provided that the damage was caused to property so used. Secondly, the Korean draft provides that damage to other property owned by either party be settled by a sole arbitrator. Thirdly, it is provided that claims based upon damage to third Parties arising out of act or omission done in the performance of official duty shall be dealt with under the Korean law. Fourthly, the Korean draft provided that calims arising out of tortious acts or omissions not done in the performance of

0503

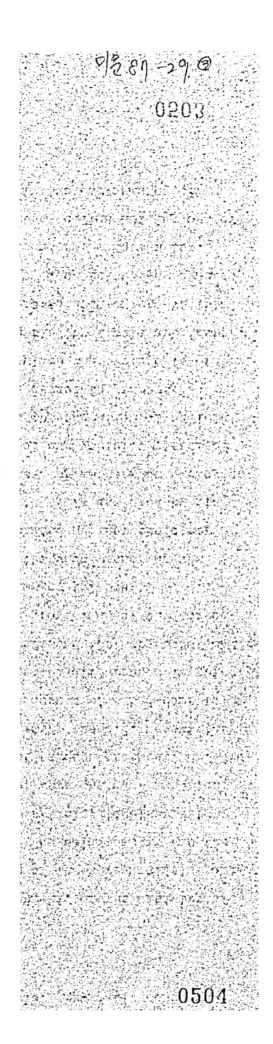

official duty shall also be dealt with under the Korean law and that claims arising from the unauthorized use of a vehicle shall be handled in the same manner. Fifthly, it is provided that a dispute as to whether damage was done in the performance of official duty or as to whether the use of vehicle was unauthorized shall be submitted to an arbitrator for decision. Sixthly, in the Korean draft, the provision of the prospective agreement governing contractual disputes was included in the claims article for the sake of convenience.

5. Mr. Chu said that the Korean draft article was clearer and more logical than its U.S. counterpart, and would result in the more speedy and successful settlement of claims. Mr. Chu said that the Korean draft had been based upon the formula concept for the settlement of scope-of-duty claims. He said the Korean people desires the inclusion of the formula concept in the claims article of the prospective Agreement, and that inclusion of formula concept would further strengthen friendly relations between Korea and the United States and permit the removal of possible misunderstanding. Mr. Chu said he hoped the full agreement upon the Korean draft article. Mr. Chu suggested that the negotiators' discussion on the subject of claims proceed on the basis of the Korean draft article; before doing this, however, the Korean side would appreciate a general explanation by the U.S. side of its draft article.

6. Mr. Habib said that the U.S. side had studied the Korean draft article carefully. There appeared to be one common point between the two sides' drafts on the subject of claims: that claims should be paid. The U.S. side had approached the problem of providing for the payment of claims from the point of view that claims should be paid equitably and promptly, within

한·미국 간의 상호방위조약 제4조에 의한 시설과 구역 및 한국에서의 미국군대의 지위에 관한 협정(SOFA)
전59권. 1966.7.9 서울에서 서명 : 1967.2.9 발효(조약 232호) (V.50 실무교섭회의 합의의사록, 제10-37차, 1963) (2/2)   351

the frame-work of a workable administrative system. The U.S. side in its draft had departed from the older claims formula which guided the drafting of the articles on claims in the North Atlantic Treaty Organization and Japanese Agreements, and which has obviously guided the Korean side in the drafting of its article. It was important to recognize why this departure had been made.

7. Mr. Habib said that the formula concept for the payment of claims, that is, the system whereby the host country bears a share of the cost of each scope-of-duty claim, was first worked out in the NATO Agreement. The United States had at that time wanted the sharing of claims costs for several reasons. There was during this period widespread inflation, particularly in Western Europe, and the United States wished to prevent sky-rocketing claims costs by the insertion of a provision which would give the host nation a financial interest in each scope-of-duty claim paid. Something of the same philosophy had been carried over into the Japanese Agreement for much the same reasons. The United States had found, however, during the course of its ten years experience with administration of the formula concept that it is time consuming and expensive to administer, compel the host nation to establish an expensive bureaucracy, and often engenders ill-will between the host nation and the United States.

8. Mr. Habib said that in some cases administration of the formula concept for claims settlement had approached the unworkable. In Japan, the formula concept was currently being administered in a manner much different from that described in the actual Agreement. In Korea, the United States had a claims procedure in operation which had the benefit of background and experience acquired in four years of operation. This procedure

is administered by experienced Korean and American personnel who quickly and efficiently adjudicate and pay claims. The U.S. side felt that the continuation of this system would be in the best interests of Korea and the United States.0210

9. Mr. Habib suggested that the Korean negotiators consider the advantages of the continuation of the present system of claims payment as against the disadvantages of the system proposed by the Korean side. The Korean draft article provides that scope-of-duty claims shall be paid according to the procedures and system employed by the Korean Armed Forces. The Korean Armed Forces do not have a system for the payment of claims which meets the requirements of the situation. It would, therefore, be necessary for the Korean Government to establish such a system, staffing the institutions with experienced people who have a backround in law, a knowledge of damages awards in Korea, and investigative ability. The new system would require constant recourse to the Korean courts for adjustments, for the Korean system for the payment of claims relies upon the court system.

10. Mr. Habib said that in addition to the increased costs to the Korean Government which would result from the establishment and staffing of a new claims payment system, the Korean draft article on claims would require that the Korean Government bear fifteen per cent of the cost of scope-of-duty claims. It should be noted that under the Japanese Agreement, the Government of Japan bears twenty-five per cent of the cost of such claims. The continuation of the present system of paying scope-of-duty claims would not, however, cost the Korean Government anything.

0509

미분 87-2-①

0203

0510

11. Mr. Habib said that the payment procedure proposed by the Korean side would be time-consuming, and result in the delay of payments. It now requires approximately three months for the payment of a scope-of-duty claim by the U.S. Forces in Korea. In Japan, payment of a similar claim requires approximately six months, with all that such a delay implies by way of ill-will toward the United States and the host country. The U.S. side had operated a system such as is proposed in the Korean draft, and knew that this system carried with it the ever-present chance for the generation of ill-will.

12. Mr. Habib noted that the draft article on claims tabled by the U.S. in the present negotiations did not mark the first departure by U.S. negotiators from the NATO -Japan Agreements formula concept. The U.S. had departed from the formula concept in a number of agreements in the past, and would depart from it in other agreements to be negotiated in the future, for the reasons which had just been mentioned. It was the hope of the U.S. side that the Korean Agreement would be among those agreements which set the pace in this regard for the future. Departures from the formula concept had been made in the philipines, Ethiopian, Pakistan, and Libyan Agreements, and a departure from the formula concept was currently being negotiated with the Government of the Republic of China.

13. Mr. Habib said that in order that the Korean side might better understand what the U.S. negotiators were proposing, he had asked Lieutenant Colonel Charles Nye to come to the meeting to explain in detail the manner in which the U.S. Forces presently pay claims in Korea, and the results of the operation of the present system. He then turned the floor over to Colonel Nye, who gave a summary of the paper which

appears as an attachment to this record.

14. Following the completion of Colonel Nye's presentation, Mr. Habib said that he wished to remind the Korean negotiators that the Colonel had presented merely the operations of his agency, and there were also hundreds of personnel who receive and process claims as they proceed through channels to Colonel Nye's office. The Korean side had proposed a system under which the Korean Government would take over the operation of the system Colonel Nye had just explained, under the terms of regulations and procedures which the U.S. side understood do not yet exist. Not only would this constitute a tremendous administrative burden, but it would not in the end advance the main principles upon which the U.S. draft article is based: e.g., the equitable and prompt payment of claims within the framework of a workable administrative system.

15. Mr. Habib said that at this point he would like to put to the Korean negotiators certain questions, which would not necessarily have to be answered at the present session, having to do with the manner in which the Korean side would carry out the administration of the system for the payment of claims which was set forth in its draft article. How would the Korean side staff the system contemplated in its draft? Where would the Korean side obtain the people with the experience and backround needed to administer their system? How soon would the system contemplated in the Korean draft article be ready to go into operation? What advantages over the present system did the Korean negotiators see for their system, assuming that it could be put into effect? The U.S. side believed that the system it was proposing is the best way to pay just claims,

and was willing to elaborate further upon the way in which the system envisaged in the U.S. draft works. The U.S. side would be willing to take the Korean negotiators to the offices of the U.S. Armed Forces Claims Service, Korea, in order that they might better grasp the manner in which the present system operates.

16. Mr. Chu thanked the U.S. side for its explanation of its draft, and asked certain statistical questions which the U.S. side noted were answered in the statistical appendix to Colonel Nye's paper which had not been read in the interest of cutting short the time required for the paper's presentation. Mr. Chu then asked what appeal procedures were open to claimants under the present U.S. Forces Claims payment system?

17. Colonel Nye said that a claimant could appeal from the Claims Commissions of his office up through to him, acting as the Chief, U.S. Armed Forces Claims Service, Korea. If not satisfied, the claimant could appeal to Headquarters, United States Armed Forces Claims Service, in the United States. There were, in actual practice, very few appeals lodged against the awards of the Claims Commissions. The U.S. side would provide statistics upon the number of such appeals.

18. Mr. Chu said the Korean side would like to know the number of accident claims satisfied under the present U.S. Armed Forces claims system in Korea, and the proportion of amounts paid to the amounts of compensation requested. The U.S. side agreed to provide statistics upon these points. Mr. Chu said that the Korean negotiators would answer the questions put by Mr. Habib at the conclusion of the U.S. side's presentation at a later meeting.

0515

미문87-29⑨

0272

0516

19. Mr. Whang said that the exchange of views at the present session had given the Korean negotiators an understanding of the U.S. side's intentions. The Korean negotiators would study the explanation given by the U.S. side, and discuss it at the next negotiating session.

20. It was agreed that the next negotiating session would be held on September 5, 1963, at 2:00 P.M.

Attachment: Paper Presented by the U.S. Armed Forces Claims Service, Korea.

한·미국 간의 상호방위조약 제4조에 의한 시설과 구역 및 한국에서의 미국군대의 지위에 관한 협정(SOFA)
전59권. 1966.7.9 서울에서 서명 : 1967.2.9 발효(조약 232호) (V.50 실무교섭회의 합의의사록, 제10-37차, 1963) (2/2)　363

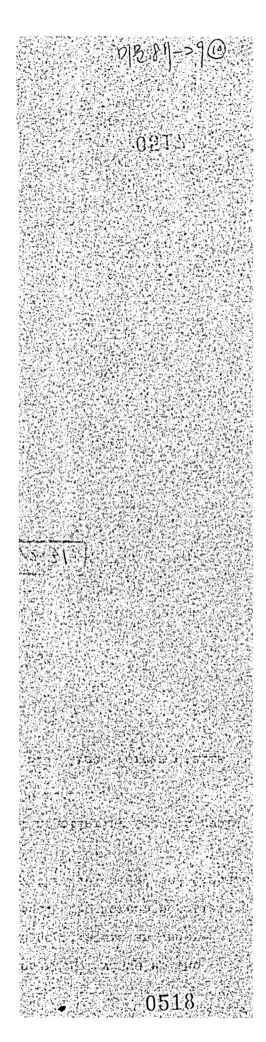

1. General.

Payment of the claims of citizens and residents of Korea is authorized by an act of the United States Congress called the "Foreign Claims Act". This law provides for the payment of meritorious claims by the inhabitants of countries in which United States troops are stationed, based on death, personal injury, or property damage caused by noncombat activities of U.S. armed forces. This law is implemented in detail by regulations of the Army, Navy and Air Force.

2. U.S. liability.

Under the foreign claims program United States liability is established when injury, death, or property damage is caused (partially or wholly) by the careless or wrongful act of a member or U.S. civilian employee of the United States Forces Korea, or by other noncombat activities of those forces. Liability also is assumed if the damages are caused by Korean civilian employees while acting within the scope of their employment. As would be expected, the United States cannot assume responsibility for damages caused by members of the Korean Army or employees of the Korean Government, even though these persons may be engaged with U.S. forces at the time in the joint mission of maintaining military readiness against a common enemy. Cognizance is taken, however, of the unique cooperation between the military forces of the Republic of Korea and of the United States by which Korean military persons are integrated into U.S. Army units, known as the Korean Augmentation

0519

0520

to the United States Army (KATUSA). Liability is assumed and compensation is paid for injuries and damages caused by these persons when acting within the scope of their assigned duties for U.S. Army units.

3. Investigation of claims.

An elaborate system is prescribed by U.S. Army directives for the investigation and reporting of detailed facts and circumstances involved in every incident in which a person suffers injury, death, or property damage as the result of military activities. Hundreds of investigating officers and commanders of Army units and installations are responsible for investigating the incidents and accidents in which members of the USFK are involved. Detailed reports of the investigations are forwarded to higher authority for approval, and a copy of each report is forwarded to the Claims Service. In some instances additional investigation and inquiry may be required in order to fairly evaluate a claim. This further investigation is more effectively handled by personnel specially trained in the law and procedures pertaining to the payment of claims Consequently, the investigation at this point is normally conducted by the claims service which processes the claims against the United States.

4. The Claims Service in Korea.

a. The Department of Defense has designated the Army to settle claims arising in Korea which are caused by the activities of members and employees of the United States Forces Korea. This is accomplished through the U.S. Armed Forces Claims Service, Korea, and Claims Commissions attached to that organization, located on

0522

the Yongsan Military Reservation. The establishment of Claims Commissions are required by the "Foreign Claims Act"; and their primary duty is to consider and settle claims submitted by the inhabitants of the country involved. A commissioner must be a commissioned officer and normally is a judge advocate officer of the military service concerned. One-member commissions are empowered to adjudge and pay claims for not more than $1000(129,500 Won) and three-member commissions may pay claims for not more than $15,000 (1,942,500 Won). Claims in excess of the latter amount are transmitted to the Department of the Army for approval by the Congress before payment may be made. Commissions of any of the military services may consider and pay claims caused by the activities and members of the other services.

b. The U.S. Armed Forces Claims Service is manned by fourteen American persons and thirteen citizens of Korea. Seven of the Korean employees are specially trained claims investigators and classified among the highest paid Korean employees of the Eighth Army. Each of the three commissioned officers (including the Chief) is appointed as a one-member commission, and together they constitute a three-member commission. In addition to the Office of the Chief and the Claims Commissions, the Claims Service is organized as follows

Administrative Branch	Investigation Branch	Claims Branch	Payment Branch
5 U.S.	1 U.S.	3 U.S.	2 U.S.
3 KN	5 KN	1 KN	2 KN

3

0523

c. The functions of the four branches are somewhat self-evident. Briefly:

(1) The Administration Branch maintains all records of claims, reports of investigation, and related files. When a claim initially is received in the Claims Service it is channeled to the Administration Branch for recording and indexing. A claim member is assigned by which the claim may be readily identified at all future times, and a portfolio prepared in which all documents are filed which pertain to the claim.

(2) The Investigation Branch is comprised of five (5) Korean national employees, all classified as senior investigators, and one commissioned officer as supervisor. Upon receiving a claims portfolio from the Administration Branch, the file is assigned to an investigator for translation of documents which are submitted in Korean and for development of the essential evidence required for complete adjudication of the claim. As a general principle the securing of evidence in support of a claim is the responsibility of the claimant. A large part of our investigators' duties, however, is to assist the claimant in securing the evidence and in many instances to secure the evidence for the claimant. When the Investigation Branch considers investigation is complete, the portfolio is transferred to the Claims Branch for further processing.

(a) The Investigation Branch also interviews all claimants who visit the Claims Service, assists them in preparing their claims on bi-lingual forms provided, and advises of the nature of evidence and formal documents (such as family registers, certificates of land ownership) that are required to support their claims.

0525

It may be noted at this point that whether a claimant desires to employ an attorney to represent him in connection with his claim is a matter solely within the discretion of the claimant. The Claims Service offers all the advice and assistance that is needed to file and establish the claim.

(3) The Claims Branch examines the claims portfolio to determine whether evidence is sufficient to support final adjudication of the claim. A resume of the claim is prepared for the benefit of the Chief and the claims commissions, including a recommendation as to the amount of compensation that should be awarded.

(4) Upon completion of the processing of a claim by the Claims Branch, the portfolio is transferred to the Chief of the Claims Service for examination and consideration. The Chief assigns claims not in excess of $1000 (129,500 Won) to the one-member commissions for final adjudication. As President of the three-member commission, he convenes the commission for consideration and adjudication of claims in excess of $1000 (129,500 Won). If the claim exceeds $15,000 (1,942,500 Won), he prepares a detailed memorandum and recommendation that is forwarded with the claim file to the Department of the Army for final action.

(5) When a commission adjudges an award in a claim, the portfolio is transferred to the Payment Branch. This Branch notifies the claimant of the amount of award and prepares a settlement agreement for the claimant to sign. Upon receipt of the signed settlement agreement arrangements are made for claimant to receive his compensation. Most claimants are paid on the Yongsan Military Reservation. In many instances, however, arrangements are made for

0527

0528

claimants to be paid at a military post near their homes. This is particularly true when claimant lives a long distance from Seoul, as in the Taegu or Pusan area. In addition, when a claimant is too old or ill to travel a representative of the Claims Service takes the compensation to him at his home. This also is done in most small claims in order that claimant may realize the full benefit of his award.

5. General criteria used in computing damages.

a. Property damage. Allowable compensation normally represents the cost of repairs to or restoration of the property damaged to its state of condition immediately prior to the time of damage. The claimant may establish these costs by receipts for amounts expended for repair, or by estimates of the cost of repair by reputable contractors or other repairmen. Compensation for los or completaly destroyed property is computed at the actual value of the property at time of loss or destruction. Value of growing crops and trees are similarly computed.

b. Compensation for personal injury and death. These computations usually are not as amenable to mathematical calculations as are costs of repair or destruction of vehicles, buildings, or other property. To obtain, however, as much consistency as may be possible standard elements are utilized in order to have a sound basis on which awards amy be computed for death and in various types of personal injury. The Claims Commission is charged with the responsibility of evaluating each case in the light of these standard elements in order to arrive at fair awards. The Chief of the Claims

0529

Service supervises the activities of the Claims Commissions for the purpose of assuring that awards to claimants are fair and non-discriminatory.

11) Personal Injury. Standard compensable items are:

    (a) Medical and hospital expenses, including immediate first aid treatment and ambulance service.

    (b) Reasonable costs of Chinese medicines which are prescribed by a doctor as treatment for the injury, or resulting illness, on which claim is based.

    (c) Loss of income for the period during which claimant is absent from work or occupation.

    (d) Pain and suffering of the injured party.

    (e) Permanent disability. A "Table of Disability Grades" is used. This table is patterned after the one provided in the Korean Labor Standard Act of 1953. The table includes four disability grades not appearing in the Korean table, and the number of days of compensation for each disability grade has been increased in recognition of the increased cost of living in Korea since 1953. If the injured party is not a wage or income earner (such as a child or house-wife), emphasis is placed on the nature (rather than grade) of disability and age and pain and suffering of the injured party in order to arrive at comparable awards.

0531

7

미트87-29 ⑰

0231

0532

(f) Disfigurement. Scars and other disfigurements of a female are considered more serious than those suffered by a male. In addition, age, social status and occupation of both the male and female are taken into account.

(g) Cost of artificial limbs, and their repair and replacement for life expectancy of the injured party.

(h) Miscellaneous expenses attributable to the injuries sustained.

(2) Death. Standard compensable items are:

(a) Medical and hospital expenses incident to and preceding death.

(b) Funeral expenses. These include preparation of body for burial, purchase and preparation of gravesite, reasonable amounts for traditional ceremonial expenses(including food and drink).

(c) Death award. Our Korean claimants frequently refer to this element as a "solatium" or "consolation award". The amount of this award varies from case to case, being affected by the age, income and social status of the deceased, as well as his family relationship (that is, whether the father, mother, minor daughter, first son, or other). Additional amounts are computed in this award for a surviving widow and for each surviving child under age of

0533

seventeen years. Our experience indicates that
average death awards range from $772.20 (
(100.000 Won) for young children to approximately $2702.70 (350,000 Won) for adults.

(d) Miscellaneous expenses attributable to the
death on which claim is based.

6. Hospitalization of claimants.

As a general rule United States law authorizes admission
to and treatment in U.S. hospitals only for U.S. persons (and
some of their dependents) who are employed by the Government.
Not all U.S. employees are eligible for this medical service.
exceptions may be made in emergency and unusual cases for a small
number of other persons, in which event the individual is charged
$37.00 (4792 Won) for each day of hospitalization and $7.00 (907
Won) for each outpatient treatment. Nevertheless special arrangements have been approved for the claims program in Korea which
operates under the "Foreign Claims Act", whereunder any Korean
citizen who is injured by the activities of United States Forces
Korea may be admitted and treated (including all necessary surgery)
in U.S. hospitals in Korea without any charge whatsoever for
the medical services. In the past few years hundreds of
Korean citizens have been treated under this program in Army
medical facilities and furnished free hospitalization for
weeks and months in our major hospitals. Several of the
patients have received this hospitalization and medical
service for more than one year in the 121st U.S. Hospital
located near Inchon.

0535

0536

7. Statistics.

The number of claims received by Claims Commissions and amounts of compensation paid since the Claims Service began its operations on 1 June 1959 are shown below:

	1959 (7 mos)	1960	1961	1962	1963 (6 mos)
Nr. Received:	517	2,125	1,163	979	378
Amount Paid:	$282,688.28	$727,696.22	$361,801.26	$187,633.75	$77,032.16

Total claims received since 1 June 1959: 5,162
Total compensation paid since 1 June 1959: $1,636,851.67 (12,639,775 Won)

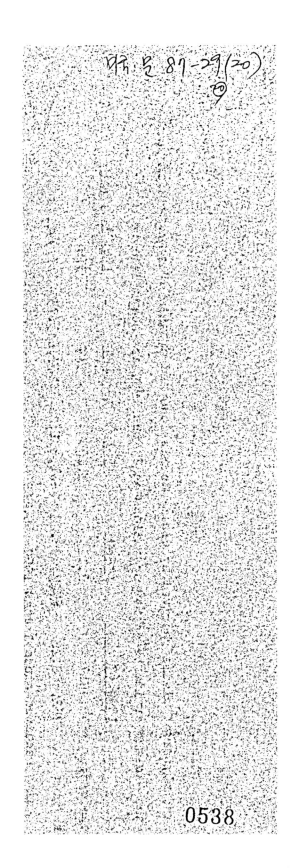

JOINT SUMMARY RECORD OF THE 30TH SESSION

September 5, 1963

1. Time and Place : 2:00 to 4:10 p.m. September 5, 1963
   at the Foreign Minister's Conference
   Room

2. Attendants:

ROK side:

Mr. Whang, Ho Eul	Director Bureau of Political Affairs Ministry of Foreign Affairs
Mr. Shin, Kwan Sup	Director Bureau of Customs Duty Ministry of Finance
Mr. Koo, Choong Whay	Chief, America Section Ministry of Foreign Affairs
Col. Lee, Nam Koo	Chief, Military Affairs Section Ministry of National Defence
Mr. Chu, Mun Ki	Chief, Legal Affairs Section Ministry of Justice
Mr. Shin, Jung Sup	Chief, Treaty Section Ministry of Foreign Affairs
Mr. Kang, Suk Jae	2nd Secretary Ministry of Foreign Affairs
Mr. Cho, Kwang Je	2nd Secretary Ministry of Foreign Affairs
Mr. Huh, Sung	3rd Secretary Ministry of Foreign Affairs
Mr. Yun, Song Yong	Prosecutor Ministry of Justice (Observer)

U.S. side:

Mr. Philip C. Habib Co	Counselor of the Embassy for Political Affairs American Embassy
Gen. G. G. O'Connor	Deputy Chief of Staff 8th U.S. Army
Mr. William J. Ford	1st Secretary American Embassy

0539

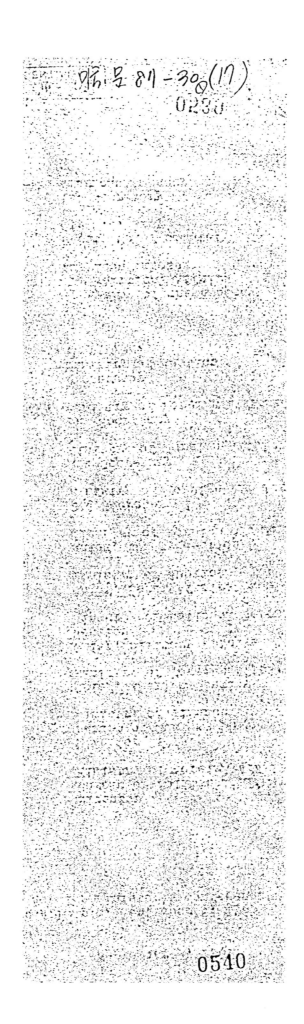

Col. Howard Smigelor	Deputy Chief of Staff UNC
Capt. R. M. Brownlie	Assistant Chief of Staff USN/K
Mr. Rodney E. Armstrong	2nd Secretary American Embassy
Mr. Robert A. Lewis	2nd Secretary and Consul American Embassy
Mr. Robert A. Kinney	J-5 8th U.S. Army
Maj. Robert D. Peckham	Staff Officer, JAG 8th U.S. Army
Lt. Col. Charles Nye III	Chief, U.S. Armed Forces Claims Service, 8th U.S. Army (Observer)
Lt. Col. Martin Drucker	Claims Service, 8th U.S. Army (Observer)

1. Mr. Hwang Ho Eul opened the meeting by introducing Mr. Yun, Song Yong of the Claims Section of the Ministry of Justice, who was to be present on the Korean side in the capacity of Observer during the negotiator's discussion of the subject of claims. Mr. Habib welcomed Mr. Yun, introduced Lt. Col. Martin Drucker, Chief-designate of the United States Armed Forces Claims Service, Korea, who was to be present for the discussion of claims as an observer for the U.S. side, and noted that Mr. Ford was attending his last negotiating session, having been transferred to Washington. Mr. Whang welcomed Colonel Drucker, and expressed regret at the departure of Mr. Ford.

2. Mr. Ford expressed regret at his imminent departure from the negotiations. He drew the attention of the negotiators to the fact that the letters SOFA have a double meaning in the English language: a Status of Forces Agreement, and an upholstered bench for relaxation. He said that in his experience participation in SOFA negotiations were not relaxing, and that the two meanings of the letters in

0541

0542

English were incompatible. He said that he had, however, enjoyed his labors, and had found good friends on both sides of the negotiating table; since all of the partici-pants in the negotiations were, in a sense, in "foreing service", it would be his hope that he might meet many of his former colleagues around the table again.

CLAIMS

3. Opening substantive discussion, Mr. Hwang noted that at the preceding meeting both sides had given ex-planations of their draft articles on the subject of claims. He said that, in response to the request of the U.S. side at the previous meeting, the Korean side would give an explanation of the system employed by the Korean Government for the settlement of claims. He asked Mr. Chu Mun Ki to present this explanation.

THE STATE COMPENSATION SYSTEM OF THE REPUBLIC OF KOREA

4. Under the terms of the State Compensation Law (Republic of Korea Law No. 231, promulgated September 8, 1951), the Government's liability is established for damage caused to individuals. This law provides that, in the same manner as would be the case with private individuals, the Government is liable for compensation when an official or a member of the Government or employee of a public corporation has caused damage to an individual or to property, either by intent or by fault, in con-travention of the laws of the Republic. The liability arises when the Government official causes damage while acting in the performance of his official duties, or when the damage arises from defects in the establishment or maintenance of highways, rivers, public utilities, or services, or when the damage arises from acts done in contravention of the civil code or other laws.

0543

5. Under the provisions of the State Compensation
Law, the Government and public corporations are liable
for compensation:

(a) When a public official (including a member
of the Army, Navy, Air Force or the Marine Corps,
or the civilian compenent of these forces, or an
employee of these entities) has caused death,
injury, or disgrace to an individual, or has caused
damage to personal property by fire or otherwise,
either by intention or by fault, in contravention
of the laws of the Republic during the course of
his performance of official duty;

(b) When personal injury or death, or property
damage has been cuased by reason of defects in the
establishment, or maintenance of highways, rivers,
or other public utilities or services (an example
of this type of damage would be the inudation of
farmlands through improper management of irrigation
facilities);

(c) When damage has been caused to personal property by an act on the part of a Government
official or agency which is in contravention of
the civil code or other laws.

6. An alien who sustains personal or property damage
from an act by a Government official or agency falling into
one of the categories descrived above is entitled to
State Compensation only if an agreement exists between
the alien's Government and the Government of the Republic
of Korea providing for the mutual satisfaction of claims

한·미국 간의 상호방위조약 제4조에 의한 시설과 구역 및 한국에서의 미국군대의 지위에 관한 협정(SOFA)
전59권. 1966.7.9 서울에서 서명 : 1967.2.9 발효(조약 232호) (V.50 실무교섭회의 합의의사록, 제10-37차, 1963) (2/2)   391

filed against the Governments for compensation owing to injured nationals of the other party.   0218

7. As described above, any person who has been damaged by the act of a Government official is entitled to claim compensation from the Government, and the Government is liable for the payment of compensation for damage caused, if the claim is just. The organization of the Korean Government for the consideration of claims is described below.

8. Since the promulgation and effectuation of the Law Governing Procedures for Claims for State Compensation (Law No. 1223, promulgated December 24, 1962), claims against the Government have been filed with the Ministry of Justice. For the purpose of implementing the law, a State Compensation Committee was established within the Ministry. There had already existed in the Ministry a Claims Section which had examined claims (and in the past, had also decided upon the amounts payable in compensation for these claims). When claims are filed with the General Affairs Section of the Ministry, they are immediately sent to the Claims Section. Upon receipt of the claim, the Claims Section, which is in charge of administration and investigation, immediately starts the investigation of the claim. There are now 13 investigators in the Claims Section. Two of these investigators hold the rank of prosecutor and have qualifications equivalent to those of judges in the Korean judicial system. The other personnel of the Section are: one legal officer, two Class Three Public Officials, and eight other officials. The investigators of the Section develop facts bearing upon whether any official act in question was done in

한·미국 간의 상호방위조약 제4조에 의한 시설과 구역 및 한국에서의 미국군대의 지위에 관한 협정(SOFA)
전59권. 1966.7.9 서울에서 서명 : 1967.2.9 발효(조약 232호) (V.50 실무교섭회의 합의의사록, 제10-37차, 1963) (2/2)   393

0548

the performance of official duties, and whether the damage which is alleged was caused by the act in question; they also collect evidence and gather information required for establishment of the amount of compensation to be offered. When their investigation is completed, the investigators prepare reports and forward them, together with the claims, to the State Compensation Committee for its consideration. The processing of claims is carried out with efficiency, and with the skills and knowledge which the investigators have gained in performing their duties for over ten years. The processing is carried out with the positive cooperation of other entities of the Korean Government: Prosecutors' Offices, the Korean Armed Forces, and the various investigation agencies of the Korean Government.

9. The State Compensation Committee carefully examines the claims and the investigation reports attached to them in the light of applicable laws. The Committee decides whether the Government is liable for compensation, and, if so, in what amount compensation shall be offered. The Committee is composed of a Chairman and six Committee Members. The Committee has a Secretary and a few clerks assigned to it for the performance of administrative tasks. At present, the Vice-Minister of Justice holds the appointment as Chairman of the Committee, and three Bureau Directors of the Ministry of Justice, one judge, and one attorney at law hold appointments as Members of the Committee. In addition, one representative (of the rank of Section Chief or above) from the Ministry concerned with the claim being considered sits as an ad hoc Member of the Committee during its sessions. The Committee is empowered to consider and decide upon claims regardless

0549

of the amounts involved. The Members of the Committee
are all in possession of legal experience extending
over ten years, and have qualifications comparable with
those possessed by Judges of the Supreme Court of Korea.
The Ministry involved is allowed to take part in the
consideration of a claim in which it is involved; for
example, in a Committee session called to consider the
case of a death caused by an Army truck, one of the senior
judge advocates of the ROKA would probably be nominated
as the representative of the Ministry of National Defense.
The Representative from the concerned Ministry is usually
a legal specialist, such as a legal counsel, selected
from among the high-ranking officers of the Ministry
involved.

10. After having considered a claim and decided upon
the amount of compensation, the State Compensation Committee reports to the Minister of Justice. The Minister
makes the final decision on the amount of compensation,
based upon the report prepared by the Committee.

11. The claimant is notified of the amount of compensation decided upon by the Ministry of Justice. He
may then apply, if the decision is satisfactory to him,
for the payment of the compensation. If the claimant is
not fully satisfied, however, he may bring a suit against
the decision in the courts.

12. When an application for claims payment is received
from the claimant, the Ministry of Justice requests the
Ministry of Finance or the Ministry of National Defense
to effect payment without delay.

미읍 8か2의 ①

0552

13. It is imperative that the final decision of the Minister of Justice, and all the processing upon which this decision is based, must be effected within two months from the date of the receipt of the claim. The notification of the Minister's decision and the claimant's acceptance or rejection of the award have to be made within seven days and three weeks, respectively. Therefore, the maximum length of time required for the settlement of a claim is less than three months. As for the minimum length of time required, however, there has been a case which was settled within 25 days from the date of the receipt of the claim.

14. The Korean courts also have a role in the settlement of claims. The Korean court system consists of the Supreme Court as the highest court and the courts of appeal, district courts and their branches as the lower courts. These courts are established in various parts of the country, and are manned by 350 judges appointed from among those individuals who have graduated from a university, have passed a strict national examination for the judiciary, and have finished a period of probation in excess of two years.

15. Any claimant may bring a suit at a District Court (or to one of its branches) directly, without recourse to the Committee, or when he has a complaint against the amount of compensation decided upon by the Minister of Justice on the basis of processing by the State Compensation Committee. If the claimant is not satisfied with the adjudication of the District Court, he may appeal to the court of second instance, which in this case would be the court of Appeal. If the claimant

0553

is still unsatisfied, he may appeal to the Supreme
Court. When the claimant is either satisfied with the
judgement of a lower court or a final adjudication of
the matter has been made by the Supreme Court, the
payment of compensation will be made immediately to
the claimant.

16. It is imperative that the judgements of the
three levels of courts which may be involved in the
settlement of a claims case be delivered within a
period of five months, four months, and three months
respectively. The decision upon the part of the claimant
as to whether the judgement of a lower court is acceptable
should be made within a period of two weeks from the
date of the judgement in question. The maximum period
of time necessary for the settlement of a claim through
the courts is, therefore, one year and one month. In
the Ministry of Justice's experience, however, claims
have been settled through the courts in as little as
two months.

17. Turning to the subject of the determination of
the amount of compensation to claimants, the sub-topic
of compensation for death will be discussed first. The
factors upon which compensation for death is based
are listed below.

(a) The amount of income based on life expectancy.
In judging the weight to be given this factor,
the Hofmann formula and schedule is utilized.
Under the terms of this formula, the amount of
award is given by the deduction of interest from
the amount that is given by the multiplication
of the deceased person's life expectancy (as given
by the mortality tables of the Ministry of Health

미문8257830 ①

0556

and Social Affairs) by the amount of the yearly
income of the deceased. For example, in the
case of the death of an attorney at law aged 30,
with a yearly income of won 500,000 (US $3,846 at
the official rate of exchange), the amount of
compensation, based upon this individual's life
expectancy of 65, will amount to won 10million
(US $76,923). There are, however, exceptional
cases in which the deceased has no earnings.

(b) Medical and hospital expenses incident to a
death. When a claim is based upon the death of
a person after serious injury, the amount compensable will include, in addition to the amount
based upon the deceased person's predictable
earnings, all of the medical and hospital expenses
incident to medical treatment preceding death,
plus the full amount which might otherwise have
been earned by the family of the deceased person
during the period they were obliged to be in
attendance upon the deceased.

(c) Ex gratia payments. These payments are provided to the surviving parents, widow or children,
if any, of a deceased person. The amounts of
awards of this nature are varied, being effected
by such factors as the age, education, income and
social status of the deceased, as well as by the
family relationship and circumstances of the
person who will receive the award. Until the
present, the Ministry of Justice's experience has
been that when the death of one person is involved,
the award generally ranges from won 300,000

0557

(US $2,308 at the official rate of exchange) to won 500,000 (US $3,846), with a maximum of won 150,000 and a minimum of won 30,000 distributed to each surviving family member entitled to an award.

(d) Funeral expenses. Funeral expenses are paid, including all expenses incurred for the interment. The amount paid in this category are related to the income and social status of the deceased.

18. In determining the amount of compensation for personal injuries, the following factors are relevant:

(a) Medical and hospital expenses, including all expenses of first aid treatment, and of hospital and medical care.

(b) Other treatment expenses, including all of the costs of medicine and recreation, when the injured person is not fully recovered, and requires continuous treatment or recreation, oven after leaving the hospital, at home or at resorts, or needs the continous application of Chinese or other medicines prescribed by a doctor.

(c) Loss of income during the period in which the claimant is absent from work, and the amount of income foregone (whether only a partial or complete loss of earning power) because of physical incapacity, minus interest.

(d) Ex gratia amounts in compensation for injuries, varied according to the degree of injury, age, sex and social status of the injured. The maximum amount is paid for scars and other disfigurements sustained by an unmarried female, particularly when these injuries are sustained on the legs.

0559

(e) Awards for miscellaneous expenses are also
made to injured persons. For example, compensation is paid for the cost of obtaining artificial limbs and for the cost of maintaining
these limbs during the expected life of their
wearer. Awards are made for travel expenses
incurred by an injured person in going to and
from school. Awards are also made for expenses
incurred in arranging for special tuition to
make up for time lost from educational acitivitios
because of injuries.

19. In determining the amounts of allowable compensation for property damage, allowable compensation includos
the cost of repairs necessary to restore the property to
its condition prior to the damage. Awards of this nature
also include compensation for the loss of income to the
owner of the property resulting from his inability to
utilize the property while damaged. For example, when
a civilian taxi is damaged by the wrongful act of a
vehicle of the Korean Armed Forces, compensation will
include the cost of repairs to the taxi, an amount in
lieu of the loss of income to the owner while the taxi
was under repair, as well as amount reimbursing the taxi
owner for his payment of taxes and driver's wages during
the period the taxi was inoperable.

20. The compensation system now in operation in the
Republic of Korea consists of five different stages of
consideration and adjudication designed to ensure a
speedy as well as satisfactory settlement of claims.
Thus, an claimant is assured of equitable and just
compensation. Furthermore, the claimant, if not fully
satisfied, can procede in the Korean court system up

0561

미흡하기30. ㉠

0562

through three levels of judgement. Therefore, the claims compensation system of the Republic of Korea is deemed to be efficiently and soundly instituted, and is well harmonized to effect speedy and satisfactory compensation.

21. Mr. Habib thanked Mr. Chu for his presentation. There followed an extended exchange of questions and answers in which additional information concerning the Korean system for the settlement of claims was developed. This information is summarized in the paragraphs below.

22. At the present time, there are no local offices to which a Korean claimant can present a claim against his Government, and the claim may be mailed or directly submitted to the General Affairs Section of the Ministry of Justice in Seoul. There is, however, under consideration the formation of a network of local offices which might handle certain civil affairs such as claims at the local level. For the transmission of a claim to the Ministry of Justice, the claimant is required to furnish such information as his personal references (name, address, age and occupation), amount of compensation requested and the facts involved in the accident.

23. The State Compensation Committee is empowered to settle all claims against the Korean Government arising out of acts or omissions of employees of the Korean Government acting within the scope of their official duties, as well as any claims arising out of an act or omission which constitutes a violation of the civil or other special codes. Claims arising from the expropriation of property by the Korean Government, or from the exercise by the Korean Government of the

right of eminent domain are not within the purview of the State Compensation Committee. The State Compensation Committee, in arriving at its judgement, takes into account the general principles of Korean law: for example, the doctrine of contributory negligence. The State Compensation Committee follows precedents established by the Korean courts in determining the amounts allowable as part of its awards for the payment of court costs and attorneys' fees.

24. Under the Ministry of Justice's interpretation of Article 24 of the Korean Constitution, any Korean citizen may litigate any problem he might have with his Government in the courts. The Ministry of Justice, therefore, interprets that this provision as permitting any claimant to take up his claim diredtly with the courts without recourse to the State Compensation Committee. The utilization of the claims procedure descrived above is, therefore, entirely voluntary on the part of the claimant, and the claimant may discontinue the procedings at any point if he is dissatisfied, and seek redress in the Korean courts. The Ministry of Justice hopes, however, for an increasing reliance by claimants upon the procedures developed under the terms of the State Compensation Law, and is undertaking efforts to publicize nationally these procedures. At present, roughly 70 per cent of the claims filed against the Government are being pressed under the terms of the procedures available under the State Compensation Law, and number of claims taken up with the courts is gradually decreasing.

25. If an unsatisfied claimant rejects the decision of the State Compensation Committee, and takes his claim

한·미국 간의 상호방위조약 제4조에 의한 시설과 구역 및 한국에서의 미국군대의 지위에 관한 협정(SOFA)
전59권. 1966.7.9 서울에서 서명 : 1967.2.9 발효(조약 232호) (V.50 실무교섭회의 합의의사록, 제10-37차, 1963) (2/2) 411

to the courts, the judge hearing the case is, under the terms of the Korean Constitution, bound only by the provisions of Korean law ans by his conscience. The proceedings and determinations of the State Compensation Committee, while available to him for review, are not dispositive of the issue when it comes before the court. There have been cases in which dissatisfied claimants have gone from the State Compensation Committee to the courts; one such case now in the courts involves a claim arising out of a maritime accident which was disallowed by the State Compensation Committee because of difficulty of finding reliable evidence due to the place where the accident took place.

26. The State Compensation Committee operates under the terms of generalized regulations which do not, however, apply to each claim on an equal basis because each claim presents its own somewhat unique aspects which require different modes and procedures for settlement. For example, the Korean regulations do not set forth in detail the types of evidence required by the State Compensation Committee to support a claim for a giving awards because in each case the relevant material evidence will be different, e.g., hospital bill receipts, family registration papers, etc. The State Compensation Committee does, however, in practice require the submission of all the relevant material evidence which it considers necessary. If false evidence is submitted by the claimant, he is subject to punishment under the terms of the criminal code and other Korean laws.

27. The factors used by the State Compensation Committee in fixing each award are related to the individual requirements of the claim being satisfied, and

한·미국 간의 상호방위조약 제4조에 의한 시설과 구역 및 한국에서의 미국군대의 지위에 관한 협정(SOFA)
전59권. 1966.7.9 서울에서 서명 : 1967.2.9 발효(조약 232호) (V.50 실무교섭회의 합의의사록, 제10-37차, 1963) (2/2) 413

may include such matters as occupation, income, age, sex, the social status and family role of the injured party, etc. In making lump sum awards in lieu of prospective earnings, the State Compensation Committee relies upon the Hofmann formula described in the Korean presentation above. In determing its award the Committee does not take into account the amounts paid the injured party under the terms of pension and workmen's compensation programs, or amounts paid to the injured party from any private insureance policies he might hold because such payments are fundamentally different in nature from an award made in compensation for a wrongful injury and damage.

28. The State Compensation Committee relies upon the Claims Section of the Ministry of Justice (as well as, of course, the claimant) for the development of evidence with respect to each claim which it handles. The Claims Section does not, however, have the authority to disallow claims for lack of evidence or for any other reason; disallowment is the perogative of the Committee itself.

29. The State Compensation Committee commenced operation in December, 1962. Claims to be acted upon did not, however, come in any quantities until May of 1963. In the three months previous to this meeting, more than 80 claims have been filed, of which more than 70 have been settled. The total compensation paid thus far by the Committee to claimants is approximately won 6 million (US $46,154)at the official rate of exchange). The Ministry of Justice estimates that the State Compensation Committee is paying awards whi

0569

approximately 45 per cent of the amount requested by claimants. The Korean negotiators offered to provide the U.S. side with statistics concerning the exact number of claims settled by the courts and by the Committee and the awards of compensation paid claimant utilizing both systems, in the past three months.

30. It was agreed that, if it is felt desirable, Korean and American claims specialists would meet to continue discussions on the subject of Korean claims procedures outside the formal negotiating sessions.

OTHER BUSINESS

31. It was agreed that the next negotiating session would be held on September 20, 1963, at 2:00 p.m.

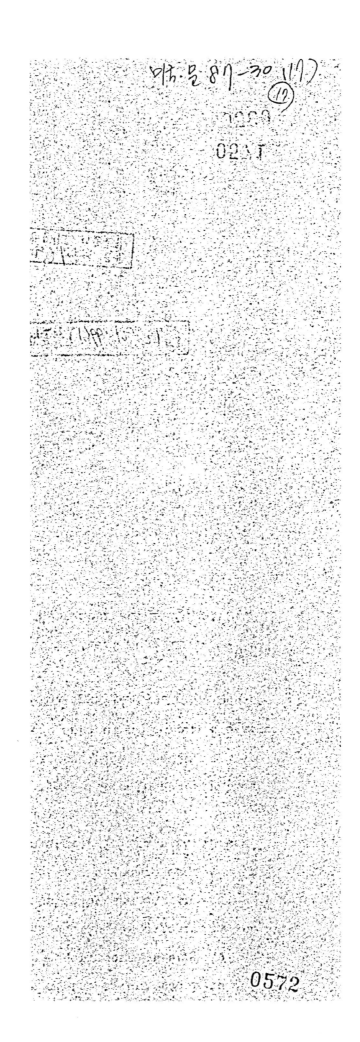

분류문 87-30 (17)
(12)

0220
0221

0572

September 20, 1963

1. Time and Place: 2:00 to 4:20 p.m. September 20, 1963
                     at the Foreign Minister's Conference
                     Room

2. Attendants:

ROK Side:

Mr. Whang, Ho Eul	Director Bureau of Political Affairs Ministry of Foreign Affairs
Mr. Shin, Kwan Sup	Director Bureau of Customs Duty Ministry of Finance
Mr. Koo, Choong Whay	Chief, America Section Ministry of Foreign Affairs
Col. Lee, Nam Koo	Chief, Military Affairs Section Ministry of National Defense
Mr. Chu, Mun Ki	Chief, Legal Affairs Section Ministry of Justice
Mr. Shin, Jung Sup	Chief, Treaty Section Ministry of Foreign Affairs
Mr. Kang, Suk Jae	2nd Secretary Ministry of Foreign Affairs
Mr. Cho, Kwang Jae	2nd Secretary Ministry of Foreign Affairs

U. S. Side:

Mr. Philip C. Habib	Counselor for Political Affairs American Embassy
Brig. Gen. G.G. O'Connor	Deputy Chief of Staff 8th U. S. Army
Col. Howard Smigelor	Deputy Chief of Staff UNC
Capt. R. M. Brownlie	Assistant Chief of Staff USN/K
Mr. Robert A. Lewis	2nd Secretary and Consul American Embassy
Mr. James Sartorius	2nd Secretary American Embassy
Mr. Rodney E. Armstrong	2nd Secretary American Embassy

0573

Mr. Robert A. Kinney   J-5
                            8th U.S. Army

Maj. Robert D. Peckham   Staff Officer, JAG
                            8th U.S. Army

1. Mr. Whang Ho Eul opened the meeting by saying
that he wished to note that the thirty-first session marked
the first anniversery of the reopening of the negotiations
for a ROK-US Status of Forces Agreement on September 20,
1962. Many difficult problems have been tackled coopera-
tively and with sincerity. The complexities of the
negotiations are now understood more thoroughly. The
Korean side hopes that the negotiations will be carried
forward with continued sincerity and good intent, and
that the negotiations will be successfully completed at
the earliest possible date.

2. Mr. Habib responded that the negotiators on both
sides of the table know better than anyone else that the
discussions deal with a complex instrument. The U.S.
side considers that the discussions have made exceptional
progress and is pleased with the spirit in which this
progress has been made. As intimated in some of the
early public statements by the U.S. side, the negotiators
have taken up some of the less complex topics first, and
have now gotten these subjects pretty much out of the
way. In the discussion of some of the more difficult
articles and clauses which still remain for negotiation,
the U.S. side pledges a continuation of the sincerity
which has thus far characterized its approach to the
negotiations. Mr. Habib then introduced James Sartorius,
Second Secretary of Embassy, who replaces Mr. William
Ford on the U.S. negotiating team.

3. Mr. Whang welcomed Mr. Sartorius, and expressed
his confidence that Mr. Sartorius would continue Mr.

0575

Ford's contribution to the progress of the negotiations.

FACILITIES AND AREAS - Grant of and Return

4. Opening substantive discussion, Mr. Hwang asked
if the U.S. side had any new thoughts on the draft
article dealing with the grant of and return of facilities
and areas (US draft Article I, or "A").

5. Mr. Habib recalled that the negotiators have
reached agreement upon paragraphs 2, 3, and 4 of the U.S.
draft article, and that the remaining points of difference
all have to do with those points covered in paragraph 1
of the US draft article. The U.S. side had considered
the points made by the Korean side in previous discussions
of this paragraph. First, the Korean draft provided in
paragraph 3 for a new survey of the facilities and areas
used by the U.S. Forces after the coming into force of
the Agreement as an alternative; the Korean side had
suggested that language embodying the substance of paragraph 3 of their draft article might be added at the end
of paragraph 1b. of the U.S. draft. The U.S. side wished
to point out that the U.S. Forces in Korea had under
way a comprehensive survey of the facilities and areas
This survey was begun in 1959
in use by them and is scheduled to be completed by 10
October, 1964. The results are being transmitted to
the Korean Government as they become available, and it is
estimated information on 95% of the areas and facilities
surveyed thus far has been supplied the Korean Government.
The U.S. side sees no good reason to include language in
the prospective Agreement requiring that a new survey be
made at great expense of time and money to do essentially
what has already been done and to replace information
which is already or will shortly be in the hands of the
proper Korean authorities.

0577

6. Continuing his review of the points of difference in paragraph 1 of the U.S. draft, Mr. Habib said
that the U.S. side had been able to take into account
the desire of the Korean negotiators expressed in an
earlier meeting that the Joint Committee be given a
role as the custodian of the records concerning the
facilities and areas in use by the U.S. Forces. In
considering this point, the U.S. side discovered a
gap in its draft which it would like to remedy. This
gap concerns the lack of any provision in the prospective agreement concerning those areas and facilities,
mostly airfields, which the U.S. has returned to Korea
with the reserved right of re-entry. There exist
mutual understandings between the U.S. and Korea
concerning these facilities and areas where the U.S.
has a reserved right of re-entry (Mr. Habib quoted
one such agreement, with respect to the Suwon Auxiliary
Air Field), but such agreements do not specify that
the facilities and areas, once re-entered, shall be
considered as part of the facilities and areas specified
in the prospective Status of Forces Agreement.

7. Mr. Habib thereupon tabled a new paragraph 1b.
of the draft U.S. article on the grant of and return
of facilities and areas. He said that this revision
sought to accomplish two purposes: take into account
Korean desires concerning the role of the Joint
Committee in the maintenance of records concerning the
facilities and areas utilized by the U.S. Forces, and
regularize the relationship of the existing re-entry
agreements between the two Governments to the prospective
Status of Forces Agreement.

한·미국 간의 상호방위조약 제4조에 의한 시설과 구역 및 한국에서의 미국군대의 지위에 관한 협정(SOFA)
전59권. 1966.7.9 서울에서 서명 : 1967.2.9 발효(조약 232호) (V.50 실무교섭회의 합의의사록, 제10-37차, 1963) (2/2)　　425

8. Mr. Whang said the Korean side would study
the new draft language taking into account the explanation
just offered by Mr. Habib, and would give its views at a
forthcoming meeting. It was agreed to pass on to a
review of the draft article on measures which may be
taken in facilities and areas (U.S. draft article III or
"B").

FACILITIES AND AREAS -Measures Which May be Taken in

9. Mr. Habib recalled that in the course of previous discussions of this article the Korean side
suggested that the second sentence of the first paragraph of the U.S. draft article might more appropriately
be handled as an agreed minute to the article. The U.S.
side accepted this suggestion and now table a draft
agreed minute embodying the substance of the second
sentence of paragraph 1 of the U.S. draft article.

10. Mr. Whang recalled that at a previous meeting
the Korean negotiators had suggested that the phrase
"within the extent that Korean nationals and their
property are not unduly impaired" be added at the end
of the sentence in the Agreement dealing with emergency
measures. At the time this suggestion was made, the
U.S. side had responded that there was no intent to
take measures which would have any of the effects
contemplated by the suggested Korean language. Mr.
Whang suggested that this understanding be supplemented
by an agreed minute to the article under consideration.

11. Mr. Habib objected that the phrase proposed
by the Korean side is indefinable. The problem to be
met by the language dealing with this matter is obvious;
since by definition the language deals with emergency

0281

0580

situations, it should set forth a clear principle
and not one incapable of definition with precision.
The emergency doctrine of the U.S. Forces, as set
forth in their regulations, is to take only such
actions as are necessary for the resolution of a given
emergency. The Korean language would disregard the
only real measure of actions to be taken in any emergency situation: necessity. The Korean side would
agree that it is most essential that in an emergency
the U.S. Forces should be given the necessary scope
of action to fulfill their mission. Mr. Habib asked
that the Korean side consider the U.S. draft, bearing
in mind the emergency doctrine of the U.S. Forces.

12. Mr. Whang said that the Korean side would
study the U.S. draft and would give its views at a
forthcoming meeting. He recalled that in the course
of previous discussions of this article the Korean
side was uncertain that the language of the U.S. draft
paragraph 1 adequately set forth the Government-to-
Government nature of requests for Korean measures to
provide access to facilities and areas. The Korean
negotiators had, however, studied the article thoroughly,
and now considered that, given the language of the U.S.
draft conerning "consultation between the two Governments
in the Joint Committee", the requests made under the terms of
paragraph 1 of the U.S. draft article could be considered
as requests by the Governmentoof the United States. The
Korean side therefore wished to withdraw its objections
to this aspect of the U.S. draft article.

13. Mr. Habib said that the understanding just set

0582

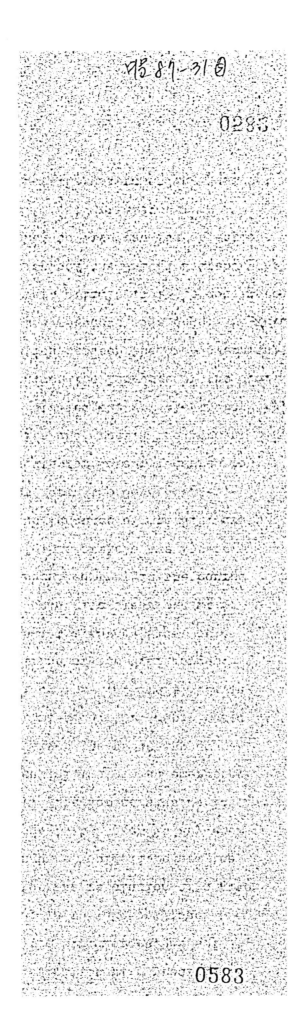

forth by Mr. Whang was shared by the U.S. side. He
noted that paragraphs 2 and 3 of the U.S. draft article
had previously been agreed upon.

FACILITIES AND AREAS -Return of

14. Turning to the draft article on the return of
facilities (U.S. draft article IV, or "C"), Mr. Whang
suggested a discussion of paragraph 1 of the U.S. draft
article. Mr. Habib responded that the U.S. position
upon the matters covered in paragraph 1 is unchanged, and
that the U.S. side still considers that the question of
compensation for the use of facilities and areas is
outside the scope of an agreement such as the prospective
Status of Forces Agreement.

15. Mr. Whang recalled that the U.S. side at a
previous meeting had tabled a new paragraph to be added to
the article on return of facilities and areas, specifying
the fact that Korea has no obligation to pay for the
residual value of improvements made to facilities and
areas returned to Korea by the U.S. In the course of
the discussion following the tabling of this new paragraph, the Korean side suggested the inclusion in the
paragraph of a phrase which provided that "supplies or
other materials" were among the objects for which Korea
would not be required to compensate the U.S. The Korean
side felt that the topic of non-liability for residual
value should be covered in the text of the article dealing with the return of facilities and areas. The Korean
side therefore proposed that the U.S. side agree to drop its paragraph 2 in favor of the text of paragraph 14 of the Korean
draft article, minus the language concerning "supplies
or other materials" which the U.S. negotiators had

0584

previously found objectionable. The proposed paragraph 2 (following the U.S. side's numbering)would read: "The
Government of the Republic of Korea is not obliged to make any compensation to the Government of the United States for any improvements made in facilities and areas or for the buildings or structures left thereon on the expiration of this Agreement or the earlier return of the facilities and areas."

16. Mr. Whang went on to say that the topics covered in paragraph 2 of the U.S. draft article on the return of facilities and areas seemed to the Korean negotiators to be matters of common sense. It was common sense that the items specified in this draft paragraph, if the property of the U.S., could be removed at will from the Republic of Korea. The Korean side therefore suggested the deletion of this paragraph or alternatively its relegation to an agreed minute.

17. Mr. Habib said that the U.S. side would study the Korean proposal with respect to the arrangement of the provisions concerning residual value. As for the Korean suggestion with respect to paragraph 2 of the U.S. draft article, however, it was the feeling of the U.S. side that it was necessary to have language covering the right of re-export of the items specified in the draft paragraph included in the text of the prospective Agreement. It was agreed at this point to suspend discussion of the topic of facilities and areas and to pass on to the draft article on Military Payment Certificates.

MILITARY PAYMENT CERTIFICATES

18. Mr. Whang said the Korean negotiators had restudied the text of the U.S. draft article on Military Payment

0586

Certificates (MPC), and were willing to withdraw their suggestion that the words "within the facilities and areas in use by the United States Forces" be attached to the end of the first sentence of the article. The Korean side agreed to the deletion of this phrase because MPC transactions were internal transactions among authorized users and the additional limiting language is believed to be unnecessary. Mr. Habib welcomed this statement.

19. Mr. Whang continued that the Korean side had also reviewed its position on the language in the Korean draft article which states that the lack of obligation on the part of the U.S. to redeem MPC held by unauthorized persons is recognized only "after the date of coming into force of this agreement". The Korean side would delete this language if there is an understanding that the deletion would not affect adversely negotiations with U.S. authorities for the exchange of MPC now held by the Korean Government for U.S. dollars.

20. Mr. Whang said the Korean Government now has a certain amount of MPC in its custody. At some future time, the Korean Government may enter into negotiations with the U.S. Government for the exchange of these MPC into U.S. dollars. It was with this possibility in mind that the Korean draft article on MPC was drafted, and that the phrase quoted earlier was inserted. By agreeing to deletion of this phrase, the Korean negotiators would not wish to have their position in the prospective negotiations adversely affected. Mr. Whang continued that, while in law unauthorized persons are not supposed to utilize MPC, in practical terms MPC were often handed over in the past to Koreans by authorized users in payment for goods and services provided to the authorized user. The Koreans had no choice; it was a question of either

0588

accepting the MPC, possibly without knowledge of the illegality of the transaction, or receiving no payment at all. In the future, the Korean Government intended to publicize the illegality of such transactions, but in the meantime large quantities of MPC had come into the hands of Koreans, some of which was turned over to the Korean Government in response to its call for a declaration of holdings of foreign currency. A way should be found to redeem this MPC in usable foreign exchange, in order to make up the loss now outstanding to the original recipients, and in order to repair the loss of good will which will otherwise accrue to the U.S.

21. Mr. Habib inquired what amount of MPC the Korean Government is currently holding in custody. Mr. Whang replied that he had no exact figures on the Government's holdings.

22. Mr. Habib asked whether the Korean side would agree to deletion of the phrase quoted by Mr. Whang if the understanding with respect to non-prejudice to any future negotiations were made reciprocal; that is, if the negotiating record also included a statement that the US has no obligation to redeem any amounts of MPC held by the Korean Government. Each side to the present negotiations would, under the terms of such an understanding, retain its independence with respect to a matter which should properly be discussed outside the present negotiations.

23. Mr. Whang said that the answer to Mr. Habib's proposal was complex and difficult, and that he wished to withdraw his offer of the deletion of the phrase under discussion. The Korean side would stand on its original draft language.

24. Mr. Habib said he regretted Mr. Whang's retreat from a proposal which seemed to offer a solution by which the interests of both sides to the present negotiations could be preserved and the negotiation of a Status of Forces Agreement advanced. The U.S. is, of course, not prepared to agree to compensation for MPC illegally acquired and was not willing to assist in the ex post facto legalization of illegal transactions just because they had taken place on a broad scale. Mr. Whang had, unfortunately, in the preceding discussion made clear that the Korean side wished to impose an obligation upon the U.S. side to agree at some time in the future to exchange the Korean Government's holdings of illegally acquired MPC for dollars. In these circumstances, he was compelled to table a draft agreed minute which rules out the possibility of any future negotiations for the conversion of Korean Government holdings of illegally acquired MPC. Mr. Habib tabled the draft agreed minute he had just described, and it was agreed to turn to the topic of local procurement.

LOCAL PROCUREMENT

25. Major Peckham presented a detailed explanation of the manner in which the U.S. side envisaged that the exemptions from Korean taxation specified in the U.S. draft article on local procurement would be granted. He stressed that the key to a proper understanding of the U.S. draft article is a close reading of U.S. draft agreed minute number 3 to the U.S. draft article, which sets forth in detail the procedures by which the U.S. Forces would obtain the exemptions specified in the article above. Examples of the manner in which these procedures would be implemented were set forth. Major Peckham also emphasized

0592

한·미국 간의 상호방위조약 제4조에 의한 시설과 구역 및 한국에서의 미국군대의 지위에 관한 협정(SOFA)
전59권. 1966.7.9 서울에서 서명 : 1967.2.9 발효(조약 232호) (V.50 실무교섭회의 합의의사록, 제10-37차, 1963) (2/2)

that the U.S. Forces in Korea are already receiving exemptions, for both direct and "ultimate use" procurement, from most of the taxes specified in the U.S. draft article under the terms of existing Korean legislation. The implementation of the U.S. draft article would require only a broadening and formalizing of the existing procedures, and not the development of any new procedures.

26. Mr. Sin Kwon-sup, replying to Major Peckham's presentation on behalf of the Korean side, expressed certain reservations about certain points, and said that a broadening of the present system for the exemption of U.S. Forces procurement from Korean taxation would increase the cost of tax administration appreciably. He suggested that the matters touched upon in Major Peckham's presentation be discussed between specialists from the two negotiating teams outside the formal negotiating sessions. The U.S. negotiators agreed to this suggestion.

OTHER BUSINESS

27. It was agreed that the next negotiating session would be held on October 4, 1963, at 2:00 P.M. The negotiators having remained in session almost three hours, the meeting was thereupon adjourned.

0594

JOINT SUMMARY RECORD OF THE 32ND SESSION

028

October 4, 1963

1. Time and Place: 2:00 to 3:15 p.m. October 4, 1963
   at the Foreign Minister's Conference
   Room

2. Attendants:

ROK Side:

Mr. Whang, Ho Eul	Director Bureau of Political Affairs Ministry of Foreign Affairs
Mr. Shin, Kwan Sup	Director Bureau of Customs Duty Ministry of Finance
Mr. Koo, Choong Whay	Chief, America Section Ministry of Foreign Affairs
Col. Lee, Nam Koo	Chief, Military Affairs Section Ministry of National Defense
Mr. Chu, Mun Ki	Chief, Legal Affairs Section Ministry of Justice
Mr. Shin, Jung Sup	Chief, Treaty Section Ministry of Foreign Affairs
Mr. Kang, Suk Jae	2nd Secretary Ministry of Foreign Affairs
Mr. Cho, Kwang Jae	2nd Secretary Ministry of Foreign Affairs

U.S. Side:

Mr. Philip C. Habib	Counselor for Political Affairs American Embassy
Brig. Gen. G.G.O'Connor	Deputy Chief of Staff 8th U.S. Army
Col. Howard Smigelor	Deputy Chief of Staff 8th U.S. Army
Mr. Benjamin A. Fleck	First Secretary American Embassy
Col. L. J. Fuller	Staff Judge Advocate United Nations Command
Capt. R. M. Brownlie	Assistant Chief of Staff USN/K
Mr. James Sartorius	2nd Secretary American Embassy
Mr. Robert A. Lewis	2nd Secretary and Consul American Embassy

0596

한·미국 간의 상호방위조약 제4조에 의한 시설과 구역 및 한국에서의 미국군대의 지위에 관한 협정(SOFA)
전59권. 1966.7.9 서울에서 서명 : 1967.2.9 발효(조약 232호) (V.50 실무교섭회의 합의의사록, 제10-37차, 1963) (2/2) 443

Mr. Robert A. Kinney   J-5.
                                        8th U.S. Army
Maj. Robert D. Peckham   Staff Officer, JAG
                                        8th U.S. Army

1. Mr. Whang opened the meeting by welcoming back
to the negotiating table Col. Fuller and Mr. Fleck, both
of whom had been absent on leave.

Facilities and Areas

2. Mr. Whang then opened the substantive discussion
by reviewing previous discussion of Paragraph 1 of
Article "A" dealing with facilities and areas. He reminded the negotiators that they had not resolved the
remaining differences in language between the U.S. draft
and the Korean draft. The Korean negotiators had given
careful study to the two drafts and were now prepared
to accept the U.S. draft of Paragraph 1(a). They did so
with the specific understanding that the words "wherever
located, used" in the third sentence of the U.S. draft
have substantially the same meaning as the words "necessary
to" in the Korean draft. Mr. Habib assented to this
understanding and agreement was reached on paragraph 1(a).

3. With regard to paragraph 1 (b), Mr. Whang said
that the Korean side understood the U.S. side to have
said that a survey of existing areas and facilities
currently is being conducted by the U.S. armed forces
and will be completed about 10 October 1964. About 95%
of the results of this survey to date have been furnished
to the ROK Government. Pointing out that a similar survey
was being conducted concurrently by the ROK armed forces,
he said that the results of the two surveys should be
identical. If there were any significant differences in
the results of the two surveys, the Korean negotiators

0598

0599

believed a joint survey should be made with regard to the facility or area in question. With the understanding that this would be done, the Korean side accepted the revised paragraph 1(b) which had been tabled by the U.S. side at the previous meeting.

4. Mr. Habib replied that the U.S. negotiators had always been of the view that adjustments of the kind referred to by Mr. Whang should be made through the Joint Committee. Full agreement having been reached on the text of Paragraph 1, it was noted that agreement had previously been reached on Paragraphs 2, 3, and 4 of this Article.

5. Mr. Habib stated that the U.S. side wished to propose a slight change in paragraph 4(b). This paragraph refers to facilities and areas which are to be used by the U.S. armed forces for only limited periods of time. As it now reads, it provides that the Joint Committee shall decide the extent to which the SOFA shall apply to these facilities and areas. The U.S. side wished to make a slight change in method but not in principle by inserting the word "not", so that the language would read "the extent to which the provisions of this Agreement shall not apply". Mr. Habib pointed out that this change would make the task of the Joint Committee much simpler, since it would not be necessary for the Joint Committee to list all of the provisions of the SOFA which would apply to any given facility or area but only those provisions which would not apply.

6. Mr. Habib asked the negotiators to consider the case of a specific area which the U.S. armed forces proposed to occupy for a limited period of time. If such occupation was

0600

acceptable to the ROK Government, the Joint Committee would then draw up a special agreement applicable to that specific area. This procedure would be followed in every case of a limited occupancy facility. It would be much simpler for the Joint Committee to specify in each such case only those provisions of the SOFA which would not apply. The proposed change in language would not alter the requirement that the Joint Committee draw up a special agreement; it would merely simplify the Committee's task in drawing up the agreement. The change would in no way alter the understanding already reached by the negotiators with regard to this paragraph.

7. Mr. Whang replied that the change proposed by the U.S. negotiators did not appear to alter the substance of the paragraph. The Korean side would consider the matter and give its views at the next meeting.

8. Turning to draft Article "B" dealing with facilities and areas, Mr. Whang recalled that at the previous meeting the U.S. side had tabled a proposed Agreed Minute in lieu of the second sentence of paragraph 1 of the U.S. draft. The Korean negotiators had suggested the addition at the end of the second sentence of the phrase "within the extent that Korean nationals and their property are not unduly impaired". With the understanding that the substance of this phrase will be respected by the U.S. armed forces, Mr. Whang continued, the Korean negotiators agreed to paragraph 1 of the U.S. draft and to the Agreed Minute. Paragraphs 2 and 3 of the U.S. draft having been agreed upon previously, it was noted that complete agreement had now been reached on the text of Article "B".

9. Turning to draft Article "C" dealing with facilities and areas, Mr. Whang recalled that the Korean negotiators had proposed to add to paragraph 1 of the U.S. draft the

한·미국 간의 상호방위조약 제4조에 의한 시설과 구역 및 한국에서의 미국군대의 지위에 관한 협정(SOFA)
전59권. 1966.7.9 서울에서 서명 : 1967.2.9 발효(조약 232호) (V.50 실무교섭회의 합의의사록, 제10-37차, 1963) (2/2)　447

last sentence of paragraph 13 of the Korean draft. They had also proposed that paragraph 2 of the U.S. draft be deleted or converted into an Agreed Minute

10. Mr. Habib stated that the U.S. negotiators had consistently opposed payment of compensation. Furthermore, the question of compensation should not properly enter into this article, inasmuch as the question of compensation is the subject of the next article. Therefore, the U.S. side proposed the deletion of the last sentence of paragraph 13 of the ROK draft from this article. The U.S. side, he added, is favorably inclined to consider conversion of paragraph 2 of the U.S. draft into an Agreed Minute but has not yet received approval from Washington.

11. Mr. Whang agreed that the last sentence of paragrph 13 of the ROK draft related to the following article. However, the ROK side would reserve its position on deletion of the sentence until agreement was reached on draft Article "D", which deals with the subject of compensation.

12. Mr. Habib stated that the U.S. side would state its views concerning the new paragraph 2 proposed by the ROK side following the receipt of the views of the U.S. Government.

13. Mr. Habib then sought the agreement of the ROK side to the division of the facilities and areas portion of the SOFA into various separate articles, as in the U.S. draft. Mr. Whang replied that the Korean negotiators had agreed, as a matter of convenience, to discuss the various items as separate articles, as in the U.S. draft. However, the Korean side preferred to defer final decision on this matter until negotiation of substantive matters had been completed.

14. Each side then indicated that its position with regard to the question of compensation had not changed and it was agreed to defer further consideration of U.S. draft Article "D" and paragraphs 4 and 5 of the Korean draft article.

0603

15. Mr. Whang stated that the drafts dealing with invited contractors had been discussed at many meetings and that each side knew the position of the other. With regard to paragraph 1, the difference in positions lay in the definition of invited contractors. He said the Korean position had not changed.

16. Mr. Habib stated that the U.S. side understood the Korean position. He said the U.S. side was in the process of studying this paragraph to determine which provisions were absolutely necessary to the performance of the mission of the U.S. forces. He suggested deferment of further discussion of this paragraph until completion of the study.

17. The Korean side agreed to defer discussion of paragraph 1. Mr. Whang noted that paragraph 2 of the U.S. draft had previously been agreed upon. He then requested the U.S. side to reconsider subparagraph (i) of the revised paragraph 3 of the U.S. draft.

18. Mr. Habib stated that since agreement had been reached on the article dealing with the licensing and registration of motor vehicles subsequent to the last discussion of the article dealing with invited contractors, the Korean side should now find subparagraph (i) acceptable.

19. Mr. Whang stated that the Korean position had not changed and that the Korean negotiators considered contractors to be in a different category from those to whom the provisions of the article on licensing and registration of motor vehicles would apply. He said that contractors would be permitted to register vehicles and obtain drivers licences under the same conditions as ordinary aliens.

20. Mr. Habib asked if the Korean side made any distinction between personally-owned vehicles and vehicles owned by the contracting companies. Mr. Whang replied that no distinction was envisaged.

한·미국 간의 상호방위조약 제4조에 의한 시설과 구역 및 한국에서의 미국군대의 지위에 관한 협정(SOFA)
전59권. 1966.7.9 서울에서 서명 : 1967.2.9 발효(조약 232호) (V.50 실무교섭회의 합의의사록, 제10-37차, 1963) (2/2)   451

21. Mr. Habib stated that while the Korean negotiators appeared to be basing their position on the provisions of the Japanese SOFA, the provisions of Korean law were quite different from those of Japanese law in regard to these matters. He was sure that the Korean negotiators did not wish to create difficulties. He then asked the Korean negotiators a series of questions regarding the application of Korean law to the invited contractors' vehicles with respect to: taxation, registration fees, insurance requirements, and whether or not there would be a limitation imposed on the number of such vehicles. Mr. Whang stated that the Korean side would state its position with regard to these points at the next meeting.

22. Mr. Whang stated that the Korean side had generally agreed to paragraph 6 of the U.S. draft, except for the phrase "other business in Korea". He said the Korean side was now prepared to agree to paragraph 6 of the U.S. draft, with the understanding that the phrase "other business in Korea" refers to business other than that conducted under contract with the U.S. armed forces. Mr. Habib stated that this understanding was correct and agreement was there-upon reached on paragraph 6.

23. Mr. Whang stated that the only outstanding point of difference between paragraph 7 of the U.S. draft and paragraph 6 of the Korean draft was the sentence in the U.S. draft providing for exemption from taxation on income derived outside of Korea. He said the Korean side had not included such a provision in its draft because it had not been thought necessary. The Korean side agreed to paragraph 7 of the U.S. draft.

한·미국 간의 상호방위조약 제4조에 의한 시설과 구역 및 한국에서의 미국군대의 지위에 관한 협정(SOFA)
전59권. 1966.7.9 서울에서 서명 : 1967.2.9 발효(조약 232호) (V.50 실무교섭회의 합의의사록, 제10-37차, 1963) (2/2) 453

24. Mr. Whang noted that paragraph 7 of the Korean draft related to criminal jurisdiction over contractors. He said the Korean side assumed that the missing paragraph 8 of the U.S. draft dealt with the same subject. The Korean side hoped that the U.S. side would table this missing paragraph as soon as possible. Mr. Habib confirmed Mr. Whang's assumption concerning the subject matter of paragraph 8 and said that it would be tabled as soon as possible.

25. Mr. Habib recalled that the Korean side had asked what U.S. organizations other than the U.S. armed forces would let contracts to invited contractors. He said the U.S. Operations Mission and the U.S. Embassy were the only organizations other than the U.S. armed forces which might utilize the services of invited contractors.

26. Mr. Whang stated that he understood that the use of such contractors by the Embassy and USOM would be based respectively, on the status, immunities and privileges accorded diplomatic organizations under international law and practice and on those accorded USOM under the pertinent agreement between the two governments of the ROK and the U.S.A. However, exempting the contractors from payment of taxes on income derived from contracts with these two organizations was quite another matter. Therefore, the Korean side proposed that the provisions of paragraph 7 be excluded from the application of the Agreed Minute. If that were done, the Korean side would accept the Agreed Minute. Mr. Habib replied that the U.S. side would study this matter further.

27. It was agreed to hold the next meeting on October 18 at 2:00 p.m.

0609

맹 론 해-경(위)

0030

0610

October 18, 1963

1. Time and Place: 2:00 to 3:25 p.m. October 18, 1963
   at the Foreign Minister's Conference
   Room

2. Attendants:

ROK Side:

Mr. Whang, Ho Eul	Director Bureau of Political Affairs Ministry of Foreign Affairs
Mr. Shin, Kwan Sup	Director Bureau of Customs Duty Ministry of Finance
Mr. Koo, Choong Whay	Chief, America Section Ministry of Foreign Affairs
Mr. Chu, Mun Ki	Chief, Legal Affairs Section Ministry of Justice
Lt. Col. Do Joon Pak	Military Affairs Section Ministry of National Defense
Mr. Shin, Jung Sup	Chief, Treaty Section Ministry of Foreign Affairs
Mr. Kang, Suk Jae	2nd Secretary Ministry of Foreign Affairs
Mr. Cho, Kwang Jae	2nd Secretary Ministry of Foreign Affairs
Mr. Huh, Sung	3rd Secretary Ministry of Foreign Affairs

U.S. Side:

Mr. Philip C. Habib	Counselor for Political Affairs American Embassy
Brig. Gen. G.G. O'Connor	Deputy Chief of Staff 8th U.S. Army
Col. Howard Smigelor	Deputy Chief of Staff 8th U.S. Army
Mr. Benjamin A. Fleck	First Secretary American Embassy
Col. L. J. Fuller	Staff Judge Advocate United Nations Command
Capt. R. M. Brownlie	Assistant Chief of Staff USN/K
Mr. Robert A. Lewis	2nd Secretary and Consul American Embassy

0611

좋은 법규집(8)

0612

Mr. Robert A. Kinney	J-5
	8th U.S. Army
Maj. Robert D. Peckham	Staff Officer, JAG
	8th U.S. Army
Mr. Kenneth Campen	Interpreter

1. Mr. Whang opened the meeting by announcing that Colonel Lee Nam-koo had been assigned as Chief of the Seoul Area's Military Affairs Office. He then introduced Lt. Colonel Pak Do-joon, ROKA, who will temporarily replace Colonel Lee on the Korean negotiating team. Mr. Habib expressed regret at the departure of Colonel Lee, who had been a member of the Korean team from the beginning, but heartily welcomed Lt. Colonel Pak to the negotiations.

Facilities and Areas

2. Taking up the first item on the agenda, Mr. Whang stated that the Korean side had fully considered the proposal made by the U.S. side at the previous meeting to insert the word "not" before the word "apply" in the final sentence of subparagraph (b), paragraph 4, Article "A", dealing with the granting and return of facilities and areas. The Korean side accepted this insertion and full agreement was thereupon reached on the text of Article "A".

Taxation

3. With regard to the article dealing with taxation, Mr. Whang reminded the negotiators that agreement had already been reached on the first paragraph of the U.S. draft. With respect of paragraph 2, the Korean side had previously proposed that the second sentence be deleted and its substance included in an Agreed Minute. However, inasmuch as agreement had subsequently been reached on the relevant paragraph of the article dealing with invited

0613

contractors, the Korean side now believed that for the sake of consistency the second sentence should be retained in paragraph 2. Therefore, in order that the language of this article conform with that of the contractors article, the Korean side accepted paragraph 2 of the U.S. draft, subject to later resolution of the conflict between the use of the words "organizations" and "activities" in the two drafts. Mr. Habib stated that the U.S. side had been prepared to agree to the Korean side's earlier proposal to convert the second sentence of paragraph 2 into an Agreed Minute. However, the U.S. side agreed that retention of that sentence in paragraph 2 was consistent with the language in other articles and, therefore, was preferable. Subject to later decision in favor of either "organizations" or "activities", full agreement was reached on the text of the U.S. draft of this article.

Invited Contractors

4. Turning to the article dealing with invited contractors, Mr. Habib indicated that the U.S. side would like to hear the views of the Korean side regarding subparagraph (i) of paragraph 3. In turn, the U.S. side was prepared to provide a fuller explanation of the proposed Agreed Minute, which had been the source of some misunderstanding at the previous meeting.

5. Mr. Habib referred to the series of questions asked by the U.S. side at the previous meeting concerning the applicability of Korean laws to vehicles imported into Korea by contractors and their employees. Mr. Whang stated that the Korean side was still engaged in the process of studying with the appropriate Korean authorities the applicability of Korean laws and regulations regarding the

한·미국 간의 상호방위조약 제4조에 의한 시설과 구역 및 한국에서의 미국군대의 지위에 관한 협정(SOFA)
전59권. 1966.7.9 서울에서 서명 : 1967.2.9 발효(조약 232호) (V.50 실무교섭회의 합의의사록, 제10-37차, 1963) (2/2) 461

licensing of motor vehicles to vehicles belonging to
contractors. However, at this meeting he would like to
provide some preliminary information concerning the relevant laws, fees and taxes.

6. Mr. Whang stated that the relevant law is the
Local Taxes Law, promulgated as Law No. 827 on December 8,
1961, and amended on December 29, 1962 as Law No. 1243.

7. Mr. Whang stated that there is an acquisition tax
of 2 percent on the current value of the taxed vehicle and
a vehicle tax of Won 160,000, payable in quarterly instal-
ments.

8. Fees include an initial registration fee of Won
1,000; a renewal, transfer, and termination fees of Won
500 each; and a fee of Won 250 for obtaining a copy of
an original document. Vehicle owners are also required to
purchase a national savings bond in the amount of Won 500
at the time of initial registration of the vehicle and in
the amount of Won 400 when each inspection of the vehicle
takes place.

9. Mr. Whang stated that insurance requirements for
alien-owned vehicles should be subject to the relevant
Korean law. Under the existing laws, there is no provision
for compulsory enforcement of the requirement that all
alien-owned vehicles be insured by a Korean insurance
company. However, the matter is the responsibility of the
Ministry of Transportation and, therefore, is left to that
Ministry's discretion. The Korean negotiators presume that
at present, nearly all alien-owned vehicles are insured with
foreign insurance companies. However, none of these firms
is officially licensed by the Ministry of Finance. A
decision will have to be taken, therefore, whether to license

0617

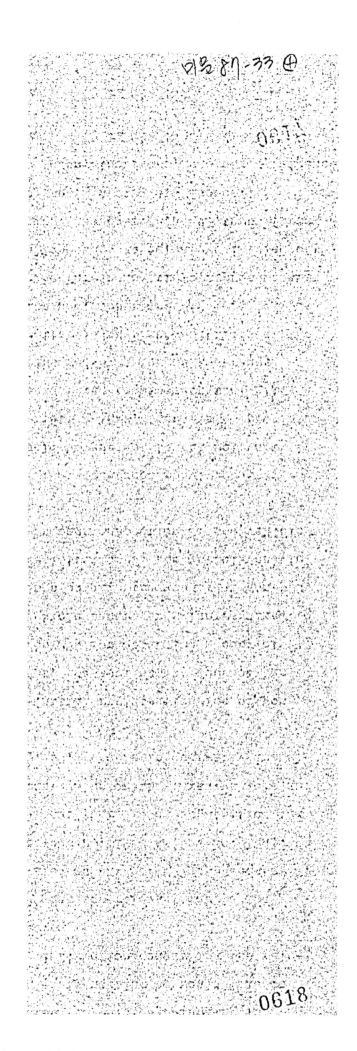

the foreign firms or to enforce the requirement that all insurance be issued by Korean firms. A decision in favor of the latter course would require further legislation.

10. Mr. Whang stated that with regard to the question of the U.S. side whether or not the Korean side was thinking of imposing a limitation on the number of vehicles to be imported by the contractors, the answer was that the Koreans had no intention of causing any inconvenience. They were ready to admit a reasonable number of vehicles for the performance of duty by the contractors and the convenience of their families. He pointed out that the present practice of the Ministry of Commerce is to impose no limitation on the number of vehicles imported, provided that no imported vehicle is transferred to persons not authorized to import vehicles.

11. Mr. Habib pointed out that there are three types of vehicles operated by the invited contractors: (a) those vehicles which are owned by the U.S. armed forces and which are furnished to the contractors for the use of the latter in carrying out their contracts; (b) those vehicles which are owned by the contractors; and (c) those vehicles which are owned by individual employees of the contractors. Mr. Habib pointed out that there are currently very few vehicles in category (c). He asked whether the Korean side intended to make any differentiation in the application of Korean laws and regulations to these three types of vehicles.

12. Mr. Whang replied that this matter had not yet been discussed with the Ministries concerned. He asked for clarification of the type of vehicle furnished to the contractors by the U.S. armed forces. Major Peckham replied that a primary factor determining the type of vehicle is

the geography of the site where the contract is to be carried out. In remote sites, such as mountain tops, army trucks and jeeps are made available to the contractors, inasmuch as normal civilian-type vehicles would be unable to traverse the rugged terrain.

13. Mr. Whang expressed his personal opinion that ownership of army trucks and jeeps made available to the contractors would remain with the United States Government. However, the Korean side would discuss this question with the Ministries concerned and would comment further at a later meeting.

14. Mr. Habib then informed the Korean side that contractors currently were operating over 400 U.S. Government-owned vehicles, 141 contractor-owned vehicles, and 13 privately-owned vehicles.

15. Mr. Whang asked if there were any difference between the types of vehicles owned by contractors and those which were privately-owned. Mr. Habib replied that the contractor-owned vehicles consisted primarily of panel trucks and pickup trucks.

16. Mr. Habib then asked if the Korean side were thinking of insisting on the right to impose a limitation on the number of vehicles to be imported by the contractors. Mr. Whang replied that it was a question of common sense and that so long as the quantities of vehicles imported were normal, there would be no intention by the Korean authorities to impose any limitation. He said that if one employee imported ten privately-owned automobiles, that would be considered excessive. Mr. Habib stated that not only would the U.S. armed forces agree that the example cited by Mr. Whang was excessive — they would not permit such importation to take place.

0621

미등허-33 ①

0051

0622

17. In response to Mr. Habib's question whether the Korean side was speaking only of privately-owned vehicles, Mr. Whang stated that limitations would also be imposed on contractor-owned vehicles and that determination of the number of vehicles to be imported by any one contractor would depend upon the nature of the contract which was being carried out. Mr. Habib agreed that the number of vehicles needed by a contractor for the performance of a contract would depend upon the nature of the contract. He said the U.S. side would await the Korean side's explanation at a later meeting of the latter's views regarding the applicability of Korean laws and regulations to vehicles operated by invited contractors and their employees.

18. Mr. Habib said the U.S. side wished to clear up the misunderstanding which had apparently occurred at the previous meeting regarding the sense of the Agreed Minute proposed in the U.S. draft. He said that the purpose of this Agreed Minute is to provide that contractors who may perform work for the Embassy or USOM in addition to the work which they perform for the U.S. armed forces, shall not be barred from the benefits of this article because they perform this additional work. The Korean side apparently had interpreted this Agreed Minute to convey upon the contractors involved the benefits of this article for this additional work. This is not a correct interpretation of the Agreed Minute. Mr. Habib asked the Korean side to study paragraph 7 of the U.S. draft, particularly the first sentence, which is qualified by the final clause "in connection with the construction, maintenance or operation of any of the facilities or areas covered by this agreement." He said the Korean side apparently believed that the Agreed Minute would provide exemption from payment of taxes on work performed by a contractor for the Embassy or USOM. This is not a correct interpretation of

the Agreed Minute, which is intended solely to prevent a contractor from losing the benefits of this article for work performed in connection with ... facilities or areas covered by this agreement.

19. Mr. Habib pointed out that acceptance of the Korean proposal to add the phrase "except for paragraph 7" to the Agreed Minute would deprive a contractor performing work for the Embassy or USOM of all the benefits of paragraph 7 with regard to work which that contractor was performing for the U.S. armed forces. Mr. Habib added that at the present time there is no contractor who is performing work for the Embassy and USOM in addition to his work for the U.S. armed forces, although in the past the Vinnell Corporation had performed some additional work for USOM. He urged the Korean side to reconsider its proposed addition to the Agreed Minute, in the light of the explanation just given of the intent of the Agreed Minute. Mr. Whang stated that the Korean side would take this matter under further consideration and give its views at a later date.

20. It was agreed to hold the next meeting on October 30 at 2:00 p.m.

한·미국 간의 상호방위조약 제4조에 의한 시설과 구역 및 한국에서의 미국군대의 지위에 관한 협정(SOFA)
전59권. 1966.7.9 서울에서 서명 : 1967.2.9 발효(조약 232호) (V.50 실무교섭회의 합의의사록, 제10-37차, 1963) (2/2) 471

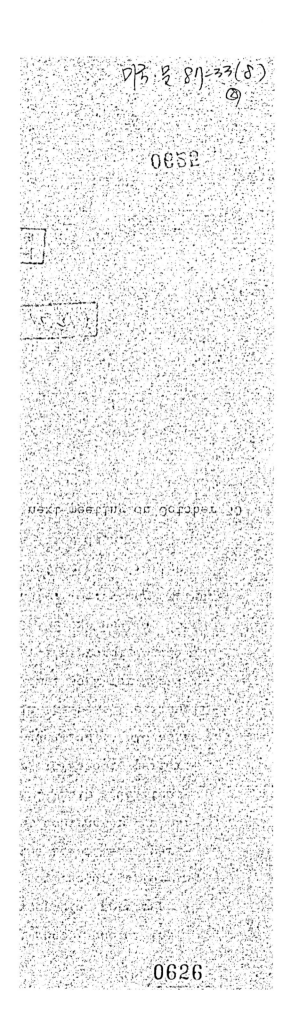

November 7, 1963

1. Time and Place: 2:00 to 4:00 p.m. October 30, 1963
   at the Foreign Minister's Conference
   Room   0638

2. Attendants:

ROK Side:

Mr. Whang, Ho Eul	Director Bureau of Political Affairs Ministry of Foreign Affairs
Mr. Shin, Kwan Sup	Director Bureau of Customs Duty Ministry of Finance
Mr. Koo, Choong Whay	Chief, America Section Ministry of Foreign Affairs
Mr. Chu, Mun Ki	Chief, Legal Affairs Section Ministry of Justice
Lt. Col. Do Joon Pak	Military Affairs Section Ministry of National Defense
Mr. Shin, Jung Sup	Chief, Treaty Section Ministry of Foreign Affairs
Mr. Kang, Suk Jae	2nd Secretary Ministry of Foreign Affairs
Mr. Lee, Chung Bin	3rd Secretary Ministry of Foreign Affairs

U.S. Side:

Mr. Philip C. Habib	Counselor for Political Affairs
Brig. Gen. G. G. O'Connor	Deputy Chief of Staff 8th U.S. Army
Col. Howard Smigelor	Deputy Chief of Staff 8th U.S. Army
Mr. Banjamin A. Fleck	First Secretary American Embassy
Col. L.J. Fuller	Staff Judge Advocate United Nations Command
Capt. R. M. Brownlie	Assistant Chief of Staff USN/K
Mr. James Sartorius	2nd Secretary American Embassy
Mr. Robert A. Lewis	2nd Secretary and Consul American Embassy

0628

```
Mr. Robert A. Kinney               J-5
                                   8th U.S. Army

Maj. Robert D. Peckham             Staff Officer, JAG
                                   8th U.S. Army

Mr. Kenneth Campen                 Interpreter
```

1. Mr. Whang opened the meeting by introducing Mr.
YI Chong-bin, of the Treaty Section of the Foreign Ministry,
who has been designated a member of the Korean negotiating
team replacing Mr. Ho Sung. Mr. Habib welcomed Mr. Yi to the
negotiations.

Air Traffic Control and Navigational Aids

2. Taking up the draft article dealing with air traffic
control and navigational aids, Mr. Whang commented that paragraph 1 of the Korean draft included a reference to communications systems. In view of the fact that paragraph 2 (b)
of Facilities and Areas Article "B", the text of which had
already been agreed to, provides for arrangements regarding
communications systems, the Korean side now agreed to the
deletion of the reference to communications systems from the
Air Traffic Control article. With this change, there remained
no difference in substance between the two drafts of paragraph
1. However, the Korean draft referred to coordination "between
the two governments" and spoke of "mutual security interests".
Since there was no real difference in substance, he urged
the U.S. side to agree to the Korean draft.

3. Mr. Habib replied that the U.S. negotiators were
under the impression that fundamental agreement had previously
been reached on the U.S. draft, subject only to agreement on
Facilities and Areas Article "B", which had subsequently been
reached as Mr. Whang had just pointed out. The language of
the U.S. draft is intended to relate this article to the
Status of Forces Agreement as a whole, which in turn is
related to the Mutual Defense Treaty. The SOFA itself, 0629

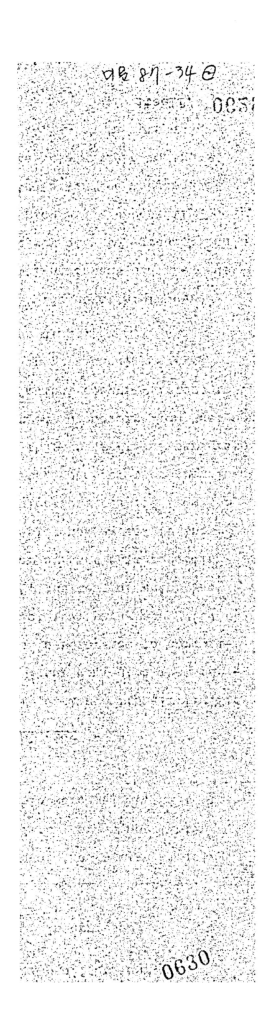

therefore, is related to our mutual security interests and there is no need to repeat in each article this fundamental concept. In the Preamble, which has already been agreed to, there is specific reference to the Mutual Defense Treaty and the desire of both governments to strengthen "the close bonds of mutual interest". Inasmuch as anything done under the provisions of the SOFA will be done for mutual security interests, there is no need to make such a specific reference in this article when it has not been included in other articles.

4. Mr. Whang replied that the wording contained in the Korean draft appeared in some other status of forces agreements. However, the Korean side agreed that this Agreement as a whole will be based on the mutual security interests of the two governments. With this understanding, the Korean side accepted the text of paragraph 1 of the U.S. draft.

5. Turning to paragraph 2, Mr. Whang stated that the chief difference in the two drafts lay in the use of the words "in territorial waters adjacent thereto or in the vicinity thereof" in the Korean draft, while the U.S. draft used the words "throughout the Republic of Korea and in the territorial waters thereof". Inasmuch as the U.S. draft, in the Agreed Minute provides that installation of navigational aids should be in accordance with the procedures established under paragraph 1 of Facilities and Areas Article "A", the Korean side accepted the first sentence of the U.S. draft and the accompanying Agreed Minute.

6. Referring to the use of the word "generally" in the second sentence of paragraph 2 of the U.S. draft, Mr. Whant stated that the Korean side accepted this sentence, inasmuch as certain U.S. systems are somewhat different from systems being used by the ROK Government.

0631

7. In view of the possibility of the establishment of temporary or emergency navigational aids, Mr. Whang stated that the Korean side accepted the third sentence of the U.S. draft, which provides for mutual notification of positions and characteristics of navigational aids which have been established and advance notification "where practicable" before making any changes or establishing additional aids.

8. It was noted that full agreement had thereupon been reached on the text of this article, subject to possible later editorial changes of a stylistic nature.

Customs

9. Taking up the Customs Article, Mr. Whang suggested that the negotiators defer discussion of the unresolved question of whether to use the word "activities" or the word "organizations", since the Korean negotiators had not yet reached full agreement with the Ministries concerned. He asked whether the U.S. side had any comments to make regarding other points at issue in paragraph 2 of the article.

10. Mr. Habib replied that in this paragraph and elsewhere in the article there existed a difference of opinion regarding the inclusion of references to the U.S. armed forces authorized procurement agencies and their non-appropriated fund activities. The U.S. side had already proposed that the references to them in the U.S. draft be placed in parentheses to emphasize the fact that they form an integral part of the U.S. armed forces. What the Korean side was suggesting, by omitting activities from the provisions of the article, was that the U.S. armed forces should penalize themselves merely because of the organizational and administrative framework under which the armed forces operate. This framework superficially appears to set these

한·미국 간의 상호방위조약 제4조에 의한 시설과 구역 및 한국에서의 미국군대의 지위에 관한 협정(SOFA)
전59권. 1966.7.9 서울에서 서명 : 1967.2.9 발효(조약 232호) (V.50 실무교섭회의 합의의사록, 제10-37차, 1963) (2/2)   479

agencies apart, whereas in actual fact they are an integral part of the armed forces. This is the only fundamental difference of opinion remaining with regard to paragraph 2.

11. Mr. Whang stated that the Korean side would consider the explanation given by Mr. Habib and would be prepared to discuss this issue as soon as agreement was reached with the appropriate ministries.

12. Mr. Whang noted that the introductory section of paragraph 3 had already been agreed upon, with the understanding that the word "charges" does not refer to charges by c civilian firms, such as unloading charges, storage charges, and charges by customs brokers. Mr. Habib agreed with this understanding.

13. Noting that subparagraphs (a) and (c) had already been agreed upon, Mr. Whang stated that at the 19th negotiating meeting, the Korean side had proposed that subparagraph (b) be modified by providing for a 6-month exemption from payment of duty on imported vehicles, with no time limitation on the importation of spare parts.

14. Mr. Habib replied that the U.S. negotiators continued to be reluctant to agree to the imposition of any time limit on the importation of duty-free vehicles. At previous meetings, the Korean negotiators had indicated a willingness to recognize problems arising out of delays in shipment and other causes of late arrival of vehicles. The basic issue is whether members of the U.S. armed forces should be expected to pay customs duty on normally available personal property. The establishment of a time limit does not answer this basic question.

15. Mr. Whang replied that the point made by Mr. Habib required further consideration by the Korean negotiators.

한·미국 간의 상호방위조약 제4조에 의한 시설과 구역 및 한국에서의 미국군대의 지위에 관한 협정(SOFA)
전59권. 1966.7.9 서울에서 서명 : 1967.2.9 발효(조약 232호) (V.50 실무교섭회의 합의의사록, 제10-37차, 1963) (2/2) 481

16. Turning to paragraph 5, Mr. Whang noted that the Korean side had previously suggested the substitution of the word "units" for the word "members" in subparagraph (a) of the U.S. draft. Mr. Habib replied that it was a fact that, in general, the members of the U.S. armed forces entered Korea as individuals and not as members of units. Therefore, the change proposed by the Korean negotiators would not be an accurate description of the actual process of entry and exit. The rotation of personnel and the granting of leave are both accomplished on an individual basis. Mr. Whang took note of Mr. Habib's explanation and proposed that further discussion be postponed until a later meeting.

17. Taking up subparagraph (b), Mr. Whang noted that the Korean negotiators had previously proposed the insertion of the word "official" before the word "mail", so as to provide for exemption from customs inspection of only official mail. He pointed out that agreement had already been reached on paragraph 3 (c), which provides for duty-free entry of "reasonable quantities" of personal effects and household goods mailed through U.S. military post offices. Therefore, provision should be made in paragraph 5(b) for inspection of personal mail to insure that only reasonable quantities of such goods were being imported through the mail channel.

18. Mr. Habib replied that this article was not intended to include provisions for verification of violations. The U.S. armed forces do not wish to misuse the military postal channels and are prepared to see, through the use of proper controls, that such channels are not misused. The right of inspection, even if granted to Korean customs authorities, would not give them adequate control over violations. Attempts to keep records of each soldier's personal mail would be an administrative nightmare which could not possibly be carried out, except perhaps at the cost of extended delays

0637

in the delivery of mail which would be unreasonable. Misuse of the mail channel is a disciplinary matter, which is covered in other portions of the Status of Forces Agreement. In order to meet the psychological needs of the Korean side and to form the basis of compromise, the U.S. side proposed the addition of the phrase "under official postal seal". Stating that the U.S. side did not wish to confuse the Korean regotiators, Mr. Habib explained that most mail addressed to members of the U.S. armed forces, including personal mail, arrives in Korea under official postal seal.

19. In response to Mr. Whang's request for a fuller explanation, Mr. Habib stated that there is a small seal on each incoming container of mail which identifies the contents of that container as mail within official U.S. postal channels. Mr. Whang stated that the term "official documents under official seal" was understood. He asked whether any difference existed between mail under official postal seal and ordinary mail.

20. Mr. Habib replied that the major portion of the mail being discussed was personal mail. He said the U.S. negotiators were trying to provide language which would make this provision of the article more palatable to the Korean negotiators. The Korean proposal for customs inspection of mail could not be carried out in a practical or administratively sound manner. It would result in delay and interference with the delivery of mail which would be unwarranted. He asked if the Korean negotiators were proposing to station a customs officer at every battalion and regimental military post office. The Korean proposal would only create confusion and was not the proper way to control violations. An alternative method of carrying out the Korean proposal would be to open the incoming mail at the ports of entry. This also would result in confusion and delays in delivery. In the end, the right of inspection would never be exercised. If the U.S.

0640

negotiators thought that the proposal had a useful purpose, they would agree, even though the implementation proved to be cumbersome. However, the Korean proposal does not protect either the ROK Government or the U.S. armed forces against violations.

21. Mr. Whang stated that the Korean negotiators by no means intended to delay or confuse delivery of mail to the U.S. armed forces. In the past, unauthorized goods had been imported through military postal channels. The Korean authorities, therefore, wished to maintain preventive measures but these were not intended to confuse or delay the delivery of mail. He said the Korean negotiators had photographs of cases in which the military postal channels had been misused. In the past, the Korean authorities have not had the opportunity to examine mail passing through these channels and they suspected that there had been unauthorized importation of goods. The adoption of this provision in the SOFA might itself prove to be an effective preventive measure.

22. Mr. Habib replied that the question of policing the use of the mails was a disciplinary matter. This was true also of misuse of privileges with regard to post exchanges, commissaries, and similar activities. The photographs in the possession of the Korean negotiators were probably taken in conjunction with the U.S. authorities, since there was close cooperation between the U.S. military police and the Korean police.

23. Mr. Whang stated that the Korean negotiators realized that the bulk of the incoming mail was from the families in the United States of the members of the U.S. armed forces. However, some dishonest persons had abused this privilege and the Korean negotiators desired, through this provision of the SOFA, to warn them that military postal channels cannot be abused. He said they had parcels primarily in mind.

0641

0642

They did not propose to send customs inspectors to every b. battalion and regimental post office, since this would exceed the personnel resources of the Customs Bureau. What they were proposing was to station customs inspectors at the ports and airports to make spot checks of incoming parcels. The U.S. negotiators had explained that misconduct would be discovered through joint action b. Korean and U.S. police and the violators arrested and disciplined. However, since the minconduct was carried out in secret, it would be im- possible to uncover all offenders. Therefore, therershould be some means by which to give a psychological warning to offenders that their misdeeds may be discovered and punished.

24. Mr. Habib stated that he gathered from "r. Whang's remarks that it was the intention of the Korean negotiators that letter mail should not be inspected and that they were interested primarily in inspecting non-letter mail.

25. Mr. Whang replied that under the provisions of the ROK Constitution, personal letters are sacrosanct and accord- ingly the secrecy of the personal letters of Korean nationals is protected. The Korean authorities, therefore, could not think of examining letter mail of members of the U.S. armed forces.

26. Mr. Habib stated that letter mail is known in the United States as "first class mail". He said he gathered that if suitable language could be found to exempt letter mail from customs inspection the Korean negotiators would look upon it favorably. He said the U.S. negotiators would consider the statements made by Mr. Whang and would discuss this matter further at a later meeting.

27. Turning to subparagraph (c), Mr. Whang noted that at a previous meeting, the Korean negotiators had proposed the deletion from the U.S. draft of the phrase "and their non-appropriated fund organizations provided for in Article--".

0643

주한미군지위협정(SOFA) 서명 및 발효 20

Mr. Habib replied that these activities form an integral part
of the U.S. armed forces and should be so described, not only
in this subparagraph but throughout the article.

28. Mr. Whang stated that in paragraph 2 it had been
agreed in principle that equipment and supplies imported by
these organizations may be imported free of duty. In this
subparagraph, the Korean negotiators wished to provide only
that such imports be subject to customs inspection. Mr. Habib
replied that Agreed Minute #1 limits such importations to
"the extent reasonably required". There was no reason to
examine what are, in the U.S. view, official cargoes. If
questions arose, the Joint Committee could be asked to look
into the matter. In view of the tone of the article, the
U.S. negotiaotrs were not prepared to agree to examination
of official military cargoes.

29. Mr. Whang stated that the Korean negotiators would
reply to this statement at the next meeting. He noted that
agreement had previously been reached on paragraphs 6,7,8,
and 9.

Revision of the Agreement

30. At this point, it was agreed to adjourn the meeting. Before adjourning, the two sides exchanged drafts of
the article providing for Revision of the Agreement.

31. The next meeting was scheduled for November 14
at 2:00 p.m.

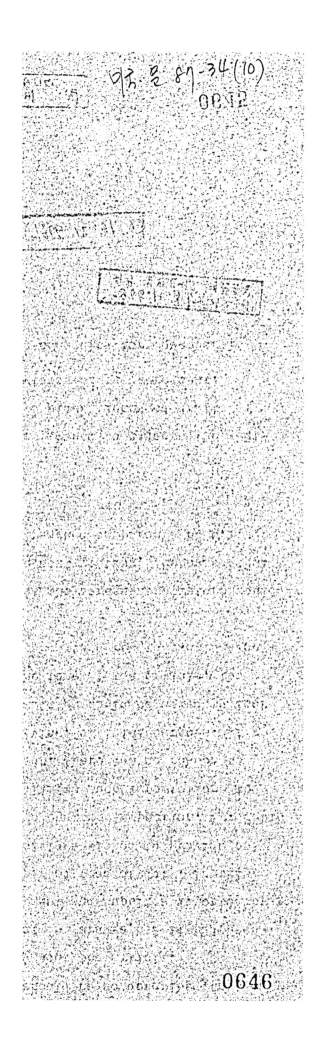

November 23, 1963 8

1. Time and Place: 2:00 to 4:30 p.m. November 14, 1963
   at the Foreign Minister's Conference
   Room

2. Attendants:

ROK Side:

Mr. Whang, Ho Eul	Director Bureau of Political Affairs Ministry of Foreign Affairs
Mr. Shin, Kwan Sup	Director Bureau of Customs Duty Ministry of Finance
Mr. Koo, Choong Whay	Chief, America Section Ministry of Foreign Affairs
Mr. Chu, Mun Ki	Chief, Legal Affairs Section Ministry of Justice
Lt. Col. Do Joon Pak	Military Affairs Section Ministry of National Defense
Mr. Kang, Suk Jae (Rapporteur and Interpreter)	2nd Secretary Ministry of Foreign Affairs
Mr. Lee, Chung Bin	3rd Secretary Ministry of Foreign Affairs

U.S. Side:

Brig. Gen. G. G. O'Connor	Deputy Chief of Staff 8th U.S. Army
Col. Howard Smigelor	Deputy Chief of Staff 8th U.S. Army
Mr. Benhamin A. Fleck (Rapporteur and Press Officer)	First Secretary American Embassy
Col. L. J. Fuller	Staff Judge Advocate United Nations Command
Capt. R. M. Brownlie	Assistant Chief of Staff USN/K
Mr. Robert A. Lewis	2nd Secretary and Consul American Embassy
Mr. Robert A. Kinney	J-5 8th U.S. Army
Maj. Robert D. Packham	Staff Officer, JAG 8th U.S. Army

0647

0648

<u>Discussions</u>

<u>Customs</u>

1. Mr. Whang opened the meeting by suggesting resumption of discussion of paragraph 5 of the Customs Article but asked if the U.S. side cared to make any comments on paragraph 1, 2, 3, or 4. Gen. O'Connor replied that the U.S. side had no further comment to make regarding those paragraphs. However, it might be useful to review the remaining points of difference. Full agreement had already been reached on paragraphs 1 and 4. Regarding paragraph 2 there were still two points at issue. First, it had still not been decided whether to use the word "organizations" or the word "activities" in this paragraph and in paragraph 5(c) and Agreed Minutes 1 and 3. Secondly, the Korean side had suggested the deletion of references to the U.S. armed forces' non-appropriated fund activities from this paragraph, while the U.S. side had proposed placing the references to these agencies and activities in parentheses in order to emphasize the fact that they form an integral part of the U.S. armed forces. Although agreement had been reached on subparagraphs (a) and (c) of paragraph 3, the substance of subparagraph (b) was still in dispute.

2. With regard to paragraph 5(b), Mr. Whang noted that the Korean side had stated that there was no intention on the part of the Korean authorities to inspect official mail or private letters addressed to members of the U.S. armed forces by members of their families in the United States. However, the Korean side desired to have the paragraph so worded that it would give the Korean authorities the right to inspect parcel mail.

3. General O'Connor replied that at the previous negotiating meeting, the Korean side had stated that un-

한·미국 간의 상호방위조약 제4조에 의한 시설과 구역 및 한국에서의 미국군대의 지위에 관한 협정(SOFA)
전59권. 1966.7.9 서울에서 서명 : 1967.2.9 발효(조약 232호) (V.50 실무교섭회의 합의의사록, 제10-37차, 1963) (2/2)　495

authorized goods had been imported into the Republic of
Korea through military postal channels. The Korean side
had emphasized that the Korean authorities did not wish
to inspect first class mail or to delay or confuse delivery
of parcel mail. However, the Korean side had expressed
the view that the inclusion in the SOFA of a provision
authorizing the inspection of parcel mail by ROK customs
authorities might prove to be an effective preventive
measure to check abuses of the military postal channels.
The Korean side had stated that they did not propose to
send customs inspectors to every battalion or regimental
post office but rather to station customs inspectors at
ports and airports to spot-check incoming parcels.

4. In veiw of the these statements by the Korean
side, General O'Connor continued, he wished to give a
more detailed explanation of how the military postal system
operates. U.S. military mail arrives in Korea in large
metal containers, eight feet by six feet by seven feet
in demensions, or a total of approximately 330 cubic feet
each. These sealed containers are not opened at the port
of entry but are sent directly to one of the 17 main
military post offices which are located in various parts
of the Republic of Korea. These containers are opened at
one of these main military post offices and the mail is
then distributed in sealed mail sacks to 32 unit distribution centers. It is at these unit distribution centers
where effective surveillance of parcels received by an
individual addressee can be maintained. U.S. military
postal authorities at these individual postal units are
continuously on the lookout for any abuse or violation of
postal or customs regulations. Thus far in 1963, a total
of 60 individuals have been denied further use of APO mails

0651

주한미군지위협정(SOFA) 서명 및 발효 20

in Korea because they were found to have abused their
APO privileges. Stern punitive action will be taken
against any other personnel who may be discovered abusing
their APO privileges.

5. As indicated by the foregoing explanation, General
O'Connor continued, it would be very complicated, if not
impossible, to maintain surveillance of parcels at ports
of entry. Attempts to maintain surveillance at these
points would be an administrative nightmare which could
only result in extended delays and confusion and probable
damage to the goods as the result of inadequate repacking.
U.S. military postal authorities are aggressively implementing a program designed to eliminate any abuses in the
APO system as they may arise. This surveillance program
focuses on the point of parcel distribution, at the end of
the line, where unusual or repeated shipments of parcels
to individuals can be easily spotted and the violators
punished. This is a practical program that works,
whereas the proposed program of spot inspection at ports
of entry would be impracticable. Therefore, the U.S.
side continued to propose acceptance of the following
language for paragraph 5(b): "Official documents under
official seal and mail in United States military postal
channels under official postal seal".

6. Mr. Whang thanked General O'Connor for his explanation and stated that the Korean side now understood
that the mail was not opened at ports of entry but only
at the 17 main military post offices and the 32 unit
distribution centers. He said the Korean side would study
the matter and explore the possibility of sending Korean
customs inspectors to the post offices and unit distribution centers. He said the Korean authorities had no

한·미국 간의 상호방위조약 제4조에 의한 시설과 구역 및 한국에서의 미국군대의 지위에 관한 협정(SOFA)
전59권. 1966.7.9 서울에서 서명 : 1967.2.9 발효(조약 232호) (V.50 실무교섭회의 합의의사록, 제10-37차, 1963) (2/2) 499

미물 87-35④

0654

intention of causing unnecessary confusion or delays. However, since there had been in the past quite a few abuses, the Korean side wished to give a warning to prospective violators and make apprehension and punishment possible. To that end, Korean customs inspectors should be given the authority to inspect the parcel mail.

7. General O'Connor stated that the U.S. authorities believed the present inspection system to be effective. He said the U.S. military postal authorities take a special look at packages mailed to members of the U.S. armed forces from Hong Kong and Japan. The U.S. side was of the opinion that the proposals set forth by the Korean side would creat confusion and delay the delivery of the mail.

8. Mr. Whang said the Korean authorities were grateful for the actions taken by the U.S. military authorities in preventing abuses. However, the SOFA must provide for an orderly administration of Korean customs regulations. He said the Korean side was prepared to agree to the U.S. position with regard to certain other points at issue in this article if the U.S. side would accept the Korean position with regard to paragraph 5(b). General O'Connor replied that the U.S. side would take the Korean position under further consideration.

9. Turning to paragraph 5 (c), Mr. Whang stated that the Korean side continued to desire the deletion of the reference to non-appropriated fund activities from this subparagraph. He stated that if the U.S. side were willing to agree to so limit the provisions of this subparagraph, the Korean side was prepared to agree to use the word "activities" instead of the word "organizations" throughout

한·미국 간의 상호방위조약 제4조에 의한 시설과 구역 및 한국에서의 미국군대의 지위에 관한 협정(SOFA)
전59권. 1966.7.9 서울에서 서명 : 1967.2.9 발효(조약 232호) (V.50 실무교섭회의 합의의사록, 제10-37차, 1963) (2/2) 501

미문87-35①

0622

0656

the article. Furthermore, if the U.S. side agreed to
the Korean position regarding subparagraphs (b) and (c)
of paragraph 5, the Korean side would not only agree to
use of the word "activities" but would also agree to the
U.S. text of paragraph 3(b). General O'Connor replied
that the U.S. side would not change its position with
regard to paragraph 5(c) because cargoes assigned to
authorized procurement agencies and their non-appropriated
fund activities are military cargoes.

10. Reverting to paragraph 5(a), Mr. Whang urged the
U.S. side to accept the ROK text. He said that use of
the word "units", as proposed by the Korean side, did not
mean that the Korean authorities intended to conduct a
customs examination of every individual member of the
U.S. armed forces entering or leaving the Republic of
Korea. He said the intention was to grant exemptions
from such examination in almost every case. However, the
ROK authorities wanted the SOFA to grant them the right
of inspection, even though they did not intent to inspect
in every case in actual practice. He further stated that
there is a fundamental idfference between the granting of
exemptions from inspection while retaining the right to
inspect and not retaining any right to inspect at all.
General O'Connor replied by reiterating the fact that
members of the U.S. armed forces enter and leave the
Republic of Korea as individual members of the armed forces
and not as members of units. He said the U.S. side would
take the Korean position under further consideration.

11. Returning to paragraph 5(c), Mr. Whang pointed out
that in this subpragraph and Agreed Minute 3, according to
the U.S. draft, "all cargo" includes cargo assigned to
non-appropriated fund organizations. In paragraph 2, it
has already been spelled out that such imports shall be

0657

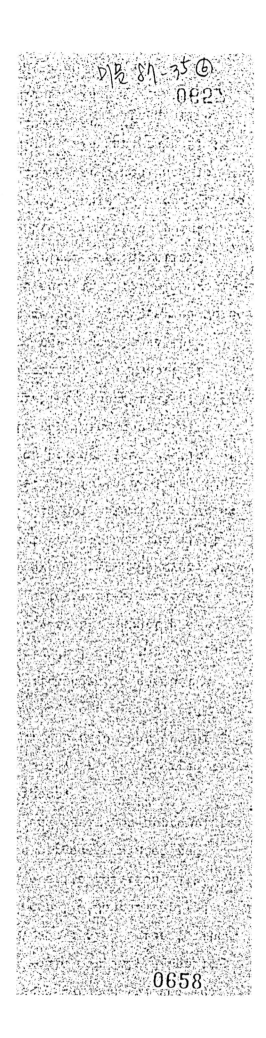

permitted entry free of customs duty. However, cirgaret-
tes, tobacco, and similar items consigned to non-appropriated fund organizations, cannot be construed as military cargo. The Korean authorities wish to have an idea
of the types of cargo and the quantities shipped so that
they can discuss unusual shipments with the U.S. authorities. Therefore, they wish to exclude cargo consigned
to non-appropriated fund organizations from the provisions
of this subparagraph.

12. General O'Connor replied that since the Korean
side had already agreed that such cargo should be admitted
free of customs duty, the U.S. side failed to see the
point of conducting customs examination of such cargo.
He pointed out the difficulty of differentiating between
certain types of rations issued directly by the armed
forces and good sold in the post exchanges. He said the
proper time to deal with infractions is when the goods
are sold or disposed of illegally in the Republic of Korea.
He pointed out that the inclusion of non-appropriated
fund cargo as military cargo is not a situation peculiar
to Korea but is worldwide U.S. military practice.

13. Mr. Whang stated that while it was true that
agreement had been reached on importation of these goods
duty-free under the provisions of paragraph 2, importation
of such goods in excess of consumption needs could result
in their sale on the black market. Therefore, the Korean
customs authorities should be in a position to know the
quantities of such goods actually imported.

14. General O'Connor replied that control over the
sale of goods imported by non-appropriated fund activities
is maintained through rationing of purchases at the post
exchanges. He displayed a sample ration card and pointed

한·미국 간의 상호방위조약 제4조에 의한 시설과 구역 및 한국에서의 미국군대의 지위에 관한 협정(SOFA)
전59권. 1966.7.9 서울에서 서명 : 1967.2.9 발효(조약 232호) (V.50 실무교섭회의 합의의사록, 제10-37차, 1963) (2/2) 505

out that the sale of such items as soap, soft drinks, and stockings is strictly rationed. With regard to items which are imported in bulk, he pointed out that adequate supplies must be maintained in the pipe line and that it would be difficult for individuals not in supply operations to know what constitutes a "reasonable quantity". He added that the rationing system is under continuing review. Mr. Whang stated that this question had been fully discussed and suggested that both sides give further consideration to the other side's position.

Military Post Offices

15. Turning to the article on Military Post Offices, Mr. Whang recalled that at the 19th negotiating meeting, the both sides had agreed to convert paragraph 2 of the U.S. draft into an Agreed Minute. Final agreement on this article must await agreement on the text of paragraph 5(b) of the Customs Article. Mr. Whang proposed deletion of the words "and their dependents" from paragraph 2 (or the Agreed Minute) and as an alternative he further proposed if the U.S. side would agree to the Korean position regarding paragraph 5(b) of the Customs Article, the Korean side would then be prepared to agree to the retention of the word "and their dependents" in paragraph 2. General O'Connor indicated that the U.S. side would respond when thise Article is taken up again, after Agreement on paragraph 5(b) of the Customs Article.

Utilities and Services

16. Taking up the drafts regarding Utilities and Services, Mr. Whang recalled that the U.S. side had proposed in the first sentence the deletion of the phrase "whether publicly or privately owned", the insertion of the word "owned" before the word "controlled", and the substitution of the phrase "local administrative subdivisions" for the phrase "political subdivisions". Mr. Whang stated

0661

that the Korean side accepted the U.S. draft of the first sentence with the proposed changes.

17. Recalling that the Korean side had proposed the deletion of the phrase "however produced" from the second sentence of the U.S. draft, Mr. Whang asked for comment by the U.S. side. Colonel Fuller replied that this phrase was included in the Utilities and Claims Settlement Agreement and had been included in the first Korean draft of this article. The U.S. side was unable to understand why the Korean side now wished to delete the phrase from this article.

18. Mr. Whang replied that inasmuch as the phrase "however produced" was contained in the Utilities and Claims Settlement Agreement, the Korean side agreed to its inclusion in this article of the SOFA, with the reservation that subsequent revision of the Utilities and Claims Settlement was not precluded and that if such revision should result in the elimination of the phrase from the latter agreement, the language of the SOFA would be changed accordingly. Colonel Fuller replied that the U.S. side would have to consider the implications of the proposed reservation by the Korean side before it could agree to the Korean side's conditional acceptance of the second sentence of paragraph 3(a) of the U.S. draft.

19. Mr. Whang stated that the Korean side accepted the revised third and fourth sentences of the U.S. draft. If the U.S. would agree to the Korean reservation with regard to the second sentence, full agreement could be reached on paragraph 3(a) of the U.S. draft.

20. Passing on to paragraph 3(b) of the U.S. draft, Mr. Whang noted that the first sentence had been agreed to and that the original second sentence had been deleted.

With regard to the original third sentence, now the second
sentence of this paragraph, which deals with emergency
operating needs of the U.S. armed forces, the needs in
question should be those which the ROK Government recognizes
to be reasonable and justifiable. Mr. Whang stated that
the Korean side would like to have the record clearly
show that the ROK Government must also agree that emergency
operating needs exist before it will take measures to
assure provision of utilities and services necessary to
meet these needs. He said the Korean side would prefer to
transfer the substance of this sentence to an Agreed Minute.

21. In response to Colonel Fuller's request for
clarification, Mr. Whang stated that the Korean side
understood this provision to mean that when an emergency
operating need arises, the U.S. armed forces will notify
the ROK Government. However, the Korean side held that
the ROK Government, after receiving such notification, must
agree that such a need exists before taking action. In
other words, the Korean side could not agree to a provision
which would provide for unilateral determination by the
U.S. armed forces that an emergency operating need existed.
The Korean side also wished to move the netire sentence
to an Agreed Minute. Colonel Fuller replied that the U.S.
side would take these proposal under consideration.

22. Mr. Whang stated that some misunderstanding
appeared to have arisen regarding paragraph 4 of the U.S.
draft and paragraph 2 of the Korean draft. He said that
Mr. Ku explain the views of the Korean side. Mr. Ku stated
that the U.S. draft provided only for accounting arrangements,
whereas the Korean draft specifically provided that specific
arrangements entered into by the U.S. armed forces for the
use of, and payments for, utilities and services would
continue in effect. Such arrangements include those contracts

0664

already in effect with the Seoul City Water Supply, the Korean Electric Company, and the national railways. The U.S. draft gives the impression that the two governments must enter into arrangements in addition to the SOFA in order to continue such financial transactions in the future. And there is no mention in the U.S. draft of existing arrangements for such transactions. Assuming that the U.S. side agrees that existing arrangements should continue after the SOFA enters into force, it is necessary to say so in the Agreement. This could be done either in an Agreed Minute or by agreement on paragraph 2(b) of the Korean draft.

23. Colonel Fuller replied that the U.S. side believed that the existing arrangements would continue in effect after the SOFA came into force. The U.S. draft of paragraph 4 was intended to provide only for the establishment of an accounting system. The U.S. side would give further consideration to paragraph 2 of the ROK draft but it appeared that some changes of language would be desirable. For instance, the ROK draft used the phrase "public utilities", which is not used elsewhere in the article. In fact, it had already been agreed to delete the phrase "whether publicly or privately owned".

24. Mr. Ku replied that the misunderstanding referred to earlier by Mr. Whang had been cleared up and the Korean side was hopeful that appropriate and mutually acceptable language could be found. The Korean side would take under consideration Colonel Fuller's explanation. Colonel Fuller stated that paragraph 4 of the U.S. draft was originally intended to refer to paragraphs 1 and 2 of the U.S. draft article, as well as paragraph 3. It was difficult to split the article into two separate articles, as the Korean side had suggested, since this would create

0666

a somewhat awkward situation with regard to paragraph 4. Mr. Ku replied that the decision whether to have a separate utilities and services article could be made at a later date.

25. Turning to the Agreed Minutes in the U.S. draft, Mr. Ku noted that at the 24th meeting it had been agreed to delete the phrase "increase in utility or service" from Agreed Minute #1. He added that the Korean side had proposed a further change in this Minute which would replace the reference to prior consultation with a provision for notification to the U.S. armed forces within fifteen days after the effective date of any change in priority or rates.

26. Colonel Fuller stated that it made a great difference whether the U.S. armed forces were consulted before a change was effected or notified afterwards. Any change in rates was so important a matter for the armed forces that they should be consulted beforehand. Mr. Ku replied that this was an important matter for both governments. The impact of any change in rates on the Korean economy and the people in general was enormous. In the past, there had usually been consultation on all matters of mutual concern. Such an important matter must be profoundly studied before any change was implemented. There would possibly be discussion by the Joint Committee. In any case, the final decision would be communicated to the U.S. authorities.

27. Colonel Fuller pointed out that prior consultation does not necessarily imply prior agreement. The U.S. side believed that use of these utilities and services by the U.S. armed forces was somewhat different than use by private users in Korea. It was so important a matter for the armed forces that they should be consulted

0668

about any pending change, not merely notified after the [ ]
change was put into effect.

28. Mr. Ku stated that the treatment accorded the
U.S. armed forces in this regard has always been equal
to, or better than, that accorded to agencies of the ROK
Government. Proposed changes will be considered from
every angle with all prudence. The U.S. forces would
continue to receive favorable consideration. Mr. Whang
stated that he wished to supplement Mr. Ku's remarks.
He said the Korean side did not intend to exclude prior
consultation. Since any change would have a profound
effect on both the Korean economy and the U.S. armed
forces, prior consultation would be held with the armed
forces. However, the Korean side did not believe that
this provision of the SOFA should make prior consultation
obligatory. Colonel Fuller remarked that perhaps more
suitable language could be found after both sides had
given this matter further consideration.

29. Regarding Agreed Minute #2 in the U.S. draft, Mr.
Ku stated that the Korean side intended that existing
arrangements should be continued, including those falling
under the provisions of the Utilities and Claims Settlement Agreement. Colonel Fuller stated that the U.S. side
had the same intention. He asked what the Korean side was
proposing with regard to Agreed Minute #2. Mr. Ku replied
that the Korean side accepted the substance of Agreed
Minute #2. However, they proposed that some specific
mention should be made of existing arrangements, either
in this Agreed Minute or in a separate Minute.

Revision of the Agreement

30. Turning to the drafts of the article dealing
with revision of the Agreement, Mr. Whang stated that
the Korean side agreed to accept the words "any Article"

0670

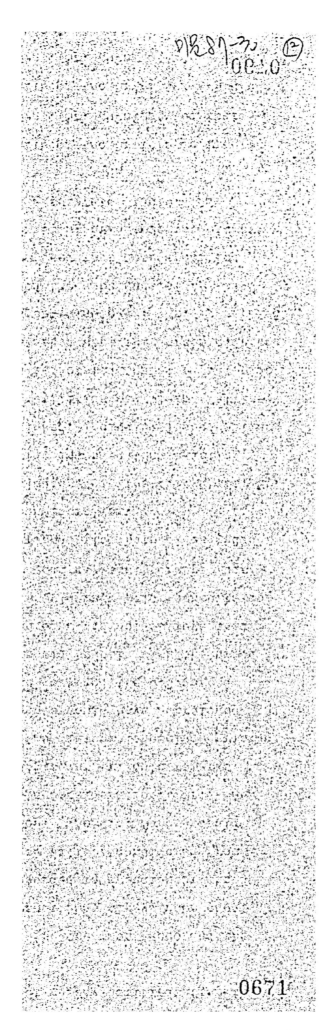

and "negotiations" as used in the U.S. draft article.
However the Korean side believed the term "diplomatic
channels" in the Korean draft to be better than the term
"appropriate channels" in the U.S. draft, since it is
quite logical to assume that negotiations for revision of
any agreement should also be entered into by the same
authorities which have originally neogitated the agreement.
General O'Connor replied that the term "appropriate" was
broader and therefore included the term "diplomatic" but
was not restricted to the latter. He pointed out that
there might be occasions on which channels other than
diplomatic channels might be more appropriate. In response
to Mr. Whang's query, General O'Connor stated that the
Joint Committee itself might be the appropriate body to
negotiate revision, or in time of war diplomatic channels
might not be available, in which case the U.S. military
commander might be the appropriate authority on the U.S.
side to negotiate revision. Mr. Whang stated the Joint
Committee was intended only to settle disputes, not to
negotiate changes in the Agreement. Even if diplomatic
channels were not available in wartime, the U.S. Government
would be the party with which the ROK Government would
negotiate revisions. General O'Connor observed that no
matter who did the negotiating, any revisions would have to
be approved by the two governments. It was agreed to give
further consideration to this matter.

31. It was agreed to hold the next meeting on December
3 at 2:00 p.m.

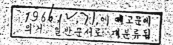

0672

한·미국 간의 상호방위조약 제4조에 의한 시설과 구역 및 한국에서의 미국군대의 지위에 관한 협정(SOFA)
전59권. 1966.7.9 서울에서 서명 : 1967.2.9 발효(조약 232호) (V.50 실무교섭회의 합의의사록, 제10-37차, 1963) (2/2)   519

JOINT SUMMARY RECORD OF THE 36TH SESSION

December 23, 1963

1. Time and Place: 3:00 to 5:00 p.m. December 5, 1963
                    at the Foreign Minister's Conference
                    Room

2. Attendants:

ROK Side:

Mr. Whang Ho Eul   Director
                                  Bureau of Political Affairs
                                  Ministry of Foreign Affairs

Mr. Koo, Choong Whay   Chief, America Section
                                  Ministry of Foreign Affairs

Mr. Park, Bong Chin   Chief, Customs Section
                                  Ministry of Finance

Mr. Choo, Moon Ki   Chief, Legal Affairs Section
                                  Ministry of Justice

Col. Kim, Won Kil   Chief, Military Affairs Section
                                  Ministry of National Defence

Mr. Oh, Jae Hee   Chief, Treaty Section
                                  Ministry of Foreign Affairs

Mr. Kang, Suk Jae   2nd Secretary
(Rapporteur and   Ministry of Foreign Affairs
    interpreter)

Mr. Cho, Kwang Jae   2nd Secretary
                                  Ministry of Foreign Affairs

Mr. Lee, Chung Bin   3rd Secretary
                                  Ministry of Foreign Affairs

U.S. Side:

Mr. Philip C. Habib   Counselor for Political
                                  Affairs
                                  American Embassy

Brig. Gen. G. G. O'Connor   Deputy Chief of Staff
                                  8th U.S. Army

Col. Howard Smigelor   Deputy Chief of Staff
                                  8th U.S. Army

Mr. Benjamin A. Fleck   First Secretary
(Rapporteur and   American Embassy
    Press Officer)

Col. L. J. Fuller   Staff Judge Advocate
                                  United Nations Command

Capt. R. M. Brownlie   Assistant Chief of Staff
                                  USN/K

0674

Mr. James Sartorius   2nd Secretary
                                    American Embassy

Mr. Robert A. Lewis   2nd Secretary and Consul
                                    American Embassy

Mr. Robert A. Kinney   J-5
                                    8th U.S. Army

Maj. Robert D. Peckham   Staff Officer, JAG
                                    8th U.S. Army

Mr. Kenneth Campen   Interpreter.

1. Mr. Whang opened the meeting by introducing Mr.
Park Bong Chin, Chief of the Customs Section, Ministry of
Finance, who was attending in place of Mr. Shin Kwan Sup,
and two new members of the Korean negotiating team: Colonel
Kim Won Kil, replacing Colonel Lee Nam Koo; and Mr. Oh
Chae Hee, newly appointed Chief of the Treaty Section,
Ministry of Foreign Affairs, replacing Mr. Shin Chung Sup.
Mr. Habib welcomed these gentlemen to the negotiating table
on behalf of the U.S. negotiators.

Customs

2. Taking up the Customs Article, Mr. Whang stated
that it had been the subject of discussion at many previous
meetings and many portions of it had been agreed upon.
However, there still remained some paragraphs concerning
which agreement had not yet been reached. He asked whether
the U.S. side had any comment to make regarding any of
these.

3. Mr. Habib replied that the U.S. side wished to
confine duscussion of this article at this meeting to paragraph 5(b), which relates to mail. He recalled that at
the previous meeting, the Korean side had indicated a particular interest in examining parcels because of concern over
the possible importation of illegal items. The Korean side
had indicated that the Korean authorities had no interest
in examining the personal letter mail of the U.S. troops.

0676

The U.S. side had explained the manner in which the mail arrives in Korea - in sealed containers which are sent directly from the ports of entry to individual postal units, where they are opened and the mail distributed. He recalled further that the question of how the Korean authorities proposed to implement any right of inspection also came up. The U.S. side had inquired whether the Korean authorities intended to send customs inspectors to each of the individual postal units or, alternatively, planned to open the sealed containers at the ports of entry, thus disrupting the swift and efficient distribution system now in effect. He asked the Korean side to explain how they proposed to carry out any right of inspection.

4. Mr. Whang replied that initially the Korean authorities had intended to inspect parcels at the ports of entry. However, after hearing the explanation of how the mail is handled, given by the U.S. side at the previous meeting, the Korean authorities now realized that examination at the ports of entry would be inconvenient. They were thinking, therefore, in terms of dispatching customs inspectors to the individual postal units. However, the Korean authorities did not intend that the inspectors would examine every parcel. From the point of view of the Korean side, the important thing was that the Korean authorities be given the right of inspection. The existence of that right in the SOFA would act as a deterrent. He pointed out that there is a difference between possession of a right and not exercising it and not having the right at all.

5. Mr. Habib stated that apparently the Korean side had in mind what is known in the United States as "spot inspection" of parcels. He also understood Mr. Whang's comments to mean that the Korean side is concerned that the distribution of mail not be held up by any system of inspection which might be established. He pointed out that the U.S.

0678

authorities felt very strongly that the mail should not pile up because of delays caused by such inspection. He said he believed Mr. Whang's comments to indicate that the Korean side has no intention of delaying the delivery of mail. Mr. Whang replied that this was the correct interpretation of his remarks.

6. Mr. Habib stated that, with the understanding that the Korean authorities had no intention or desire to delay the distribution of mail to the U.S. armed forces, the U.S. side was prepared to modify the language of paragraph 5(b) in the U.S. draft to read as follows:

> "5(b). Official documents under official *seal* and First Class mail in United States military postal channels under official postal seal;"

He added that it was also the understanding of the U.S. negotiators that the Korean side was proposing that inspection would take place at the individual postal units and not at the ports of entry. He stated that the proposed change in language would provide to the Korean authorities a right that they would not exercise except as deemed necessary and through the exercise of which they would not interfere with the prompt delivery of mail. He said the details of administering this provision of the SOFA could be worked out by the Joint Committee.

7. Mr. Whang stated that it was the understanding of the Korean side that: (1) there would be no inspection of official letters or personal letters; (2) Korean customs officials would have the right to inspect parcels; and (3) there would be no inspection at the ports of entry.

8. Mr. Habib said that what is known in the United States as "parcel post" is not first class mail. The great bulk of the packages come as parcel post. Mr. Whang stated that the Korean side understood that first class mail excluded parcels and consisted only of letter mail.

0680

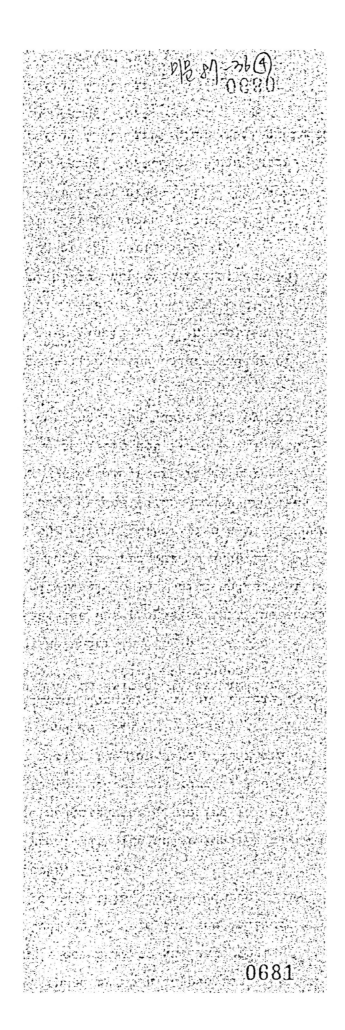

0681

9. Mr. Habib replied that this was not the case and that it is possible for parcels to be sent as first class mail, although unusual. He explained that the system described by the revised language just porposed by the U.S. side was actually the system which is in effect in Japan, although it is not spelled out specifically in the SOFA with Japan. In practice, this is the system which has evolved in Japan, through arrangements made with the Japanese authorities.

10. Mr. Whang inquired whether there is any limitation on the size of parcels which may be included in first class mail. Mr. Habib replied that there are limitations on the size of parcles, which he did not have immediately available at the meeting but would procure for the information of the Korean side. He pointed out that there is also a very real limitation imposed by the postal rates, which are higher for first class mail than for parcel post. As a result, it is so expensive to send parcels by first class mail that very few are sent. He promised to report at a subsequent meeting on the size limitations.

11. Mr. Whang then asked whether there was any difference in the markings which appear on the various classes of mail. Mr. Habib replied in the affirmative. Mr. Whang stated that the Korean side would give its views on the U.S. proposal after receiving more information about size limitations and methods of marking.

Non-Appropriated Funds

12. The negotiators then turned their attention to the Article dealing with Non-Appropriated Fund Organizations. Mr. Habib said that before beginning paragraph by paragraph discussion, the U.S. side wished to make a general statement regarding the role of non-appropriated fund activities in the U.S. armed forces, in an effort to clarify the nature

0682

and scope of these activities. He pointed out that the non-appropriated fund activities are an integral and essential part of the United States armed forces world-wide and of their civilian component abroad. Although in many countries, such activities are covered by appropriated funds, in the U.S. armed forces they are carried out through the use of non-appropriated funds. This difference in structure does not in any way make the non-appropriated fund activities any less an integral part of the U.S. armed forces. Such forces are designed to promote and provide a well-rounded morale, welfare, and recreational program for the armed forces and their civilian component.

The U.S. side feels sure, Mr. Habib continued, that the ROK Government agrees that such activities, which help to insure the mental and physical well being of U.S. personnel in Korea, is in the interests of both the ROK and U.S. Governments.

The U.S. side wished to point out again that the key words in paragraph 1 (a) of the U.S. draft of this article are the words : "authorized and regulated by U.S. military authorities". These words should provide the necessary assurance to the ROK side that activities covered in the article include only those officially authorized and regulated by U.S. military authorities. Such activities are under the close and continuing supervision of these authorities, just as are the appropriated fund activities. As an example, Mr. Habib called the attention of the Korean side to the case of an officers culb and a company mess. The former is a non-appropriated fund activity while the latter is an appropriated fund activity, and yet the supervision, control, and regulation is as close for one as for the other. There is nothing strange about these activities, he continued. They are normal activities to which the troops of any military

0684

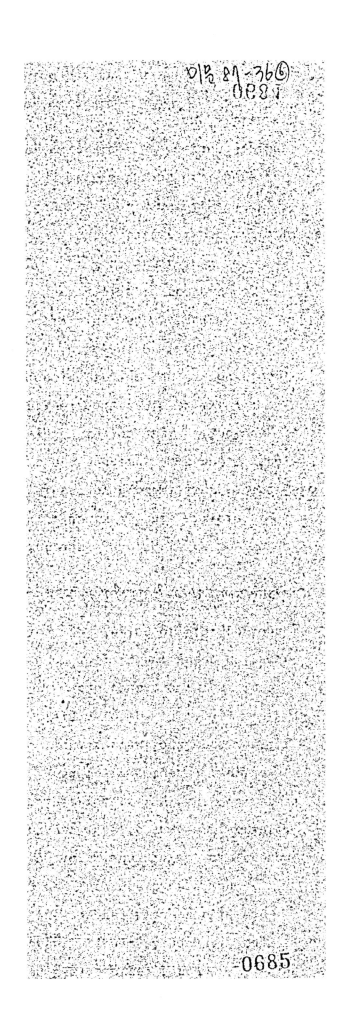

한·미국 간의 상호방위조약 제4조에 의한 시설과 구역 및 한국에서의 미국군대의 지위에 관한 협정(SOFA)
전59권. 1966.7.9 서울에서 서명 : 1967.2.9 발효(조약 232호) (V.50 실무교섭회의 합의의사록, 제10-37차, 1963) (2/2)　531

force are entitled.

13. Mr. Hwang replied that as a result of Mr. Habib's explanation, the Korean side clearly understood the nature and scope of the non-appropriated fund organizations. The Korean side agreed that such organizations were very necessary for the morale and welfare of the members of the U.S. armed forces. He stated that both sides recognized and accepted the fundamental spirit and intention of this article. The Korean side, he said, was not trying to interfere with, or cause unnecessary inconvenience to, non-appropriated fund organizations. However, the Korean side had maintained that ROK customs authorities should be authorized to inspect goods imported by these organizations. This was not intended as interference in their operation. The Korean side had explained again and again that it is necessary for the Korean customs authorities to know the quantity of goods imported because of the current state of the Korean economy. The proposal that customs inspection be authorized was made not because of a lack of understanding on the part of the Korean side but because of the state of the Korean economy.

14. Mr. Habib replied that agreement had already been reached in principle that the amount of goods imported by these activities should be limited to reasonable quantities. He pointed out that the only place where this question arises in this article is in paragraph 4 of the Korean draft. The language of this paragraph is identical with the language of Agreed Minute #1 to the Customs Article, U.S. draft. The U.S. side believed that there was no point in having identical wording appear in two different articles. Since

this provision appeared to be more appropriate for inclusion in the customs article, and since agreement had already been reached regarding that particular Agreed Minute, it appeared unnecessary to include this paragraph in this article.

15. Mr. Hwang replied that since the wording was duplicative, the Korean side agreed to the deletion of paragraph 4 from the Korean draft of this article.

16. Mr. Habib stated that recent discussion of the Customs Article indicated a desire on the part of the Korean authorities to inspect goods imported for the non-appropriated fund activities in order to insure that only "reasonable quantities" of such goods were imported. He said that the U.S. side was not prepared to agree that Korean authorities shall decide what constitutes a "reasonable quantity". The normal cooperative relationship prevailing between the U.S. armed forces and the Korean authorities would lead the Korean authorities to call for consultation should they wish to verify whether or not this provision of the SOFA was working. The U.S. side believed that it would be unworkable and unreasonable for the Korean authorities to attempt to determine unilaterally what are reasonable quantities. The U.S. armed forces have highly trained specialists in logistics and supply who carefully monitor the flow of military cargoes into Korea. It would be contrary to the interests and desires of the U.S. armed forces to bring in more imports than are reasonably required, for to do so would only result in uneconomical operation and supply maladjustment. The Korean side must assume that the U.S. armed forces operate these activities in good faith. The U.S. side is quite prepared to agree to a limitation in the Customs Article to "reasonable quantities". There is a mechanism provided in the SOFA to enable either side to make sure that the

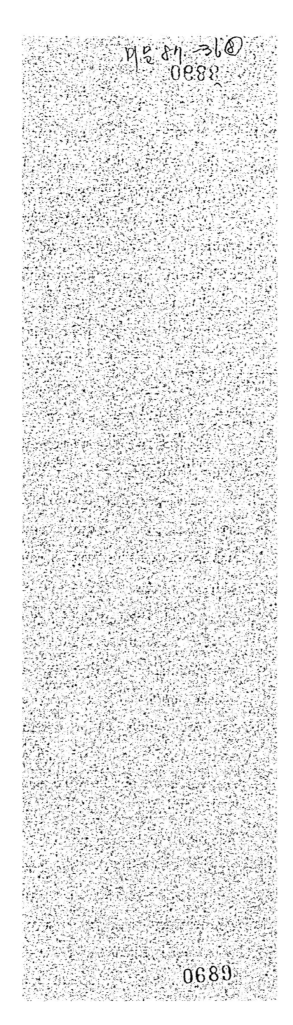

other side lives up to the Agreement. The U.S. side is convinced that the ROK authorities do not have sufficient personnel, the capability, or the desire to make a unilateral determination of what constitutes reasonable quantities. What both sides are trying to do is to draft an Agreement which will provide the framework which will enable each side to protect its interests. There should be no ambiguity in the language of the Agreement.

17. Mr. Hwang expressed agreement with the final point made by Mr. Habib. He said that in the view of the Korean side the determination of what consituted a reasonable quantity could be based on the annual consumption rate of the average American family, not the average Korean family. The Korean side appreciated the intention of the U.S. side to live up to the terms of Agreed Minute of the Customs Article. However, goods imported for the non-appropriated fund organizations of the U.S. armed forces were actually on sale in Korean markets. This would not be the case, in the view of the Korean side, if these goods were imported in the quantities actually required. Therefore, the Korean customs authorities should be enabled to confirm that the quantity imported is limited to the amounts which are reasonably required.

18. Mr. Habib replied that the two sides appeared to be discussing two different subjects. He said the U.S. side wholeheartedly shared the desire of the Korean officials to prevent such goods from being channelled into the Korean black market. The U.S. armed forces do everything possible to help check and prevent such diversions. However, the U.S. side did not agree that the way to accomplish this objective was to permit inspection of non-appropriated fund cargoes by

0690

the Korean customs authorities. The U.S. side has agreed to include provisions in the SOFA which will allow the prevention of black marketing of these goods, as well as black marketing of appropriated fund supplies and equipment. Did the Korean side wish the right to inspect cargoes of the latter type also? Non-appropriated fund cargoes are military cargoes. Diversion of military cargoes is a criminal act. In actual fact, Mr. Habib continued, the inspection of cargoes does not prevent black marketing. There are requirements on the part of the Korean authorities as well as on the part of the U.S. armed forces to control the people engaged in black marketing. The U.S. side was just as much concerned as the Korean side but was not prepared to agree to the inclusion of provisions in the SOFA which would provide no result in terms of the objective sought. An international agreement, he continued, is a set of principles which guides the parties in the carrying out of certain functions. In this present case, the SOFA was an agreement pertaining to the presence of the U.S. armed forces in the Republic of Korea.

19. Mr. Hwang thanked Mr. Habib for this presentation of the views of the U.S. side. He said that as a result of this exchange of views, each side understood the position of the other. He suggested that the negotiators proceed with a paragraph by paragraph discussion of the article. Mr. Habib agreed.

20. Mr. Hwang noted that since newspapers were the subject of paragraph 1 (b), the word "newspapers" could be deleted from the U.S. draft of paragraph 1 (a). Mr. Habib disagreed, pointing out that whereas paragraph 1 (b) sets up certain conditions under which a newspaper can be sold to the general public, paragraph 1 (a) provides the U.S. armed forces with the right to establish the newspaper. Therefore, "newspapers" should be retained in paragraph 1 (a).

0692

한·미국 간의 상호방위조약 제4조에 의한 시설과 구역 및 한국에서의 미국군대의 지위에 관한 협정(SOFA)
전59권. 1966.7.9 서울에서 서명 : 1967.2.9 발효(조약 232호) (V.50 실무교섭회의 합의의사록, 제10-37차, 1963) (2/2)　539

In this connection, Mr. Habib noted that the U.S. side
agreed to the suggestion made previously by the Korean side
that the words "except as provided in paragraph 1 (b)"
be added to the end of the first sentence of paragraph 2 of
the U.S. draft. Mr. Hwang agreed.

21. Mr. Hwang noted that the matter of "activities"
versus "organizations" was dependent upon resolution of
this question in other articles. Mr. Habib replied that
the U.S. side desired to settle this matter. He said the U.S.
side still did not understand why the Korean side objected
to the word "activities". Was it because this word was
not used in the SOFA with Japan?

22. Mr. Hwang replied that the view of the Korean side
had been made clear at the last meeting. The word "organizations"
is clearer in meaning to the Korean side and seemed more
appropriate. The word "activities" is ambiguous.

23. Mr. Habib stated that the U.S. side believed "activities"
to be a better word. However, the U.S. side was prepared to
agree to "organizations" wherever it appears in the Agreement,
if it removes ambiguity in the Korean translation, with the
clear understanding in the record that the Korean side
agrees that the word "organizations" in the Agreement includes
all non-appropriated fund functions and entities described
as "activities" by the U.S. armed forces. He pointed out
that there was no question that both sides were talking about
the same thing. Mr. Hwang agreed to this understanding.

24. Referring to the phrase "within the facilities and
areas in use by the United States armed forces" in the Korean
draft of paragraph 1 (a), Mr. Hwang recalled that at the
21st negotiating meeting, the Korean side had suggested
that whenever it is necessary to operate a temporary exchange
outside of the facilities and areas, such an exchange should
be established at the place agreed upon between the two

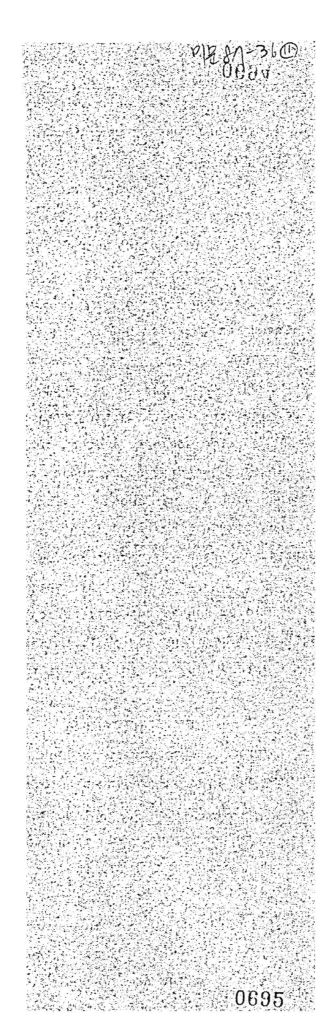

governments through the Joint Committee.

25. Mr. Habib replied that the U.S. side had considered this proposal but believed that it would establish an extra administrative burden which would not gain anything for either side. If the question ever arose, he pointed out, it could be discussed by the Joint Committee. But the adoption of this Korean proposal would not facilitate the smooth functioning of the Agreement in any way. The practical experience gained by the U.S. armed forces in the functioning of the SOFA with Japan had shown that such a provision merely imposes an extra administrative burden.

26. Mr. Hwang stated that the Korean side agreed that this provision might create an unnecessary administrative burden. The Korean side agreed to the deletion of this language, with the understanding that such matters would be raised in the Joint Committee. Mr. Habib replied that they could be raised, if the Korean side had any question; however it was not necessary to make it a requirement. If the Korean authorities wished to raise any question of this sort in the Joint Committee they were perfectly entitled to do so. Mr. Hwang stated that with that understanding, the Korean side agreed to the deletion of the phrase "within the facilities and areas in use by the United States armed forces."

27. Mr. Hwang stated that the Korean side wished to delete the word "exclusive" from the Korean draft of paragraph 1 (a), with the understanding that non-appropriated fund organizations might be utilized by members of the U.S. armed forces, their dependents, and others. The use of these organizations by "others" was defined elsewhere in the Agreement. Therefore, the word "exclusive" should be deleted in this paragraph. Mr. Habib agreed. Mr. Hwang noted that discussion of this article had not been completed but suggested that the negotiators move on to discuss the Article on Revision of the Agreement. Mr. Habib agreed.

0696

28. Mr. Hwang asked whether the U.S. side wished to make any comment on the only substantive difference existing in this article – the use of the word "appropriate" or the word "diplomatic".

29. Mr. Habib stated that "appropriate" is the more usual phraseology. Obviously, the channel for revision will be determined by the two governments when the occasion for revision arises.

30. Mr. Hwang stated that the Korean side agreed to the use of the word "appropriate", with the understanding that negotiations for revision will normally take place through diplomatic channels, except for unusual cases. Mr. Habib agreed with this understanding. Full agreement was thereupon reached on the text of this article.

31. The next meeting was scheduled for December 19 at 2:00 p.m.

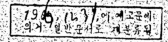

관리
번호 1567

1. Time and Place:　2:00 to 4:10 P.M. December 27, 1963
　　　　　　　　　　　at the Foreign Ministry's Conference
　　　　　　　　　　　Room

2. Attendants:

ROK Side:

Mr. Whang, Ho Eul　　　　　　　Director
　　　　　　　　　　　　　　　Bureau of Asian Affairs
　　　　　　　　　　　　　　　Ministry of Foreign Affairs

Mr. Chang, Sang Moon　　　　　Director
　　　　　　　　　　　　　　　Bureau of European and American
　　　　　　　　　　　　　　　Affairs
　　　　　　　　　　　　　　　Ministry of Foreign Affairs

Mr. Koo, Choong Whay　　　　　Chief, American Section
　　　　　　　　　　　　　　　Ministry of Foreign Affairs

Mr. Park, Bong Chin　　　　　　Chief, Customs Section
　　　　　　　　　　　　　　　Ministry of Finance

Mr. Choo, Moon Ki　　　　　　　Chief, Legal Affairs Section
　　　　　　　　　　　　　　　Ministry of Justice

Col. Kim, Won Kil　　　　　　　Chief, Military Affairs Section
　　　　　　　　　　　　　　　Ministry of National Defence

Mr. Oh, Jae Hee　　　　　　　　Chief, Treaty Section
　　　　　　　　　　　　　　　Ministry of Foreign Affairs

Mr. Kang, Suk Jae　　　　　　　2nd Secretary
(Rapporteur and　　　　　　　　Ministry of Foreign Affairs
　Interpreter)

Mr. Lee, Chung Bin　　　　　　　3rd Secretary
　　　　　　　　　　　　　　　Ministry of Foreign Affairs

Mr. Lee, Keun Pal　　　　　　　3rd Secretary
　　　　　　　　　　　　　　　Ministry of Foreign Affairs

U.S. Side:

Mr. Philip C. Habib　　　　　　Counselor for Political
　　　　　　　　　　　　　　　Affairs
　　　　　　　　　　　　　　　American Embassy

Col. Howard Smigelow　　　　　Deputy Chief of Staff
　　　　　　　　　　　　　　　8th U.S. Army

Col. L.J. Fuller　　　　　　　　Staff Judge Advocate
　　　　　　　　　　　　　　　United Nations Command

Capt. R.M. Brownlie　　　　　　Assistant Chief of Staff
　　　　　　　　　　　　　　　USN/K

0700

Mr. Benjamin A. Fleck (Rapporteur and Press Officer)	First Secretary American Embassy
Mr. James Sartorius	2nd Secretary American Embassy
Mr. Robert A. Lewis	2nd Secretary and Consul American Embassy
Mr. Robert A. Kinney	J-5 8th U.S. Army
Maj. Robert D. Peckham	Staff Officer, JAG 8th U.S. Army
Mr. Kenneth Campen	Interpreter

1. Mr. Whang opened the meeting by introducing Mr. Chang Sang Moon, newly appointed Director of the Europe and America Bureau of the Foreign Ministry. Mr. Whang stated that a reorganization within the Ministry had split the former Bureau of Political Affairs, of which he had been Director, into the Bureau for Europe and America and a Bureau for Asian Affairs. Mr. Whang had been appointed Director of the Bureau of Asian Affairs; as a result, he would no longer be associated with the Status of Forces negotiations and Mr. Chang would succeed him as Chief Negotiator for the ROK Government. Mr. Whang announced that Mr. Park was attending the meeting in place of Mr. Shin Kwan Sup, who had another engagement. Mr. Whang then introduced Mr. Lee Keun Pal, a Foreign Service Officer who had just returned from an assignment to the Korean Consulate General in San Francisco and had joined the staff of the American Section of the Foreign Ministry.

2. Mr. Habib welcomed Mr. Lee to the negotiations and stated that Mr. Park was an old friend who was always welcome at the negotiating table. Mr. Habib stated that he wished to make a few remarks in connection with the change of leadership on the Korean side of the table. He said that during the period in which Mr. Whang had served as Chief Negotiator, there had

한·미국 간의 상호방위조약 제4조에 의한 시설과 구역 및 한국에서의 미국군대의 지위에 관한 협정(SOFA)
전59권. 1966.7.9 서울에서 서명 : 1967.2.9 발효(조약 232호) (V.50 실무교섭회의 합의의사록, 제10-37차, 1963) (2/2) 549

always been great frankness and honesty of discussion
between the two negotiating team. The U.S. Side had a
feeling of deep appreciation for Mr. Whang's leadership.
During this period, the U.S. side had consistently felt that
the negotiations were a team effort, with both sides cooperating in developing a mutually satisfactory Agreement
rather than battling each other.

3. Mr. Habib said that the great regret felt by the
U.S. side at Mr. Whang's departure from the negotiating table
did not dampen the warmth with which they greeted Mr. Chang.
When the Agreement is finally signed, the great contributions
made by Messrs. Chin, Whang, and Chang will be fully
recognized. Mr. Habib pledged to Mr. Chang the fullest
cooperation of the U.S. negotiators and said that they
fully expected the continuation of the excellent negitiating
relations which had existed to date. He said they looked
forward to receiving the advice and assistance of Mr. Whang
from time to time.

4. Mr. Whang replied that this was a significant
meeting for him, inasmuch as it was the last one of 1963
and the last one in which he would participate. He thanked
Mr. Habib for his kind words and said that he had found his
association with the U.S. negotiators to be a very happy
one. He felt honored to have had the opportunity to
participate in these historic negotiations. He was also
very grateful for the close friendships which had developed
between himself and the U.S. negotiators. He said he would
continue to be concerned with the course of the negotiations
and looked forward to final agreement at the earliest
possible time. The atmosphere of the negotiations had been
very amicable and he was personally sad at leaving the
negotiating table. However, he was glad that Mr. Chang was his
successor and he felt confident that Mr. Chang would make
a great contribution to the negotiations. 0704

0705

5. Mr. Chang stated that he felt it a personal privilege and honor to participate in the SOFA negotiations, which had been in progress for long time. Mr. Whang had made a great contribution to the course of the negotiations, with the cooperation of the U.S. negotiators. He said he would try to follow Mr. Whang's example. He hoped to have the fullest cooperation of the U.S. negotiators. The presence of the U.S. armed forces in Korea was for the mutual benefit of the ROK Government and the U.S. Government and he was convinced that the negotiators could reach a mutually satisfactory Agreement.

6. Mr. Habib replied that the U.S. negotiators welcomed the spirit expressed by Mr. Chang and stated that Mr. Chang could be assured of the full cooperation of the U.S. negotiators.

Non-Appropriated Fund Organizations

7. Turning to the first item on the agenda, Mr. Whang stated that with regard to the article dealing with non-appropriated fund organizations, it had been agreed at the previous meeting to use the word "organizations" rather than the word "activities" throughout the article and the entire Agreement. It had also been agreed to insert the phrase "except as provided in paragraph 1(b)" at the end of the first sentence of paragraph 2 of the U.S. draft. Mr. Habib confirmed Mr. Whang's statements.

8. Mr. Whang stated that the second sentence of the U.S. draft of paragraph 2 was similar to the Korean draft, except that the U.S. draft contained the phrase "Korean taxes to which other purchasers of such merchandise and supplies are subject and at rates no less favorable than those imposed on other purchasers". In this connection, he said,

0706

the ROK Government has no intention of imposing taxes on
these organizations at less favorable rates. The existing
taxation system is one of indirect taxes and, therefore,
there cannot be different rates for different purchasers.
This language in the U.S. draft is therefore irrelevant.
Furthermore, it does not appear in the SOFA with Japan.
The Korean negotiators believe that details of this nature
should be worked out by the Joint Committee. The SOFA is
supposed to provide a broad framework of principles and not
include details of this nature. Therefore, the Korean side
suggested that this language be deleted.

9. Mr. Habib replied that U.S. side was under the
impression that the language of this paragraph had already
been agreed to at previous meetings. However, the U.S.
negotiators welcomed the statement by Mr. Whang that no
discriminatory tax rates exist and that the ROK Government
has no intention of establishing discriminatory rates in
the future. This is what the language of the U.S. draft is
intended to insure. The fact that this language does not
appear in the SOFA with Japan is no reason to leave it out
of the Agreement under negotiation, particularly if it will
spell out the point at issue. If the ROK Government has no
intention of imposing discriminatory taxes, then it should
have no objection to including this language in the Agreement.
The U.S. negotiators believe its retention is desirable in
order to make certain that no discriminatory taxes will be
imposed.

10. Mr. Whang replied that the Korean negotiators
understood the intention of the U.S. side. However, it
would be impossible to include every detail in the SOFA.
The Agreement should consist of a broad framework of

principles, with the details left for subsequent working out by the Joint Committee. He suggested that the language in question be deleted, with the negotiating record clearly showing the understanding of both sides that the present system of taxation is one of indirect taxation under which there are no different rates for different purchasers and the understanding that the ROK Government has no intention of imposing discriminatory taxes on the organizations covered by this article.

11. Mr. Habib replied that the U.S. negotiators agreed that the SOFA should avoid getting into details. However, the point at issue was not a detail such as the rates, levels, or methods of taxation to be imposed by the ROK Government. The point at issue was a statement of principle. The U.S. negotiators appreciated the explanation and assurances given by the Korean negotiators. The U.S. negotiators were not trying to avoid the payment of taxes by non-appropriated fund organizations but were trying to have included in the SOFA the principle that there shall be no discriminatory taxation. This is a well understood principle, on which the U.S. negotiators thought that agreement had already been reached.

12. At Mr. Whang's suggestion, it was agreed to give further consideration to this question and discuss it further at a subsequent meeting.

13. Mr. Whang pointed out that paragraph 4 of the U.S. draft and paragraph 5 of the Korean draft provide for the provision of tax information required by Korean legislation. Requests for such information would be made through the Joint Committee. Since no unnecessary request would be made, the Korean negotiators considered unnecessary the clause "after consultation between the representatives of the two governments

0710

in the Joint Committee" in the U.S. draft. He suggested
the deletion of this language.

14. Mr. Habib replied that the language of the U.S.
draft was very positive in that it bound the U.S. authorities
to provide required information to the Korean authorities.
The language is intended to establish the framework of a
system which will enable the U.S. authorities to assist
the Korean authorities through the provision of the desired
information. It would enable the Joint Committee to perform
a valuable function. With regard to a matter as complicated
as the provision of tax information, the U.S. negotiators
believe that the Agreement should indicate the manner in
which the information is to be presented. The language of
the U.S. draft would provide a channel for facilitating the
provision of the desired information, and would bind the
U.S. authorities to provide the information.

15. Mr. Whang expressed appreciation for Mr. Habib's
explanation and suggested substitution of the word "through"
for the word "after". Mr. Habib said "through" would not be
as good English as "after". Perhaps the Korean side meant
"upon consultation". The U.S. side believed "after
consultation" was the best usage. It was not intended to be
a preventive device but merely a time factor. As he had
already pointed out, the word "shall" would bind the U.S.
authorities to provide the requested information.

16. Mr. Whang replied that "after consultation" implies
that the information will be provided only after the
consultation has been completed. Therefore, the Korean
side would prefer "through consultation". Mr. Habib pointed
out that the U.S. negotiators wanted to provide for the
opportunity for discussion of the requests in the Joint
Committee. The language does not say "after agreement";

0712

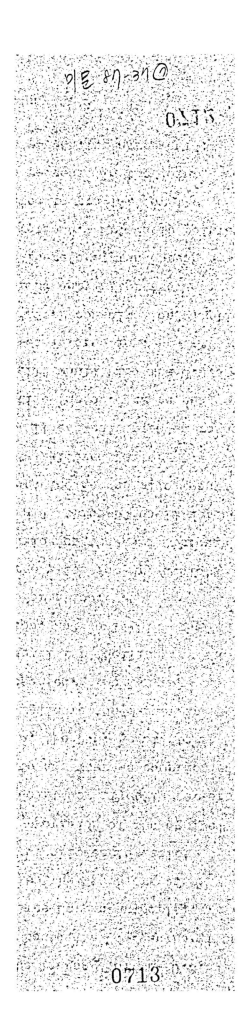

한·미국 간의 상호방위조약 제4조에 의한 시설과 구역 및 한국에서의 미국군대의 지위에 관한 협정(SOFA)
전59권. 1966.7.9 서울에서 서명 : 1967.2.9 발효(조약 232호) (V.50 실무교섭회의 합의의사록, 제10-37차, 1963) (2/2) 559

it merely says "after consultation". It was thereupon agreed to consider this matter further.

17. Mr. Whang then stated that paragraph 5 of the U.S. draft provided for use of the facilities of non-appropriated fund organizations by persons other than members of the U.S. armed forces. For this reason, it constituted an exception to the provisions of the remainder of the article. The Korean negotiators suggested, therefore, that it be converted into an Agreed Minute and be rewritten in simpler language.

18. Mr. Habib replied that the U.S. negotiators agreed that this paragraph was exceptional and also agreed to its conversion into an Agreed Minute. He said the U.S. side had given a great deal of additional consideration to this problem and had redrafted the paragraph in an effort to make the language much more specific and less susceptible to conflicting interpretations. Mr. Habib thereupon tabled a proposed Agreed Minute to be substituted for paragraph 5 of the U.S. draft and gave a brief explanation of the new language.

19. As the Korean negotiators were aware, Mr. Habib said, the presence of U.S. officials and other official and private organizations and individuals has created a unique situation in the Republic of Korea. This paragraph constitutes an attempt to meet this situation in a manner which will be mutually satisfactory. He pointed out that the right to use non-appropriated fund facilities is customarily given to other officers and personnel of the U.S. Government, as provided in item (a) of the paragraph. This is common practice worldwide and is a simple concept. The same is true of items (c) and (d), which provide for contractors

0714

한·미국 간의 상호방위조약 제4조에 의한 시설과 구역 및 한국에서의 미국군대의 지위에 관한 협정(SOFA)
전59권. 1966.7.9 서울에서 서명 : 1967.2.9 발효(조약 232호) (V.50 실무교섭회의 합의의사록, 제10-37차, 1963) (2/2) 561

and service organizations, respectively. However, the situation in Korea is a bit more complicated than usual because of the presence of non-Korean forces other than the U.S. armed forces, which receive logistical support from the latter. These forces include the Thai and Turk troops and the liaison officers of various nations assigned to the UN Command. These forces are covered by item (b). Inasmuch as it is impractical to try to provide such privileges for the principals and not for their dependents, the dependents of all the categories of persons covered by items (a) through (d) are covered by item (e). Item (f) would provide non-appropriated fund privileges to other entities such as the United Nations Commission for the Unification and Rehabilitation of Korea (UNCURK), the United Nations Technical Assistance Board (UNTAB), other UN agencies, non-American diplomatic personnel, certain missionary organizations, and others. The language of the paragraph provides that privileges would be extended under item (f) only"with the express consent of the Government of the Republic of Korea". Summing up, Mr. Habib stated that this paragraph provided for the extension of non-appropriated fund facilities to three general groups: (a) U.S. Government personnel ordinarily accorded such privileges; (b) those organizations and individuals who are integral parts of the U.S. armed forces; and (c) such other organizations and individuals as the ROK Government will expressly agree to.

20. Mr. Whang stated that the Korean negotiators had suggested conversion of this paragraph to an Agreed Minute and the use of simpler and clearer language. The draft tabled by the U.S. side raised certain questions. For instance, could the U.S. negotiators enumerate those persons

0716

who would be included under item (a) and what other organizations would be included under item (d) in addition to the Red Cross and the USO?

21. Mr. Habib replied that item (a) would cover non-Korean employees of the U.S. Government in Korea, including the Embassy, USOM, USIS, the Embassy military attaches, and members of the various military advisory groups. At the present time, there were no organizations other than the Red Cross and the USO that would be covered by item (d). This item was so phrased to permit the includion of additional groups at some future time and to allow for the possibility of changes in organizational structure of the two organizations specifically named. For instance, the United Service Organizations are composed of several separate groups which have banded together for this particular function but conceivably might, at some future date, decide to reorganize in some other fashion. At present, he pointed out, only handful of people would be involved under item (d). Item (f), Mr. Habib continued, was more complicated. In addition to UNCURK and UNTAB, this item would include such organizations as the Scandinavian Medical Mission (100 persons), the American-Korean Foundation, and members of the diplomatic corps. Personnel of these organizations would be covered by this paragraph only with the express consent of the ROK Government. As the Korean negotiators were fully aware, this was a very delicate problem which would have to be approached cautiously and which could only be solved by the mutual efforts of the Korean and U.S. authorities.

22. Mr. Whang stated that item (c) obviously referred to the invited contractors working for the U.S. armed

forces. He asked if anyone else would be covered by this item. Mr. Habib replied that this item was intended to cover not only invited contractors of the U.S. armed forces but also contractors working for the United States Operations Mission under specific contracts. He said that no expansion in the range of such contracts was foreseen.

23. Mr. Whang thanked Mr. Habib for his explanation of the proposed Agreed Minute. Mr. Whang said the Korean negotiators would study the Agreed Minute and give their views at a subsequent meeting.

Customs

24. Turning to the Customs Article, Mr. Whang stated that the Korean negotiators were prepared to accept paragraph 2 of the U.S. draft, with the understanding that the word "organizations" was to be used instead of the word "activities", as agreed upon at the previous meeting. Mr. Habib confirmed that the word "organizations" was to be used throughout the Agreement wherever the phrase "non-appropriated fund organizations" appeared. He said the U.S. side assumed that the Korean negotiators were also agreeing to the previous U.S. proposal to place in parentheses the phrase "including their authorized procurement agencies and their non-appropriated fund organizations provided for in Article   ". Mr. Whang asked if there was any special significance to the use of parentheses in this context. Mr. Habib replied that it was being proposed solely for the sake of grammatical clarity. Mr. Whang remarked that inasmuch as the use of parentheses did not change the substance of the paragraph, the Korean negotiators agreed to the placing of the phrase in question in parentheses.

25. Mr. Whang remarked that agreement had not yet

0720

been reached on subparagraph (b) of paragraph 3, subparagraphs (a), (b), and (c) of paragraph 5, and Agreed
Minutes 2, and 3. He suggested that the negotiators take
up paragraph 5(b) for discussion, noting that at the previous
meeting the Korean negotiators had requested information
regarding the size and markings of parcels mailed as first
class mail.

26. Mr. Habib stated that the maximum weight limitation
on parcels shipped by first class mail is 70 pounds. They
are marked to indicate the class of mail being used. First
class mail is handled separately from other classes of mail and
and parcels sent by first class mail are shipped in separate
mail bags and not mixed with first class letter mail. He
pointed out that because of the greater cost of first class
mail, the great bulk of parcels are shipped by parcel post.
As an example of the cost differential, he cited the case
of a 10 lb. parcel shipped by parcel post in Zone 8 (over
1800 miles). The cost of sending such a parcel would be
$2.16. To ship the same parcel by first class mail would
cost $8.00.

27. Mr. Whang stated that the Korean negotiators would
like to have it agreed that Korean customs inspectors would
function at the 17 main military post offices rather than
at the 32 mail distribution centers mentioned by the U.S.
negotiators at the previous meeting.

28. Mr. Habib replied that this was a detail which was
not appropriate for inclusion in the SOFA but would have to
be worked out by the Joint Committee. He said that the U.S.
negotiators understood that if the Korean negotiators agreed
to the revised text of paragraph 5(b) proposed by the U.S.
negotiators at the previous meeting, it would be with the

0722

following understandings:

a. Examinations of parcels in the MPO mails in the ROK by ROK customs inspectors will be conducted so as not to damage the contents of the parcels inspected or delay delivery of the mail;

b. Such examinations will be conducted in U.S. MPO installations at designated points of mail distribution and in the presence of U.S. officials;

c. No parcel in the MPO mails will be removed from U.S. postal channels except as mutually agreed;

d. It is understood that the right of inspection will be exercised on a "spot check" basis so as not to unduly delay delivery or increase the administrative burden of the postal authorities.

With those understandings, Mr. Habib continued, the U.S. negotiators are prepared to agree to the principle of the right of the Korean authorities to inspect non-first class mail. The Korean authorities can be assured of the co-operation of the U.S. armed forces in implementing this provision of the SOFA.

29. Turning to paragraph 6, Mr. Whang stated that although the text of this paragraph had already been agreed upon, the Korean negotiators would like to spell out the fact that disposal of imported goods in contravention of the provisions of paragraph 6 shall be dealt with under Korean laws and customs regulations.

30. Mr. Habib replied by referring to Agreed Minutes #4 and #5. Colonel Fuller pointed out that obviously, if an illegal transaction occurred involving an unauthorized person, the Korean authorities would have jurisdiction over such a person. He added that in the case of any person

0721

0725

caught disposing of goods illegally, the provisions of the Respect for Local Law Article, the Criminal Jurisdiction Article, and the U.S. armed forces' regulations would apply. Any exception to the foregoing would have to be spelled out in the Agreement.

31. Turning to paragraph 5(c), Mr. Whang pointed out that the phrase (including their authorized procurement agencies and their non-appropriated fund organizations provided for in Article   was included both in 5(c) and in Agreed Minute §3, which related to 5(c). The Korean negotiators believed the appearance of the phrase in both places was redundant and suggested its deletion from paragraph 5(c). Mr. Habib replied that the U.S. negotiators would take this proposal under consideration.

32. At this point the meeting was adjourned. The next meeting wasscheduled for January 9, 1964 at 2:00 P.M.

0726

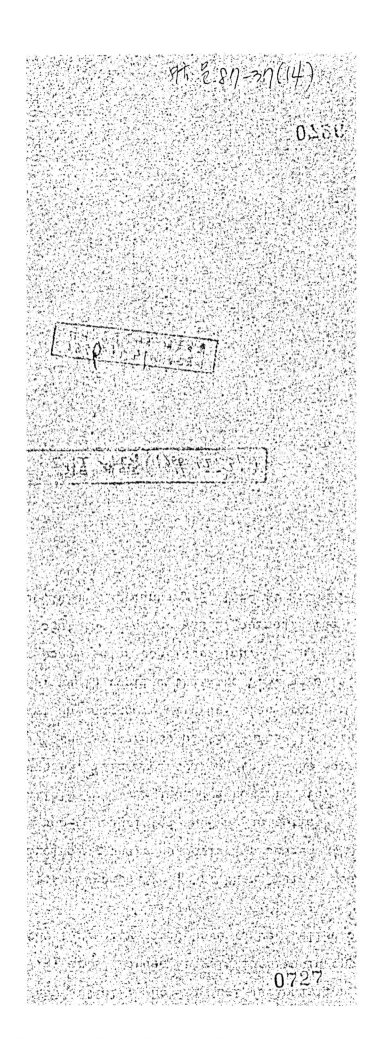

외교문서 비밀해제: 주한미군지위협정(SOFA) 20
주한미군지위협정(SOFA) 서명 및 발효 20

초판인쇄 2024년 03월 15일
초판발행 2024년 03월 15일

지은이 한국학술정보(주)
펴낸이 채종준
펴낸곳 한국학술정보(주)
주 소 경기도 파주시 회동길 230(문발동)
전 화 031-908-3181(대표)
팩 스 031-908-3189
홈페이지 http://ebook.kstudy.com
E-mail 출판사업부 publish@kstudy.com
등 록 제일산-115호(2000. 6. 19)

ISBN 979-11-7217-031-8 94340
      979-11-7217-011-0 94340 (set)